MW01003116

BEHIND THE RED VELVET CURTAIN

Behind the Red Velvet Curtain

An American Ballerina in Russia

Joy Womack
As told to Elizabeth Shockman

ROWMAN & LITTLEFIELD

Lanham • Boulder • New York • London

Published by Rowman & Littlefield
An imprint of The Rowman & Littlefield Publishing Group, Inc.
4501 Forbes Boulevard, Suite 200, Lanham, Maryland 20706
www.rowman.com

86-90 Paul Street, London EC2A 4NE

Distributed by NATIONAL BOOK NETWORK

Copyright © 2025 by Joy Womack and Elizabeth Shockman

All rights reserved. No part of this book may be reproduced in any form or by any electronic or mechanical means, including information storage and retrieval systems, without written permission from the publisher, except by a reviewer who may quote passages in a review.

British Library Cataloguing in Publication Information Available

Library of Congress Cataloging-in-Publication Data
Names: Womack, Joy, 1994- author. | Shockman, Elizabeth, 1985- author.
Title: Behind the red velvet curtain : an American ballerina in Russia /
     Joy Womack As told to Elizabeth Shockman.
Description: Lanham, Maryland : Rowman & Littlefield, [2025]
Identifiers: LCCN 2024042895 (print) | LCCN 2024042896 (ebook) | ISBN
     9781538199374 (cloth) | ISBN 9781538199381 (epub)
Subjects: LCSH: Womack, Joy, 1994- author. | Ballerinas—United
     States—Biography. | Ballerinas—Russia (Federation)—Biography. |
     Bol'shoĭ teatr SSSR. Balet—History—21st century.
Classification: LCC GV1785.W58 A3 2025 (print) | LCC GV1785.W58 (ebook) |
     DDC 792.802/8092 [B]—dc23/eng/20240925
LC record available at https://lccn.loc.gov/2024042895
LC ebook record available at https://lccn.loc.gov/2024042896

♾️™ The paper used in this publication meets the minimum requirements of American National Standard for Information Sciences—Permanence of Paper for Printed Library Materials, ANSI/NISO Z39.48-1992

CONTENTS

Author's Note vii

Prologue 1
CHAPTER 1: Womacks Win 4
CHAPTER 2: Flying 12
CHAPTER 3: Away 18
CHAPTER 4: Ballet Factory 25
CHAPTER 5: "Prove It to Me" 33
CHAPTER 6: Vertigo 43
CHAPTER 7: Cathedral of Dance 51
CHAPTER 8: Dream 58
CHAPTER 9: Return 69
CHAPTER 10: The Markings of a Ballerina 78
CHAPTER 11: Protégé 87
CHAPTER 12: The Historic Stage 98
CHAPTER 13: Soup 105
CHAPTER 14: Department of Public Services 116
CHAPTER 15: Secret Wedding 124
CHAPTER 16: Behind the Red Velvet Curtain 132
CHAPTER 17: *The Nutcracker* 141
CHAPTER 18: Acid Attack 149
CHAPTER 19: Dead End 154
CHAPTER 20: Trial 162
CHAPTER 21: Saltwater 170
CHAPTER 22: Diplomacy 182

CHAPTER 23: Santa Barbara 188

CHAPTER 24: A New Russia 196

CHAPTER 25: Murder on a Moscow Bridge 206

CHAPTER 26: Stage Fright. 211

CHAPTER 27: Art and Politics 216

CHAPTER 28: Waiting 222

CHAPTER 29: Home 227

CHAPTER 30: Culture Shock 233

CHAPTER 31: Ranching 242

CHAPTER 32: Goodbye 250

CHAPTER 33: Astrakhan 255

CHAPTER 34: American Wedding 264

CHAPTER 35: Flee 272

Epilogue 280

Notes 285

Acknowledgments 291

About the Authors 295

Author's Note

Behind the Red Velvet Curtain is a memoir by Joy Womack as told to Elizabeth Shockman via dozens of interviews and collaborative work completed between 2012 and 2024. Interviews generously given by Joy's friends, family, colleagues, and teachers were used to reconstruct timelines, events, and dialogue. Also used were diaries, social media posts, vlogs, photographs, videos, and news articles.

Everything is true, as remembered by Joy, but in some cases the names and identifying details of individuals have been changed to protect their privacy. There were also slight changes to timelines to allow for narrative continuity.

The international system for transliteration of text from the Cyrillic to Latin alphabet has been utilized in cases where Russian words are used.

Please note that this story contains reference to and description of self-harm and child abuse.

PROLOGUE

It wasn't excitement that filled my chest and pounded against my rib cage as I waited backstage. It was fear.

We were late into the dark of a January night. Orchestra music filled the air. Stage lights and shadows moved across our faces, purple and iridescent like glimmers across the weedy terrain at the bottom of the ocean.

My teacher and classmates hovered over me as I sat on the floor in a frothy pile of tulle. They watched as the school nurse bent and took my heel in her hand. She was careful, but it hurt—a pain that shot up my leg to the base of my spine.

I ground my teeth to keep from crying. My foot was battered and raw: blisters on the heel, toenails that had bruised and blackened from pools of blood under the skin. But that wasn't the problem. The injury was something invisible to us: an undiagnosed throbbing that radiated from deep within the metatarsals. It hurt to flex my foot. Pointing had become impossible.

The nurse shook a can of Biofreeze and sprayed it in a blast of cold onto my skin.

I felt a flutter of hope as if from underwater. All my focus was on the foot, lying there, suddenly numb, like it belonged to someone else.

Maybe the Biofreeze worked. Maybe I'll be able to do this.

Dancers crowded the edge of the curtain beside us. They arched their necks, kicked their legs in the air, jumping and bending to keep the blood flowing through their muscles before they took their turn, leaping into the light. The orchestra thrummed in my chest like a countdown.

My teacher, Arkhipova, stood with her arms crossed, pearls around her neck, her mouth set in a flat line over nicotine-stained teeth.

I could barely hear her words over the swell of strings and brass.

"Do this performance and then you'll rest," she said, her eyes on my foot, her shoulders rounded into a slump.

We had been rehearsing this piece for weeks.

"No one else knows these steps," she reminded me. "All the important people in Moscow are here. We have to do this."

She nodded at the scuffed slippers beside me.

She was a sort of queen at our school. You could see it in the way she moved: an inheritance of generations of music, choreography and sweat, absorbed into the memory of muscle and sinew. It was visible in the way she lifted her chin, raised her brows beneath synthetic blonde bangs.

Somehow, she had managed to convince the organizers of this gala to grant me a spot on the playbill tonight. I had seen my name there in Cyrillic: Джой Уомак. I was fifteen years old, the only first-year student, the only American who'd been allowed the privilege of performing. I wanted to prove to her I could do this. I wanted to be the type of dancer who belonged here.

I pulled the satin pointe shoe carefully over my toes, knotted the pink ribbon over the bloated skin of my ankle.

So far, so good.

The nurse bent to tuck her arms beneath my shoulders and heaved me upright. A knife of pain sliced through muscle and nerve. It streaked up my body, choked the windpipe in my throat, blurred my vision.

Crap-crap-crap-crap-crap-crap-crap.

I can't do this.

My partner came up beside me, tights on his legs, sequins on the puffed fabric of his sleeves. He took my arm, his eyebrows knit together.

"Ready?" he asked.

I ground my teeth together as if the muscles in my jaw could somehow keep me standing.

What happens to an injured foot when you perform on it? Does it break? Can my leg and core muscles keep me upright? Will my slipper be enough to keep my bone from splitting? Can satin and cardboard hold in the shards if they splinter?

I heard my partner whisper-singing a cheery-toned Soviet children's song in my ear as we moved to the golden line separating the wings from the stage.

He's trying to cheer me up. The thought came as if from far away. I didn't know what to do with it. I dug my nails into his palm and took a hobbling step forward. The tiny movements of my ankle and knee were excruciating. I could feel tears smarting at the edges of my eyes, pricking my nose.

My partner bobbed his head. His humming sounded hopeful and a little desperate.

Pain pulsed in my ears.

It's just five minutes. You just have to make it through five minutes.

The audience roared with applause as the dancers before us bounded off the stage into the dark folds of velvet curtain beside us. They glistened with sweat, muscles quivering, chests heaving.

Then there was silence. I stood, my injured foot hovering off the ground, my heart pounding in my chest.

What would have happened if I'd said no that night? If I'd asked them to find someone else, or refused to rise from the floor? If I'd screamed and sobbed when the slipper touched the skin of my foot, or if I'd clung to my teacher's legs, begged her to let me stay behind the curtain? Would they have listened? Would they have told me to leave Moscow? Sent me back to America? Would everything be different now?

But refusing to dance didn't even occur to me. I wanted to be there, was desperate to perform on the glowing stage in front of me. And this was what I'd always known ballet to be: muscle, blood, and agony, dressed in a frilly skirt, set to music, lit by a tangled web of cords and canister lamps.

CHAPTER 1

Womacks Win

When I was two years old, nearly three, my father brought me to the hospital. I can remember hurrying to keep up with his long legs until we stepped into a room under the bright and antiseptic glare of fluorescent lights. My mother waited for me there, propped in a bed, an ill-fitting pastel gown draped over her shoulders. Her dark hair was long then, pulled back behind a headband. Her smile was wide and weary. It sparkled across her face.

"Come and see, Joy," she whispered.

I can remember moving to her side in a quiet way, the string of a round, helium-inflated balloon wrapped around my hand. I was wide-eyed, like a tiny deer, when she leaned over and placed a small, warm bundle in my arms.

"Your new baby brother," she said.

The bundle was heavy and soft against my chest. I looked down and saw a scrunched-up, pink face. I smelled the clean, fuzzy wisps on the top of his head.

I held in my toddler arms Baby Womack number five. In Mom's arms was his twin, Baby Womack number six. Eventually there would be nine of us.

This is the very first thing I can remember.

The base of my reality, from the beginning of memory, is being part of a crowd. I was a Womack, set into an ever-expanding tectonic slab of family. We were numerous and indistinguishable. We were as solid as the earth, as far-reaching as a continent.

We called ourselves the Children of Wo, and we moved in a swarm through our Santa Monica neighborhood. Where we lived, the sun shone on tiled roofs and spiked palm trees and bristling green carpets of grass. Our neighbors were doctors and business owners and movie stars. They drove expensive cars, installed pools in their backyards that glistened and gurgled. They knew celebrities, invited Robert De Niro to fundraiser parties, shared classrooms with Audrey Hepburn's granddaughter. Some of our neighbors actually were celebrities, like Elijah Wood, who parked two MINI Coopers in his driveway and came to our house for dinner once when we invited him.

But we Womacks were different. Our living room overflowed with sleeping bags, shoes, bike helmets, and extra kids always either starting a sleepover or waiting to get picked up from one. The counters in our kitchen brimmed with dirty plates, water bottles, and plastic containers of Shaklee vitamins. We needed an oversized van just to make it from one destination to the next.

Even the way we shopped for groceries felt like an *SNL* skit about a weird and embarrassing family. We went to Costco on Tuesdays and Thursdays, and when we returned, Dad backed the car from the street right onto the lawn. He would crank the gears into park directly in front of the door. Then we spilled en masse from sliding doors, like an endless line of ducklings, scurrying to the front door of our home, our arms laden with giant boxes of cereal and warehouse bundles of toilet paper.

Our backyard was filled with forts we made from palm leaves, and our street was overrun with a patrol of half-sized Womacks, racing barefoot on scooters. We erected Playmobil cities in our rooms and waited on the stairs for spankings when we got in trouble. A dilapidated camper rose like a blister from our driveway to house visiting guests. We wore matching uniforms to school and spent all of our spare time in church. We were the actual Beverly Hills Hillbillies.

My parents believed in miracles. It was something they spoke about casually in conversations with other adults or mentioned out their rolled-down window, while backing the van onto the street. It was something they pleaded for aloud in prayers at the kitchen table, or in gathered chairs at church, their eyes closed, their heads bowed.

Their faith was like a tide. For my mother, it was low and placid before I arrived. But by my childhood, it had swollen and grown and flooded our daily lives.

Mom spoke in terms of divine intervention, and unseen spiritual realities. When she looked back at her marriage, at the unlikely existence of our family, filled to overflowing with eleven people, it was as a divine blessing, a supernatural grace, gifted from heaven.

My parents had met later in life, after they'd both divorced other people. Dad, a Baptist from Texas, wore a white suit and cowboy boots to their first date. Mom thought he looked like John Travolta from *Saturday Night Fever*. She was Jewish, a Democrat from New York, with a degree from Harvard Medical School. And she wanted nothing to do with him. He was a Christian hick from the South, whose niece was a country music singer. She'd grown up on the Upper East Side with a mother who was a famous attorney and kept a Picasso hanging on the wall in her living room. They didn't like the same music or the same cars. They argued about politics and music and religion in the letters they sent back and forth across the country to each other. It didn't make sense that they would end up together. But a friend convinced them to meet, then they met again, then they dated, and eventually they got married.

The plan, they'd told us, was to have one or maybe two babies. But the first time my mother got pregnant, it was with triplets—three boys.

"And after that, our math was off," Mom used to laugh—a joke she told when she explained our family to other grown-ups.

But after the triplets, I was born—another miracle, another unexpected gift from God.

I was supposed to have been a triplet myself. But at twenty-one weeks of gestation, as Mom tells it, her belly flattened, and the amniotic fluid drained from her womb. She rushed to the hospital, where doctors told her two of the triplets that had been growing inside her had died. The third, they said, would soon miscarry.

"Better to terminate the pregnancy now," they advised.

But this, as Mom tells it, is where the miracle happened.

A pastor from Texas visited her in her hospital room, where she was draped in a mesh of IV cords and monitors recording the tiny beats of my embryonic heart. This was a pastor whose seminary in Dallas had taught him that the gifts of healing, of the Holy Spirit, were a thing of the past. So it was surprising to everyone involved when he told my mother that he'd heard the audible voice of God.

"God spoke to me while I was praying for you," the pastor said. "He told me to pray for your baby's healing."

At first, my parents were skeptical. They didn't think God spoke out loud or that he performed miracles. But then the pastor put his hand on the deflated balloon of my mother's lower torso and recited words from the gospel: "Ask and you will receive," the pastor prayed, "and your joy will be complete."

Instantly, Mom's belly swelled, and the monitor beside her quickened its pace of staccato beats—the audible sound of divine intervention: an accelerated in-utero heart rate.

I was born four months later: underweight, fingers extended, unable to swallow.

They named me Joy.

For Dad, faith was less like a tide than an ocean that had always been there, shaping his life from Sunday school as a kid in Texas, to regular weekend church services in Southern California.

Dad was more focused on things you could see, things that made other people notice you. He too thought of our family as a blessing from God. But he also expected us to produce our own miracles.

"There are winners in life, and there are losers," Dad told us. "Womacks win."

These are words he said as he sat at the dinner table eating tacos, when he barreled through Santa Monica in our van, when he paced the turf sidelines at our sports tournaments, or sat on the bleachers in his baseball hat with a kid in his lap, staring down the forty-yard line.

"Second place," he told us, "is just another way of saying you're the first loser."

I believed him, and there was nothing I wanted more than to be gifted and talented and extraordinary. Dad was tall and tan and strode through the world like he owned it. I wanted to be like him, and I wanted to make him proud of me. All of us did. My three older brothers raced bikes in competitions. They pedaled up mountainsides, brought home medals, and scored touchdowns on the football field. My little sister filled her report cards with As and A+s. My little brother learned to speak Chinese.

For me, it was anything and everything I could get my hands on. I wanted to be the best at memorizing Bible verses, at designing take-home Valentines for my classmates, at dressing in a way that made the girls at school want to copy me.

Because my older brothers were on a bike team and trained every week with Dad, I wanted to do the same. I begged to be allowed to join them until Dad relented and bought me a helmet and a zip-up cycling jersey.

We trained early in the mornings, launching out of our driveway and skimming along cliff roads in a horde of wheel spokes and sweat, tasting ocean in the air. I pedaled furiously to keep up with the boys, my hair flying out from under my helmet in curly brown tangles behind me. I worked my legs into a hot liquid to go faster and faster. My brothers and their friends were taller, older, swifter. Their legs were longer, their muscles more developed.

"Too bad you won't be able to keep up," they told me.

In principle, it should have been impossible to beat them. But I was obsessed with proving myself, and this obsession erased the burn in my lungs and my thighs. I spun like mad to overtake, to leave them in the dusty spray from my tires. I ate the challenge of winning like biting into the flesh of a watermelon. And at the end of our rides, if I managed to squeak out in front of the entire swarm of boys, I would peel the sweaty helmet off my forehead, and I would relish that particular sheepish, generous, and condescending look on their faces. Then I would turn to my dad and see something glowing on his face: a pride that was visible in the glint of his eyes, the widening of his cheeks.

"That's my girl!" he would say.

I lived for these moments. And, eventually, I didn't know how to live without them.

Winning, I found, felt like being loved.

If Dad was about the headlines, the medals, and the shiny glories of first place, Mom was more exacting. Mom was about excellence.

She was small and beautiful and intense with hair that fell in waves down her back and spectacled eyes that found imperfections in our chores and seemed to see through walls to decipher trouble we'd created, trouble we were planning to create. She gave us verses from Psalms and Proverbs to memorize: instructions to obey parents, to "think of Jesus, others, and yourself in that exact order." She kept a "wisdom worker" paddle to spank us when we were naughty or rebellious. She consulted Christian parenting books for advice on infant feeding schedules, child discipline, and how to raise kids in a way approved by God.

Mom loved an essay. When we misbehaved, she sat us down with a sheet of paper and a pencil to copy out lists of the house rules. We wrote out letters of apology, examined our hearts to root out the sin, explained the errors of our ways using verses from the Bible, and wrote out plans to correct our behavior.

"Obedience is right away, all the way, and with a happy heart," she taught us to say, with smiles on our faces.

With Mom, I learned it was easiest and best to submit, to comply, to make the emotions on my face and the actions of my body match the instructions of those who were in charge.

Mom took us to school at Lighthouse Christian Academy, which was in the same white-walled building as our church—an evangelical Pentecostal foursquare congregation.

We sat in our classes wearing green and blue plaid uniforms. We learned about multiplication, cell division, phonics, the creation of the entire physical universe six thousand years ago in only six earthly days and how we might apply the teachings of Jesus in a practical way.

Sometimes Mom, with her Harvard medical training, was concerned about the gaps in Lighthouse's science curriculum. But this was a school that was all about community, all about relying on parents, especially mothers, to fill in gaps. So she sometimes volunteered to teach the occasional science class at our school. She stood at the front of the room in a long dress and told us about cell biology, anatomy, physiology.

At home, she insisted on reviewing the papers I wrote before I turned them in. After taking a look at one of my science papers once, she ripped it apart.

"There's more fluff than content in here," she said, tearing the paper into pieces. "You have to write it again."

"My teacher says it's fine!" I argued, watching my hard work disappear into shreds. "It has everything the assignment asked for. It's fine."

"Just because it's fine, doesn't mean it's good," Mom said.

I rewrote the entire thing.

Church was a place we attended every day of the week. On Sundays, we sat in rows in a sanctuary with a steepled roof, and a sign over the door that read "Jesus is Lord." We listened to sermons from our pastor, who told us that the Bible was clear: God's word, gifted to humanity. He told us that truth was black and white with no gray in it. But people were beasts, sinners, worms led astray by Satan. If we wanted to avoid hell, this pastor told us, we had to confess our sins and ask Jesus to save us and take the punishment from God that we deserved. This was what made us acceptable, we learned: Jesus bleeding enough to make God, who was righteously angry at us, so distracted that he could ignore how gross we were.

I wanted to be saved, to be excellent, to be certain. I was committed. So I listened to this preaching on Sundays, and many times, as the worship team sang songs about mountains bowing, I would lower my head and repeat what I heard: *Save me, God. Help me not to sin. Help me be respectful. Help me do what's right.*

When I was seven, my parents dressed me in white robes, and I walked to the front of the church, where I stood on seafoam-green carpet and spoke into a microphone to tell everyone how much I loved Jesus, how much I wanted him to be my savior. The people sitting in rows at church listened to me read this statement I'd prepared with smiles on their faces, like I was a shining example of everything they were doing well.

When I put the microphone down, I stepped with my pastor into a tank of water and allowed my head to be pushed fully under, totally immersed. My hair, my clothes, the pale folds of my robe went from dry to soaked, and I stopped breathing as the hand of our pastor held my head submerged.

This was what it took to acquire safety and perfection in the family and church in which I was raised: a symbolic drowning, a death, a confession of guilt, a publicly staged show.

CHAPTER 2

Flying

I was three years old when I went to my first ballet lesson. The studio was a hushed place where sunlight spilled in generous portions across white walls, the air smelled of lemon cleaner, and music played, delicate as tinsel, in the background. I can remember pushing my heels together on the burnished wood floor of this room so that the soft pink leather of my shoes touched. I bent my knees and raised my hands in the still, open air. I made shapes, like wind chimes and nodding blooms of bougainvillea, with my body.

When Mom dropped me off for lessons, it was like pressing a mute button: the van door slammed shut over the noise of my siblings, and I stepped away from everyone else into a sublime and separate world.

Like church, the world of ballet was one in which I could make visible and measurable progress toward an ideal of perfection. It was a place where achievement was measured by obedience, where music inspired conformity, and where I could see, by comparison with others in the mirror, if I was doing things right.

But it wasn't all slowness and silence. The moments I liked best were ones in which dancing felt full and alive. This usually came after we bent and dipped and raised and lowered backward and forward like pendulums in a row at the barre for minutes or hours or days. We worked our muscles into a warm and sweaty Play-Doh, and then our teacher rewarded us with choose-your-own "freestyle dance." I can remember being very young and, at her instruction, pushing off from the floor to leap, legs outstretched, from one corner of the mirrored room to another.

Dancing at those moments felt like joy and flying, like learning the words to a song that I played with my whole body. These were the times I loved—when music filled my muscles and pushed me forward, spinning me like a top across the room.

There were other benefits to dance. When I memorized all the rules, when I progressed, when I bent my body into the shapes described to me by my teachers, I got called to the center of the dance floor to demonstrate correct movements to the rest of my classmates. Eventually, I got called to go on stage. I wore a costume with sequins and tulle, put glitter and rouge on my face, drew lines around the lids of my eyes. I performed in front of hundreds of people who sat still to watch me, then clapped in unison and appreciation when I finished.

Not everyone in my life approved of dance.

There were some people at Lighthouse Church who worried it might lead to bad things. Mrs. Gavin, who went to our church and taught at our school and wore long skirts with the alphabet printed on them, was one of these people.

"This mania for ballet is immoral," Mrs. Gavin told my parents. "It's sinning. Joy is making an idol out of dancing."

Part of me worried she was right. I spent a lot of my time agonizing over whether or not I was good, whether or not whatever I was doing was correct, whether or not God approved of me.

But ballet was its own kind of perfection. It took concentration to learn new dance steps. And when I focused my mind and my muscles, I found I could make my body do miraculous things. I could embody notes of music, and stories. I could suspend myself in the air, capture a movement that raised eyebrows, fill the chests of people watching with a sort of delight.

When I applied myself, when I sweated and worked, ballet paid off. It could command the full attention and praise of my instructors and, sometimes, of my parents. Mom once made me a cake with elaborately decorated nutcrackers on top. Another time she curled my hair into spirals before a performance. And Dad encouraged me, bragged about me to our friends and family, told me I was a star. Together they attended my performances, clapped for me from the auditorium, and told me, after it was over, how well I had done, how proud they were of me.

Surely, I told myself, excellence, beauty, perfection, and obedience were their own form of worship.

There was a comfort in childhood of knowing things for certain. My dad was good, I knew, possibly a genius. So were our pastors and Olympic athletes and professional bike racers and anyone who, like my parents, saw through the lies of things that were mainstream and government-controlled. There were heroes we could point to as examples, like Peyton Manning, whom Dad loved to talk about: a quarterback who took the world by storm, who surprised everyone with his greatness.

There was my cousin, Lee Ann Womack, a country singer, who, by the sheer force and magnetism of her talent, had made an outsized name for herself. We heard her songs on the radio, impressed adults by telling them she was our relative.

And then there was my grandmother, a pioneering civil rights law-yer, a woman ahead of her time who won cases for interned Japanese Americans, and a teenager denied entry to a school because she was a girl. She inspired journalists to write her name into headlines and told judges how to read laws.

At church, there were other heroes: Jesus, of course, the King of kings who walked on water and insisted it was possible to move moun-tains by faith alone. But there was also David, who, when he was just a boy, slayed a terrible giant with a tiny pebble he picked up from the ground. Or Paul, who said he could do all things through Christ who gave him strength. Or Moses, who gave God glory by doing impressive and impossible things like parting the Red Sea, turning rivers into blood.

It was obvious to me what greatness looked like, where it came from, and how it should be used. There was no question I was supposed to aspire to outsized and remarkable things. It was something I was always aware of, something I felt urgently and carried with me at all times, like my last name.

We Womacks were meant for greatness, but we were supposed to do it right. We were supposed to somehow do it in God's power, and we were supposed to praise God when we did it. Like the football players who pointed to God in heaven when they scored touchdowns. Like Peyton Manning, who told people Jesus was his number one, who used his fame to raise money for people whose homes were flooded during Hurricane Katrina.

It was reassuring to know all of this so clearly about the world, to know that what our parents told us, what our pastor told us, was right and true. To know, undoubtedly, who was on the right side and who wasn't.

This certainty about life lasted until I was twelve. That was the year everything changed.

It happened all at once when my parents returned from a trip to Dad's family in Austin, Texas.

"We can't stay in Santa Monica anymore," Mom told me. "This church, this place isn't good for us. We're moving to Texas."

My parents had been wrestling with Lighthouse for years. Mom didn't like the ways the textbooks and classes distorted history and twisted science. She felt strangled by the heavy layers of guilt and fear the church asked her to carry. We had all felt this in one way or another—a constant, low-level pulse that if there was a problem, it was our fault. And there were other things that we didn't have words for, that we didn't talk about—things that happened at the church that made us feel frightened and hurt but that seemed impossible to describe as bad in a place that claimed to be safe and to have inherited a mantle of divine truth.

"Pastor Randy doesn't always tell the truth," Mom had started to tell us.

By the time my parents returned from Texas, where worried family members had confronted them, their concerns were filled with conviction.

"Lighthouse Church is a cult," they said.

The way their words landed in our lives was like an earthquake that rattled what I knew and shattered, like glass windowpanes, the things I'd always taken for granted.

Our pastor smiled and carried on his shoulders an unassailable authority. His family's house was a place where we'd grown up, their back door as familiar as the door in our yard, their refrigerator full of food we snacked on as our own. The rooms in their home were always clean—much cleaner than ours. And their family was one we'd been taught to mimic.

Pastor Randy had always stood at the front of our church. He'd told us how to be safe from punishment and sin, how to make ourselves into people God approved of. He was an authority whom our parents and the Bible itself had taught us to respect. He'd spoken for God.

To think otherwise felt like a seismic crack in the grass- and asphalt-covered ground beneath my feet But my parents had had enough. They stopped attending the daily services at Lighthouse Church. They unenrolled us from classes and got rid of our blue and green school uniforms. They packed our toys and plates and books and bike helmets into cardboard boxes. They loaded our furniture into a moving truck. They bought a house in Austin, Texas.

"You'll like it in Texas," Mom said. "You'll make new friends."

"Our new house is huge," Dad said. "There's a basketball court inside and a pool in the backyard."

"But I don't want to go," I said, thinking about my friends Bethany, Hannah, and Sally, who had laid friendship rocks at the beach with me every summer; thinking about Westside Ballet School and the *Nutcracker* role I'd been promised.

I cried for the entire twenty-one-hour drive from the Pacific Ocean to central Texas.

My family left our church as far behind us as we could. But there were some things I took with me from Lighthouse: a persistent sense of unease; a frantic searching of my own heart for inadequacy; an abiding, low-level anxiety that made it difficult to ask questions.

I learned a way of thinking at Lighthouse that felt like fitting fastened wheels into an iron rail. My brain got soldered to a steel groove of right and wrong, black and white, in and out—a groove along which it felt appropriate to just chug along. Critical thinking skills were not necessary to keep moving on this sort of track. Neither was compassion or questioning. Questioning, in fact, was something that could get you in trouble. It was wrong and an affront. Good kids, faithful kids, patriotic kids, kids who were going somewhere didn't ask questions.

This was a rail that helped me fit in at all sorts of ballet companies, as it turned out. It helped me fit in in Russia.

CHAPTER 3

Away

I hated Texas.

I didn't know anyone at the school my parents wanted me to attend. Our new church was ridiculous: stadium-sized, packed with strangers, vibrating with a state-of-the-art sound system. Lights flashed from its ceilings, its conference rooms were filled with multiple youth groups, and Jolly Ranchers in crinkling wrappers were handed out just for attending.

"It's corporate Jesus," my family joked.

Our new house was big, yes. But I didn't want an indoor basketball court. I wanted to walk out the door and down the street to visit friends. I wanted to bike to the ocean. I wanted to attend daily dance classes with teachers who liked me and believed I had a Balanchine-style, New York City Ballet future in front of me.

But there was none of that in Austin. There were just streets filled with McMansions and mega churches, afternoons filled with my brothers' football practice sessions, and an over-large house crawling with siblings I couldn't get away from.

For a while after we moved, I tried teaching myself to dance via YouTube. I set up a computer in the kitchen and practiced pliés with bent knees, holding on to the backs of chairs or the rims of countertops. I arabesqued on one foot in the dining room, and legged around our shiny new basketball court floors in pointe shoes like a sulky preteen heron.

I made myself difficult to my parents, refused to go to public school classes, and rushed through my homework so I could spend more time doing crunches and battements and pirouettes. I tried to make myself into a person from the stories I'd heard about training Olympians and elite athletes who started young and never stopped pursuing their dreams.

Mom was the one who eventually found me a dance studio—the Austin School of Classical Ballet. It was an unassuming workshop that looked like a converted warehouse with the smell of motor oil from a nearby mechanic's shop perfuming the air.

But Jennifer Felkner, who ran the place, had been trained by Russians. She had absorbed the Vaganova pedagogy into her muscles and bones.

"If you want a career in American ballet, you should stick with Balanchine," she said. "But if you want to dance anywhere in the world, you should learn the Vaganova style."

There was no question in my mind. Dancing internationally sounded exciting. I asked her to teach me everything she knew.

She spent time watching me: the way my femur angled into my pelvis, the way my ankle columned over my foot, the way my arms met in crescents in front of my torso.

"Your leg should extend in a straight line," she would suggest, moving my limb until it looked more Galina Ulanova than Suzanne Farrell.

She was like a road crew, meticulously filling in the potholes left in my approach by nearly a decade of Balanchine training.

"If you build a foundation of solid Vaganova technique," she would say, "you can be any kind of dancer you want to be."

I was, at times, impatient to move ahead to fancy circus-trick dance moves. But Jennifer encouraged me. She spoke to me about clocks: arms and legs extending from the torso in lines, like shining gears set with delicate instruments into a device that ran with flawlessness and precision. And she told me with reverence about all the Russian greats—dancers from the Mariinsky or Bolshoi: Mikhail Baryshnikov, Rudolph Nureyev, Natalia Makarova, Maya Plisetskaya, Natalia Osipova. After listening to her in class, I'd go home and look them up on YouTube.

This was when I really got to know the Russians: late at night in Austin, bathed in a blue glow from my screen, mesmerized by grainy black-and-white footage of Russian dancers from the 1950s and 1960s. They were unlike anything I'd ever seen before. They wheeled out from behind dark curtains and attacked the stage with what might as well have been cartwheels or full-on flying. They were like ghosts or gravity-defying ninjas from *Crouching Tiger, Hidden Dragon*. I didn't even have words for the things they could do.

I already loved ballet, but discovering these Russian dancers turned me into a heart-and-soul disciple.

"This is who I want to be," I whispered over those late-night YouTube sessions. "This is what I want to do."

Jennifer Felkner believed I could take my dancing to the next level. I'm not sure what she saw in me—an obsession, perhaps, or maybe just a flair for the dramatic.

But she told me about the Kirov Academy of Ballet, a school in Washington, D.C., filled with teachers committed to the Vaganova technique. And then she helped convince my parents to let me go there to study.

I myself didn't need any convincing. I wanted to go. Living on the other side of the country, away from my family, in dorm rooms with a bunch of other prepubescent dancers didn't sound scary. It made me feel special—the one kid in my family brave enough to strike out alone, make my way in the world. It felt the same way I remembered feeling in Santa Monica when my parents let me skip the last hour of Lighthouse classes to go to ballet lessons.

My parents had always praised us for intensity, commitment, excellence. Moving to a boarding school for dance was the most intense thing I could imagine.

I was thirteen when I left Austin to join a preprofessional ballet school in Washington, D.C.

I never lived at home with my family again.

The Kirov was a gated campus in north Washington, D.C., filled with yellow-brick and white-columned buildings, rehearsal studios, cinder-block dormitories, and a three-hundred-seat theater. Getting accepted to the school and then moving there felt more or less like gaining entrance to the ballet equivalent of Hogwarts. It made me feel chosen, promising, on my way to a bright and impressive future.

Some of the teachers at Kirov were Russian. They spoke in harsh accents, refused to pronounce *th* or *w* sounds, and were thoroughly unimpressed by half-hearted efforts at center work and sloppy port de bras.

I loved them.

They seemed funny and intimidating and surrounded by a halo of intrigue, like the distant C-list celebrity cousins of some sort of monarchy. They had touched the glow of Russian art and ballet. Being instructed by them in dance felt like having Dostoyevsky's distantly related descendant give you tips on how to write a novel.

I respected the weight and aura of old-world grandeur I was sure my Russian instructors carried. I respected their strictness and solemnity, which I was certain was somehow the key to balletic and artistic perfection. I wanted to impress them with my dedication to dance, my willingness to suffer muscle aches for art. I wanted them to see that I knew how much majesty dancers like Baryshnikov and Plisetskaya lent to the world.

I wanted to absorb whatever magnificence I could by association to all things Russian. But it had never occurred to me to actually travel there.

In my second year at Kirov, I went to New York to visit my grandmother and attend a ballet workshop. It was there that I met someone named Keenan Kampa—a beautiful and talented American teenager with blonde hair, perfect feet, high cheekbones, and an even higher grand battement. She told me she had been invited to join the Vaganova Academy in St. Petersburg and would be moving to Russia soon to attend.

Then I heard about other students from England who'd moved to Moscow to apprentice themselves at the Bolshoi Ballet Academy. They were studying in classrooms full of Russians, learning from Bolshoi instructors and living in Moscow dorm rooms. News outlets had filmed documentaries about them that I watched on YouTube.

These students were just a few years older than I was. And the thought occurred to me—if they could join an elite Russian ballet academy, why not me? Why not ask if I could study at the Bolshoi itself?

At the workshop, an actual teacher from the Bolshoi had traveled across the Atlantic to make an appearance. When I worked up the courage to ask her if she thought I could apply, she turned her head to look at me, and a smile escaped her red-lipsticked mouth.

"Of course," she said. "Send them an audition video."

I was thrilled. In some ways, it was a sort of escapism. My classes at Kirov weren't going as well as I'd hoped. There were several girls in my year who were better than I was. They were chosen for leading roles and special attention from our teachers. It made me feel insecure, worried that I wasn't doing enough, wasn't reaching high enough.

In other ways, it was desperation. I had not been accepted at the schools to which I'd sent applications. The ones that did want me were places I couldn't afford.

But Womacks didn't flounder. They didn't wait for second place. Womacks went big or they went home.

So I filmed an audition reel of me in a leotard going through barre and center work. I made sure to put a Kitri jump in there—throwing my arms up, and kicking my leg so far back it nearly hit my head. I did my very best Natalia Osipova impression. I wanted to show that I knew the Bolshoi's style and that I had the potential to be big enough to embody it. Then I sent the DVD off to Moscow, together with a letter, pleading with the Bolshoi Academy to let me in.

I hardly dared hope that anything would come of it. Sometimes, after a particularly rough day of dance conditioning at Kirov, I'd joke-complain to the other girls in my class, "Well, maybe I'll be in Moscow next year."

The idea of going to Russia felt like a fantasy. It was something to talk about. But it wasn't like I actually thought I'd be accepted.

Then, early on a spring morning, I got my answer.

I was sitting on the floor in my dorm room at the Kirov, drying my hair—the sort of mundane and unassuming spot in which life-changing news always makes itself known. A notification blinked onto my Blackberry. The sender's name was Russian: a jumble of unpronounce-able consonants. My stomach lurched.

This is it, I realized. I took a deep breath, steeled myself, clicked it open.

"Congratulations!" the email began. "I am pleased to inform you that you have been accepted to the Moscow State Academy of Choreography."

I just sat there, numb, unbelieving. The Moscow State Academy of Choreography. This was the Bolshoi's school, the school founded by Catherine the Great. The school that fed dancers into Russia's premier theater.

I scrolled to my parents' home number and pressed the call button.

"Mom!" I screamed into the receiver. "I got in, Mom!" They accepted me at the Bolshoi!"

Her response was a lot less enthusiastic than I'd hoped for. "Good for you, Joy," she said. "We'll talk about it."

At first, she asked a lot of questions. She wanted to know about safety, logistics, health insurance. My dad had fewer questions and much more excitement. He made jokes about needing to hire Liam Neeson to protect his eldest daughter like the blockbuster CIA kidnapping thriller *Taken*. But he was proud of the acceptance letter I'd received from Moscow. We all were. The Bolshoi, after all, was a school that didn't just teach people to dance—it turned out dancers of such caliber that the force of their talent was a sort of vortex. These were artists who bent not only the shape of international ballet, but the shape of international geopolitics.

I'm not sure why I was accepted. Was there something extraordinary in the way I moved? Did I happen to catch a member of the Bolshoi's staff on a good year, a year they were looking to recruit foreigners to bring in money for renovation work? Or was it just that I'd had the audacity to ask, the ridiculous temerity to even joke-imagine this as a possibility?

I didn't spend much time thinking about why I'd been invited, or what it would mean to move by myself to another country, or even whether or not it was a good idea to go. There were no other schools I'd been accepted to that I could afford. Russia was my only option. Besides, it was the Bolshoi. It was the best. It was unheard of. Of course I was going.

CHAPTER 4

Ballet Factory

I left for Russia on the last weekend of August 2009.

Dad came up to New York, where I was staying after a summer intensive run by Bolshoi teachers, to help me pack. He wanted to be there for the excitement, to be the one to launch me into my future. Mom couldn't make it—someone had to stay in Texas and watch all the rest of the Womack kids. But she sent me bags filled with beautiful new tights and leotards—dance gear more expensive than I'd ever had before, or would ever have again.

I stuffed everything into two lumpy black duffel bags, then climbed on top to knee them closed.

Dad took a picture of me perched on top, piles of clothes spilling out from under the zippered nylon lid, a huge smile on my face. It was a moment of abundance and possibility and recklessness. I posted it on Facebook.

"Moscow bound," I wrote in the caption. "Help!"

I had no idea what I was getting into. What fifteen-year-old ever knows anything about what their decisions mean, what future disasters they're signing themselves up for? I was too busy thinking about how this felt like the beginning of a fairy tale.

"You trying to fit seventy pounds into a fifty-pound suitcase here, Joy?" Dad kept joking. It was a line he'd been repeating all weekend. He said it again when we stood under the vaulted dome of the JFK departures terminal, watching the scale at the check-in desk. He looked at the gate agent then, like he expected to find her laughing along.

This was a rare moment. I had Dad all to myself—no other kids in his lap, no one else he was keeping an eye on during a football play. He was fully and completely intent on me, his mouth in a permanent smile, the remaining white hair on his head jetted like stratus clouds over his ears. I felt like an adult when he looked at me, like I was one of his business partners.

"Joy, this is a huge opportunity," he told me, striding through the terminal, towering over me, over most of the people there. "You need to go for this, make the best of it. You're brave, you're strong. If you can do this, it will make you."

This was the biggest thing I'd ever done. And Dad was the most outrageous dreamer I knew. But this was beyond anything even he had ever schemed up. I wanted to hit some sort of pause button on the moment, on the way his face shone down at me.

"I can remember when you were born," he said as we stood at the head of the security line, and he leaned in close, almost whispering. "I held you in the palm of my hand. I watched you grow up, fall down."

I heard his voice crack. I'd never heard Dad's voice crack.

"If you need to come home at any time, come home," he said. "But if you can do this, then do it. And do it to the best of your abilities."

He gave me a tight hug, then sent me off to the security line. When I turned around for a last wave, I saw tears rolling down his sunburnt cheeks.

I'd been fine up until then, but seeing his wet face, hearing his voice break, scared me. I realized what a huge decision I'd made, how far away I was about to go, how long it would be until I'd see him again.

Until I'd walked through that metal detector, it had felt like I was testing everyone, trying out the possibility of this move to Russia. At the end of the TSA line, watching my dad try to smile at me through his tears, I suddenly felt alone and frightened.

This is it, I thought.

I was on the other side of whatever decision I'd made. Now I had to deal with whatever it was I'd gotten myself into.

Nine hours later, I was on the other side of the ocean, walking up the jet bridge from an airlocked plane cabin to the hulking, gray Sheremetyevo terminal in northern Moscow. My purse was slung over my shoulder, and a queasy excitement was pitted deep in my belly.

But I was not ready to launch myself into an elite Russian dance school. This was something I felt with each painful step I took up the jet bridge.

My foot was injured with the kind of wound that made itself known in sharp throbs corkscrewing the inside of my right foot like a thorn. My entire leg, from my toes to just below my knees was gripped in a silver brace: foam padding, rigid plastic, tight Velcro, and beneath it, an aching heel. As I limped across the tiled floor of the terminal, my foot thumped and dragged.

I looked like some sort of extra from a *Pirates of the Caribbean* set.

This was an inconvenient truth I'd tried to ignore for weeks as I worked myself into shape and packed my bags. Not only was I attempting the impossibility of studying at a world-renowned ballet academy in Russia, but I was doing so with an injured foot.

In the passport control booth, a dead-eyed border guard took my documents, then stared at me through the glass pane in front of him.

I tried to smile, but felt nervous.

What kind of idiot moves to a new country to become a ballerina when they have a foot injury?

The guard looked down at his computer. He stamped my passport with a resounding *thud* and handed it back to me.

I moved to the baggage carousel. My leg felt sweaty and itchy under the brace.

The injury was irritating at best, a stabbing pain at worst. It had come from months of pushing myself too hard in class. My foot would swell in the afternoons after hours of dancing, supporting the entire weight of my body on the tip of a single rotating right toe. The pain was always sharpest when I'd fly out of a *sissone* or *jeté* jump, catching the full force of a landing on the heel and pad of my right foot. But slowing down, being careful had never felt like an option. I'd wanted to show my teachers, my parents, and anyone else who might have been watching that I was ready for Russia, that I was Bolshoi Ballet Academy material.

Finally, the pain had grown so acute, I went to a doctor.

The results were conclusive. My foot, the doctor explained, had been battered and weakened. A microscopic crack had chiseled through my bone.

Mom had reviewed the notes made by this doctor. She'd shown me how to fit the boot. The only way to heal a stress fracture, she'd warned, was with rest. Several weeks of rest.

"You can go to Moscow," she'd finally agreed. "But you need to sit out the first few weeks of classes. Don't push yourself too hard. Give your foot a chance to recover."

"I'll wear the boot," I'd promised her. "I'll be careful."

But when I dragged myself into the Sheremetyevo baggage claim on August 31, 2009, I pulled my two oversized duffel bags off the conveyor belt. Then I sat down on the floor, ripped apart the Velcro straps of the boot, pried loose the plastic shell, and slid the whole thing off. I stuffed it in my bag and forced my tender foot into a regular shoe.

I will not arrive at the Bolshoi Ballet Academy wearing an injury brace, thumping around like some kind of peg leg.

I zipped up my suitcases and dragged them past the airport screen, into the arrivals hall. I pulled my shoulders back, adjusted my hips, tensed the muscles in my leg to avoid limping. I kept walking. My foot buzzed and twinged as if a sharp pebble had wedged itself into my shoe and was burrowing like a tack into my heel. I ignored the pain.

The arrivals hall was a flurry of activity. Signs blinked from walls, flight announcements chimed in Russian and English, travelers rolled suitcases across the floor, and shuttle drivers crowded the exit in leather or nylon jackets, jostling and shouting under a cloud of cigarette smoke.

I tried to look like a grown-up, like I knew what I was doing. I searched the crowd for someone familiar. My parents had arranged for an acquaintance named Sarah who lived in Moscow to meet me.

Sarah stepped out of the crowd—tall with short, red hair and a wide, open American face. Her driver, Vitaliy, was with her. I felt a wash of relief.

"Welcome to Moscow!" Sarah smiled, expansive.

Vitaliy lifted my too-heavy bags onto a cart.

"*Spasibo!*" I thanked him as clearly as I could, using one of the few Russian words I knew.

Vitaliy answered with a waterfall of sentences. But this sort of unscripted exchange was beyond the limit of what I could understand. I shrugged my shoulders. We left the terminal, walking through sliding-glass doors onto the sidewalk.

I felt Moscow as a blast of cold air on my face, like opening the door to a refrigerator filled with dust and car exhaust.

Vitaliy loaded my bags in his car and drove us down the wide and traffic-choked Leningradskoe Highway toward Moscow's center. Out tinted windows, I saw electrical wires tangled overhead, people walking, waiting in lines at bus stops, smoking, carrying groceries in plastic bags.

I'm actually here! Moscow! If only my family could see me now!

I felt giddy, like I wanted to stick my head out the window. I started snapping pictures of cars stalled in traffic, glass office towers, shiny gold onion domes, pedestrians striding through crosswalks, the back of Vitaliy's head, Sarah laughing beside me.

We drove for nearly an hour to the center of Moscow, where, at a bend of the city's stone-walled river, we turned onto a leafy side road and rolled to a stop.

Out my window, I saw a green metal fence and a huge, soot-streaked, pale building.

I felt a thrill of panic. This was it. The place I'd dreamed of since childhood, obsessed over in late-night conversations with classmates, and studied in books and YouTube videos, the place I'd traveled thousands of miles to reach: the Bolshoi Ballet Academy.

I had seen pictures of the Bolshoi Ballet Academy before, but seeing it in person was a shock. The building, constructed in the decade when Khrushchev and Kennedy narrowly avoided nuclear war over Cuba, was hideous. It was a heavy stone box, streaked with pollution stains. Graffiti smeared the walls, grass grew up through the pavement, crumbling chunks of concrete littered the sidewalk.

It was not what I'd imagined when I'd envisioned the world's most prestigious ballet academy. Maybe I'd expected an imperial-era stone edifice, like a fairy tale born in the brain of Tchaikovsky or Petipa. But the reality I saw that day looked more like some sort of many-windowed, abandoned weapons factory.

I wasn't frightened by the ugliness. If anything, the late-Soviet-era grit and crumble felt like a patina of grandeur. This was a school founded by a Russian empress more than two hundred years ago. Although the building itself was from the 1960s, the institution was older than the entire United States of America. It had trained Russian serf children to dance for the imperial nobility when George Washington was alive. It had birthed a form of art that had outlived famine, revolution, and the collapse of a country. I couldn't see it as anything but majestic.

I stepped out of the car and walked up the dark, uneven stone steps. These were the same steps that Natalia Osipova, Maya Plisetskaya, and Svetlana Lunkina had climbed before launching themselves into the annals of international ballet stardom. It felt like a big moment. I asked Sarah to take a photo. I turned to the camera, a purse and duffel bag strapped to my shoulders, dark curly hair falling over my eyes, a wide smile on my face.

This, I thought, *is officially a place where I belong, where I have been invited.*

I walked to the top of the stairs, where the stained and weathered wooden doors to the academy were heavy. They creaked when I pushed them open. I could smell the dark basement interior of the school before I could see it: musty, cool, layered with dust. It smelled like the sediment of Russian history.

Two elderly men in ill-fitting suit jackets stood inside the entrance by rows of mostly empty coat hooks. One of them spoke to me in a land-slide of Russian. The only word I understood was "Passport! Passport!"

I handed over my documents and watched as he picked up a phone, a stern look on his face. An angry, complicated storm of consonants spilled from his mouth.

It was impossible, then, for me to untangle individual words from the onslaught of Russian sounds. I couldn't interpret the identically closed and irritated expressions I saw on the faces of these two security guards—or of anyone in Moscow. The old man staring me down, I'd later learn, was a kind and patient person, tasked with the officious job of checking the documents of everyone who walked through the academy's front doors. But to me, only hours new to Russia, he—and everyone else—seemed not only grouchy, but completely irate.

Maybe, I thought, *it will help if I smile wider?*

I stared at the guard, showing all my teeth. He looked away, furrowed his brows at the pages of my passport.

Vitaliy hauled my bags into the school. Sarah wrote a phone number on a piece of paper.

"Call any time, for any reason," she told me. "I live over by Smolenskaia metro station."

I nodded as if I knew what that meant.

Then, Sarah, and Vitaliy with her, were gone.

Standing on the musty, ground-level entrance of the school, it was possible to hear a piano pounding away from somewhere overhead and the muffled *thud* of feet landing on second-story wooden floors.

On the walls near the coatracks, framed photos of past students stared back at me. They stood in rows of black and white behind glass, their hair scraped into buns, their collarbones straight and sharp above their dance uniforms. Other photographs showed graduates of the school in full stage makeup and costume, frozen in sublime and impossible positions—flying above a stage, or with their legs locked into arcs over their heads.

Somewhere in that building, I knew that another American— sixteen-year-old Elisabeth Champion from Kentucky—was taking classes from a second-year instructor. I also knew that several years before she had arrived, Breanna Dvorak from Minnesota had trained at the academy.[1]

Other non-Russians were in the building: students who had flown in from England, Hong Kong, Japan, Korea, Finland, Singapore, Poland to enroll in the academy's foreign-study program or embed themselves in classes meant for Russian natives. All of them were there to learn the secrets and discipline of ballet from dance masters at one of Russia's oldest, most celebrated theatrical academies.

I was far from the only foreigner—I wasn't even the only American.

I'd spent months feeling special and chosen to have been invited there. But, now that I'd actually arrived, I suddenly felt small and a little panicked. The adrenaline tide that had pushed me through the day sagged, then disappeared.

I stood by myself in the hall, flanked by my oversized American duffel bags.

I had wanted to do something unusual, to be one of the first, one of the only. But now, as a current of exhaustion pulled at my face and worry pooled cold under my rib cage, I recognized something I'd been trying to ignore. It was a voice I had tried to silence with days of early morning workouts, late-night language sessions, and the buzzy thrill of a plane ride. I peered down the dim, terrazzo-floored corridors of the Bolshoi Ballet Academy, and this knowledge returned in a dark tide, flooding my stomach.

What if I can't do this?

CHAPTER 5

"Prove It to Me"

It was gray when I awoke in my dorm room on the school's third floor the next morning—my first full day as a student at the Bolshoi Ballet Academy. Dust motes floated in the air, and a pale light filtered through double-paned windows. I could hear a distant roar of traffic somewhere outside, rattling the panes.

I blinked up at the narrow ceiling. My new room was closet-sized with three narrow beds and a refrigerator-sized Soviet *shkaf*, or wardrobe, wedged against the walls. I had two roommates—one girl from Greece and another from Venezuela. Both were still fast asleep.

My oversized American duffel bags had been banished. Too large, too imperial to fit in our tiny room.

I swung my legs off the bed, winced at the loud metal screech from the springs beneath my mattress, then tiptoed out into the hallway. There were other sleepy-eyed girls there, ducking out of their dorm rooms. One girl was already dressed in workout clothes. There was a sheen of sweat on this girl's forehead.

A prick of worry spiked in my chest. *How long has this girl been up? Was there an early morning workout I missed?* I hurried down the hallway, clutching my towel and shampoo, filled with self-rebuke.

I should have been the first one awake. I should have been stretching, warming up, preparing before anyone else.

My first day of classes had barely started, and I was already behind.

I pushed open the door to the girls' bathroom and was enveloped in a damp and pungent wave of odor: sewer with overtones of metallic steam and flowery shampoo. Teenage girls with damp heads crowded the sinks and mirrors. They held toothbrushes and mascara wands. The floor tiles under their plastic sandals were moist and grimy. I was not wearing plastic sandals, and the cold ceramic under my bare feet was wet and clumped with damp wads of hair.

I was disgusted and also embarrassed to have forgotten to put something on my feet. But there was a long line for the showers, and I felt like I was already running late. I stepped into line behind the last girl.

Is this it? Are there no other showers?

All the girls around me spoke in Russian. Their voices echoed off the tiled bathroom walls. I breathed through my mouth, ignoring the stench of whatever horrific plumbing calamity was unfolding in the pipes beneath the floor. I watched the other girls walk around naked, scrub their teeth, towel their hair, and speak this other language with a sort of confidence and belonging that astounded me.

How can they be so young and so fluent?

Watching their mouths move, the looks they gave each other, I felt separated from them by an impenetrable glass wall. I could see them, they could see me, but there was no way to cross this invisible barrier. There was no way to understand them, to ask questions about the bathrooms, or about where to buy plastic slides, or what class they were in, or what was for breakfast.

When it was finally my turn at the front of the line, I moved to the single open showerhead. It was in a tiled room, mushroomy and chill, dripping with water, filled with shivering girls. There were no privacy curtains, no stalls or doors, and the floor was filthy. I saw a cigarette butt and what appeared to be the remnants of vomit congealing next to one of the drains.

I hesitated that first morning, clutching my towel.

But at my back I could feel the stares of the other girls still in line. One of them gestured and said something in Russian. I couldn't understand the words, but it seemed like this girl was upset, like she wanted me to hurry up.

I gritted my teeth, took off my pajamas, and stepped naked under the full blast of a showerhead.

The water was so cold, it took my breath away.

But I didn't retreat. I squirted shampoo into the palm of my hand, sudsed it into my hair, and stood rigid under the freezing blast of water for the moments it took to rinse away the white skein of foam.

While I was showering, then retreating to my room in a damp towel and pajamas, Moscow outside the academy walls was stirring to life. There were apples heavy on trees in courtyards, cars pulling out onto streets, women hurrying along sidewalks in scarves and light jackets, men wearing long, square-toed shoes.

Inside the dorms, nearly all the Bolshoi Ballet Academy students I saw were dressed alike in black skirts and crisp white shirts. In a mild panic, I rushed to the room where I'd left my luggage and began tearing apart my duffel bags to find a black and white outfit that would match what everyone else was wearing. My hand touched the plastic leg brace I'd stuffed in a far corner of the bag the day before. I remembered my mother's warning and, for a moment, contemplated pulling it out. But the thought passed quickly. I wanted to seem as if I belonged there, as if I was a natural fit for this elite Russian school. And that would not be possible if I were wearing an injury brace, hobbling around the academy's corridors for the whole first day of lessons.

So, when I descended the academy's stairwell, dressed for my first day, there was no brace on my leg. My foot still buzzed in pain each time I pressed it into the floor. But I tried not to let the hurt show on my face or in the movements I made as I walked.

There was a hum, by then, of Russian voices in the Academy halls. Small boys and girls swarmed the front entrance. They wore enormous backpacks and carried cellophane-wrapped bouquets of flowers. Their white shirts were pressed, and every hair on their heads was combed behind their ears, pinned into bow-decorated buns on the backs of their skulls.

I walked past them with a small smile on my face, like I knew what I was doing, like I knew where I was going.

I had signed up for a full three-year Bolshoi Ballet Academy education. This included classes not just on dance, acting, and character movement, but also on Russian language, literature, history, music theory, science, and math. There was a program the Bolshoi had designed specifically for foreigners, which included lessons designed to help non-native speakers. But I had not been admitted to this program. I had been chosen by a Russian teacher that summer, filed into a class that demanded full immersion with Russian students.

So I entered my first lesson—an introduction to some sort of advanced mathematics—and I found a seat at a rickety laminate desk. I took out a pencil and notebook and turned my attention to the teacher. He had a straightened back and an angered look on his face. He began writing on the board with chalk and speaking to us in a hurricane of rolled *R*s, *V*s, and guttural sounds, impossible to separate into words. I wanted to seem like I was paying attention, so I took my pencil in my hand and marked my paper with a series of small scribbles. The glass wall was still there for me. I couldn't understand what he was saying and couldn't take actual notes in English. And, of course, I couldn't write in Russian. But I wanted everyone to think that I belonged there. So I kept my pencil moving, kept looking to the front of the classroom, watching the teacher.

One of my new classmates, a girl with round eyes and silky blonde hair, watched me. She raised an eyebrow, quirked her mouth. She could tell I didn't understand, that my industrious notebook activity was just scribbling.

I felt embarrassed at the lengths I was going to make myself fit in. But I hoped that, if I could pretend well enough, this would not be noticed by very many people—that I would be able to hide my inadequacies for as long as it would take to erase them.

The hour for my first ballet class at the Bolshoi arrived after lunch. I changed into a Capezio leotard and Grishko slippers, then pulled on the new, beautiful, and expensive warm-up gear from Mom. I hurried down the green-carpeted corridor toward studio 9, arriving as early as possible, before anyone else from my new class could get there.

This is it! I thought—the moment when the language barrier wouldn't matter, when I would feel at home, when I would be able to dance and show everyone that, even though I couldn't understand what they were saying, I belonged there.

I sat down outside the studio door and began stretching.

Soon the other eight girls in my class showed up: Stasia, Irina, Yulia, Shoko, Boyana, Katya, Liza, and Polina. They were wearing warm-up gear, their hair pulled back in spirals.

All of them were from Russia except for Polina, who was from Finland, and Boyana, who was from Hungary. They had all been in Vaganova dance classes for much longer than I had. And they were incredible. They threw their legs over doorways, radiators, and window ledges, their legs curving upward in over-splits like flexible bowstrings. They leaned against the wall, scissor-kicking the air and lay on the floor, twisting their bodies into contortions I hadn't even known were possible.

These girls had been chosen young, handpicked for their perfect bodies, ideal proportions, for the ways their femurs angled into their pelvises; their heads rose like tiny buds above their shoulders, and their spines curved down their backs. Their bodies, their habits of movement fit a certain mold that, for centuries, Russian ballet instructors had predetermined was necessary for dancing. Some of them had been in rhythmic gymnastics lessons their entire lives. I had known all of this in theory, but sitting there in person, watching them warm up right next to me, I saw that they were perfectly polished, pointy, elastic, and toned, like sharp and shiny Swiss Army knives.

I felt a clench in my stomach. Class hadn't even started, and I could already tell that these girls would be able to out-dance me.

At the far end of the hallway, I saw our teacher, Natalia Arkhipova, approach, her frizzy blonde bangs bouncing on her forehead.

We jumped to our feet.

"*Zdravstvuite, Natalia Arkhipova,*" the other girls greeted her, nearly in unison.

"*Zdravstvuite.*" She nodded, repeating the formal greeting back to them. She opened the door to the classroom, allowed us to file past her inside.

I had met her in New York that summer during the ballet intensive she'd helped lead. She had liked me then and chosen me for her class. I felt relieved to see her familiar baggy T-shirt over plump arms, her nicotine-stained teeth, and her frizzed ponytail bound in a limp scrunchie behind her.

It was impossible to take my eyes off her. Her hands were like ribbons pulled through the air. She opened the studio door with a subtle motion; she walked with casual precision, spine rigid, face full of thoughtful kindness.

Arkhipova was a member of the old Moscow Soviet elite—a Grigorovich ballerina. In the 1980s, she had been one of the Soviet Union's premier dancers, a decorated national artist with a golden touch. Dance celebrities still spoke about her grace and her genius when they gave interviews on Russian TV. She was the one who'd taught them to dance, who'd introduced them to the stage, they said.

I had seen some of this history with my own eyes. I had watched the old videos of Arkhipova on YouTube. I'd gorged myself on them all summer after I'd met her in New York: grainy reels from when she'd been a *prima assoluta*, a celebrated People's Artist of the Soviet Union. Her *Nutcracker* had been incandescence personified: playful, fearless, childlike, ethereal with pirouettes so precise, they were like effortless flicks of a pen in the air.

And it wasn't just that Arkhipova herself was a legend, she had also proven herself as a teacher. She had launched the careers of many artists over the decades. Just last year, a student of hers, Angelina Vorontsova, had been plucked straight from Arkhipova's classroom to dance at the Bolshoi. People couldn't stop praising this Vorontsova. A bright dancer of rare talent, they said, possessed of an exceptional artistry.[1]

If there was a way for me to get on a Russian stage, I knew it would be through Arkhipova.

So when she let us into the studio, I darted ahead, quickly, to the center of the barre. This was where the top girl in the class stood. I may or may not have deserved to be there, but I wanted to take the place in hopes it would seem like a natural fit. Perhaps Arkhipova would see me there and not think to demote me.

The other girls filed in and took their places at my sides. They stood in front of a floor-to-ceiling window that looked out onto the tops of birch trees in the academy's courtyard. An apricot-colored curtain draped over the glass, turned the light in the room orange. A crooked row of theater seats slumped at the edge of the room, falling apart at the wooden seams.

Arkhipova sank into one of these chairs, the back of her frizzled hair reflected in a wall of mirrors.

I flexed my left foot and the painful chip in my heel bit back. *Still there.*

Arkhipova raised her hand and nodded to the piano player in the corner.

"If you please," she said in Russian.

The music began in rounds of calm, measured notes, and the class started its barre exercises: pliés, battements, tendus, battements glissés, *ronds de jambe a terre*, battements fondus.

I moved through the familiar routines of the barre, bending my legs, scooping my feet, arching my back. Within minutes I was breathing hard. My muscles began to tremble. Arkhipova was slowing us down, drawing out every movement, testing our strength, watching us like a hawk. She prowled the front of the room, focused and intense, chirping out corrections in Russian.

She called something to me, but I couldn't understand, so she walked over and yanked my leg into position.

"Vyvorotnost, Djoy, Vyvorotnost!" she said, calling for turnout, pulling the inside of my knees and legs until I was in the proper position. I lifted my chin high, sweat rolling down the back of my neck.

The pace Arkhipova set was excruciating. She walked up and down in front of us like a drill sergeant, tugging and bending us into our proper forms, lecturing in Russian, slapping her hands to the music. But if any of her corrections were for me, I didn't understand them.

"Battements frappes! Ronds de jambe en l'air! Petits battements! *Adage!* Grands battements!" Arkhipova called the French positions in

a sharp Russian accent, hardening the consonants, growling the vowels from the back of her throat. She demonstrated some of the movements, leading with her chin, tossing her hand in the air like a flag.

I could see the other girls out of the corner of my eye. Their technique was sparkling clean, and they were all perfectly in sync—their limbs rising and falling in perfect unison, their heads tilting and turning at the same angle, like a row of mirrored reflections in a dressing room. I felt like a deflated balloon beside them: my frame weak, my knees wilted inward, my port de bras sagged and sloppy.

"*RAZ-dva-tri*! *RAZ-dva-tri*! *RAZ-dva-tri*!" Arkhipova clapped the counts at me, spurring me to keep up with the music, the other girls.

I raised my chin, gripped the barre, lifted my arm higher, trembled as I moved behind the music.

Arkhipova shook her head at some point and waved her hand, calling us to center with what felt like an air of disappointment.

I took my hand off the barre and followed my classmates to the side of the room. My leotard was plastered to my back, my thighs burned, my rib cage heaved, my fractured foot throbbed. The barre had lasted much longer than expected. But the hardest part of the class hadn't even started.

Arkhipova began rattling off instructions for the first exercise. I caught a few familiar French words for different ballet positions. But I wasn't completely sure what Arkhipova wanted from us. Still, center combinations were my strong suit, the place where I felt best able to shine. If barre was about technique, center was about actually dancing. And I knew from the feedback she'd given me that summer that she liked the way I danced.

I stepped into line with the first group of girls, turned my body into position. I wasn't going to shrink into the back row, even if I wasn't completely sure what combinations we were supposed to do.

The pianist plunked out the first line of music. I raised my chin, set my shoulders, and launched into our combination.

The moment my foot and knee landed, compressed into a line off the floor, I could tell something was wrong. The floor was not where I expected it to be. My foot landed at an off angle, and my knee splayed in the wrong direction. I felt the rest of my body flail to compensate, keep balance.

I managed to stay upright, but the rest of my jumps were wobbly and lopsided. My pirouettes were unstable, my bends crooked. When I turned, my eyes struggled on where to land, how to steady myself in the lopsided, apricot-colored light.

The wooden floor of the dance studio was tilted. I'd never danced on anything like it. Back home in the United States, all the stages and practice rooms I'd ever been in were flat. But here, the floor was raked to four degrees. This was something I'd known about—the Academy's studios were meant to mimic the slant at the Bolshoi, which was engineered to display the entirety of the stage to the audience, like giant palms extended toward the theater seats in offering. But I hadn't expected the downward angle to be quite so severe. It felt like dancing on the sharp slope of a roof. Moving upstage was like mountain climbing and dancing downstage gave me such a push of momentum, I worried I might accidentally throw myself into Arkhipova's lap.

Plus, the wooden slats on the floor were old, warped, badly in need of repair. The dance linoleum had chips and holes, bubbles and craters. Moving across the floor felt like dancing on a bumpy, potholed parking lot. It was difficult to walk without tripping, much less dance.

My Russian classmates, however, were unfazed. They were perfectly in sync, as flexible as rubber bands, slicing through every dance move Arkhipova threw at them.

At the end of class, I faded to the side of the room, heaving to catch my breath, dizzy from exertion. I couldn't understand a word of the quiet lecture Arkhipova delivered. The thick glass wall that had kept me isolated all day was back, stronger, more impenetrable than ever.

Why am I here? I thought. *I could be in Australia right now, or Texas—it wouldn't make a difference. Or Arkhipova could be shouting into my ear—I still wouldn't understand.*

The other girls bobbed into curtsies, chimed a chorus of demure Russian thank-yous as Arkhipova finished speaking. I tried to join them, but by the time I realized it was a word I knew, it was too late. They started to leave the studio, and I turned to follow them.

"*Djoy!*" Arkhipova called me back, motioning with her hand.

I turned to see a stern look on her face.

Just then Vanya, a third-year boy I knew from the summer intensive in New York, poked his head in the door.

"*Zdravstvuite, Natalia Valentinovna,*" he greeted Arkhipova respectfully, using her patronymic, then said to me a more informal hello: "*Privet, Joy.*"

Arkhipova waved him over to interpret.

"I could tell that was difficult for you," Vanya translated her words for me.

I nodded. The numb, cold feeling in my chest had spread to my neck and face. It may have been the only thing keeping me from bursting into tears.

"You need work," Arkhipova said through Vanya. "I invited you to Moscow. I want you to dance. I have plans for you. But you need to prove that you want to be here."

I couldn't tell if Arkhipova was giving me good news or bad. But I started to beg.

"I love being in your class," I said. "I know I can do better. I'll do whatever it takes."

"You need to learn Russian," Arkhipova said.

I kept my face still so Arkhipova wouldn't know how close I was to crying. *Was she having second thoughts about keeping me in her class?*

"You can be like every other foreigner, or you can be different," Arkhipova said. "You're not in America anymore. You need to learn our school, our technique, our way of doing things. You need to speak Russian, think Russian, dream Russian, dance Russian. You need to be Russian to take this class."

Arkhipova paused to give Vanya time to interpret.

"If you don't learn Russian, I won't let you take my class," she said. "I'm giving you two months. If you can't learn Russian by then, I'm sending you home."

CHAPTER 6

Vertigo

I heard Arkhipova's warning as a call to battle. But I didn't know just how difficult answering that call would be.

Winter fell in Moscow like a stone. By October, the trees all throughout the city were jaundiced and molted. They dropped their yellow leaves until they stood bare, corpse-like, at the sides of roads. Warmth drained from the air, the light bled out, returning for shorter and shorter periods each day, and the snow blew in, silent and relentless.

I was bewildered by the change. My life had always been filled with warmth and sunshine—from the azure skies and bougainvillea of Santa Monica to the sage greens of Austin and the dampness of Washington, D.C. But the cold that descended in Moscow was shocking, like a blow to the face when it started. It was as if I'd been swallowed alive—Jonah disappearing into the belly of a whale.

In the mornings, I woke myself at 5 a.m. in the predawn cold. This was the holy hour, the hour for quiet, the time at which one rose, my mother would say, if they wanted to be close to God. This was the time at which, after being shocked awake, I stumbled out of my dorm room into a hushed hallway where Moscow waited for me out the window, glowing its eerie green light onto the undersides of dark clouds.

I sank into the floor at the end of the dorm hallway, under a single overhead lamp that shone chill and yellow in the common room. There were two other students who woke with me. They stretched, their foreheads flat on nubby beige and blue Russian carpet, their feet pulled backward by elastic bands, readying themselves for whatever agony awaited us in ballet class.

I was fuzzy-brained as I prostrated myself on the floor beside them. When I stretched forward, a sharpness cut through my legs and the folds of my abdominal muscles. My thighs were tender to the touch. Arkhipova had, in class after class, attacked us, shredding our muscles like taco meat with slow-motion knee-bend pliés, deepened toe-sweeping battements tendus, and leg-in-the-air developpés. She demanded straight lines, long necks, thighs turned out at the hip like the stilled, open wings of butterflies.

Slowly, she was destroying me. Like a mechanic diving into the belly of a machine, she was taking me apart, piece by piece, sharpened screwdriver in hand. I could feel in my legs and shoulders and the sore muscles between my ribs where she had slashed and burned: elongating, strengthening, polishing, tightening every ligament, muscle, nerve ending and bone fragment.

But it wasn't just my body that was disintegrating; it was my head. I was terrified with the sort of fear that, even in the early morning, bent on the floor in stretch, I could feel seeping into my body like ice.

I'd been in Moscow for several weeks and was beginning to understand that I had come to a place for which I had no description, no shape, no stage markers. It was as if I'd strapped myself with a cord to the back of a speedboat and been yanked along behind the reality of accomplishing goals I'd set for myself. The anxiety of rushing forward felt like wind and spray battering me in the face. It hummed like a motor beneath all my thoughts: *You can't do this. What are you thinking? You look like a fool. You're not good enough.*

I knew how to work hard, how to get up early, how to plead for mercy. But I didn't know how to change the shame-filled voice in my head. Bent over on the floor in the morning, I muttered prayers, like incantations to guard against failure: *Lord, I'm so scared. I really want to be good. Forgive me. Help me. Please, Lord, get me through this.*

Sometimes, in the dim, orange-colored light of the studio, fear would overwhelm me, and I would freeze. My muscles tensed, my mind washed blank, my feet stumbled. Arkhipova would give me a correction, and I would understand this correction with my mind, but I was incapable of translating her advice to my feet, my legs, my arms. It wasn't just that my body hadn't yet learned this new Russian way of moving; it was that my body, gripped by fear, couldn't actually learn anything new at all.

There was nowhere to go in those moments but down, and I felt the fall in my stomach, in my throat closing over and my lungs restricting.

What were you thinking? Joy, you idiot. The Bolshoi Ballet Academy? Who are you kidding? There's no way you're good enough for this. You're not a dancer, and you'll never be a ballerina.

The Academy dorm rooms began to close in on me. They were crowded with students who hung socks to dry over the frames of their beds, played techno music early in the morning and late into the night, smuggled bottles of vodka into parties. The bathrooms reeked of sewage. The shower room was splattered with vomit and littered with the brown lumps of used tampons. The doorless toilet stalls were perpetually out of paper.

In the cafeteria, where I went when I was hungry, the food was horrific. At breakfast, I stood in line while a woman wearing a white paper hat on her head dumped *kasha*—a gluey mixture of boiled oats or buckwheat—into a bowl. Then she slathered it with a melting lump of butter, and I sat at a table to choke it down before it turned cold and became impossible to swallow. Lunch was watery soup served with a greasy cutlet and dry, rectangular slices of white or black rye bread. Dinner was the worst. It was always some sort of immediately identifiable animal body part like heart or tongue—purple and gray with ventricles sticking out or oozing in a membrane on a plate, wrinkled over with the knobby gooseflesh of taste buds or boiled skin.

My body was constantly sore—especially my injured foot. Occasionally, I would think about the leg brace I had abandoned in a dusty corner of my luggage. I would remember my mother's advice to wear it, to slow my intensity in class, to allow time for healing. But I decided Mom didn't know what she was talking about. I walked bare-legged, full of pain, all over Moscow. After I got off the plane at Sheremetyevo Airport, I never put that brace on my leg again.

My clothes began to smell of mold or stale sweat. The student washing machines were never available, and there was no dryer to speak of. I washed things in the sink and left them to drip dry on lines hung from the walls. Some of my more expensive items disappeared from my duffel bags. Occasionally, I would see a girl from a different class wandering around in one of my shirts. Once I confronted someone wearing a top I knew was mine.

"I think that you maybe accidentally took my shirt?" I told her. "It's an easy mistake, no big deal, but can I have it back?"

The girl looked at me, annoyed.

"There was no name written on this shirt," she told me. Then she stared at me, as if that had solved the dilemma, as if I were the one being rude.

I stopped asking questions about the clothes, which my mother had bought for me, that were now moving around the school on the bodies of other students.

But when I Skyped home, I put a brave smile on my face.

"It's great," I told my parents. "I'm learning so much. I'm so thankful to be here."

It's not that I was lying, exactly. I wanted to be in Moscow. But it took a certain kind of self-deception to love Russia. I looked past the crumbling buildings, the rusted boats that floated on the river, the snarls of traffic that filled the city air with diesel-scented clouds, and I told myself that I had come to a beautiful place. I told myself that what I was seeing was historic, foreign, and rare and that my presence in this place, my observation of it, somehow made me rare.

These were the things I thought of when I spoke to my parents through my laptop, when I walked the dusty sidewalks near Frunzenskaia Street, when I rose on pointe over my aching feet atop the warped studio floor. But my body knew things my mind refused to acknowledge. The deception caught up to me in unexplained fits of crying and in fear that felt like a weighted punch to my solar plexus when

I lay alone on the floor in the early mornings, stretching and struggling to breathe.

Russian, at first, was impossible. It was hard-edged, gruff, relentless, and complex. It was filled with a dizzying mix of locative and partitive cases, tenses, and declensions.

I carried my textbooks down the dim hallways in the early mornings to the common room and folded them open to peer at their Cyrillic-covered pages while I stretched. But I could not memorize vocabulary fast enough in those first months to save me from embarrassment in classes. I was always second-guessing myself, especially in acting class, where the first lessons were mostly lecture.

Our teacher, Anna Malovatskaia, spoke of studying scripts, imagining histories to inform the roles we'd play, digging deep within to discover what our character longed for and how this longing would show up on stage in the movements of our arms and the stances of our feet.

"Imagine it's snowing outside," she would tell us, "and you go to the window, peer outside and look at all the flakes driving into drifts. How do your shoulders move? Can you show with your eyelashes, your fingertips, your mouth that the snow is coming down?"

Or she'd sit at the edge of the room in her chair and suddenly scream, "There's a bomb! The bomb's exploding!" She'd point to the far corner and yell, "There it is! It's exploded just now! Show me the bomb!" And we'd all react—jumping, crumpling, falling to show the power of an invisible blast in our faces and backs and outstretched legs.

I tried to guess what she meant by the tone of her voice or the occasional word that made sense, and I'd throw myself into whatever it was I thought she was asking us to do. Sometimes I guessed wrong, and I'd be acting like an angry cat while everyone else scurried around like dogs or rabbits. I'd arch my back and hiss while everyone else barked or hopped, laughing at me.

"What did she say?" I'd plead for help in whispers to my classmates. "What are we supposed to do?"

"You know," the others would say. "Dog. Be a dog. Gaff-gaff."

Sometimes their hints would be enough for me to catch up. But mostly I'd be in the middle of the studio, throwing my heart into a violent portrayal of a WWII soldier, while everyone else was rocking babies, or act-petting a dog, their brows raised in derision, laughter rising out of their throats.

In these moments, I blinked back tears. It wasn't just that I'd made myself look stupid. It was that the sky outside was dark, I hadn't hugged my dad in months, and I felt as if I'd moved to a place where I was permanently cut off from connection to other human beings.

My acting teacher could tell when I was upset.

"Put your emotions into the acting, Joy," she'd say.

My first Russian winter broke something in me. I cried at unexpected times and felt a numbness settle over my face and throat. It choked me at strange moments—lying on my bed at night, standing in the wings of a school rehearsal, listening to music while I sat in splits on the hallway floors.

I had a few friends, and they saw the way I stumbled around, like a blind person who hadn't yet learned the shape of living in a new place.

Anton, Artem, and Trofim were third-year students whom I knew from the visit they'd made to New York in the long-ago summer for a Bolshoi intensive seminar. In Moscow, at the Academy, they adopted me, rather like a trio of aristocratic nineteenth-century Russian brothers who'd taken pity on a bumbling American sewer rat.

They invited me, after classes, to their dorm room, where their floors were spread with vintage carpets, their beds perfectly made, their walls hung with red and gold icons of saints who promised intercession against injuries or blessings in the arts.

"How was class? How's your turnout?" they'd ask when I came in from another two-hour session with Arkhipova, my legs trembling with exhaustion, my feet blistered, my heel throbbing.

I perched cross-legged on their windowsill, and they poured me cups of hot tea, tore open foil packets of cheap and sugary Alyonka chocolate, and cracked the silky bars into chunks. They turned on music they'd unearthed from online archives: crackled recordings of Edith Piaf or haunted Mussorgsky symphonies. They presented, from carefully wrapped parcels, intricate, crumbling gingerbread cookies sent from grandmothers in Tula.

They lived in a world I couldn't understand. Anton played guitar, and Trofim could sing opera arias. Artem could describe the Basil- and Seraphim-named Orthodox patron saints of everything and recite from memory their stories. They held doors open for me and insisted on carrying my bags when I bought groceries. They corrected my dancing technique and warned me away from certain flirtatious male classmates. They introduced me to their favorite dill-flavored Russian salads and explained the intricacies of Russian grammar. It was as if, with each cup of tea they shared and digitized Russian symphony they played on their laptops, they were showing me: *This is it; this is how you live in Moscow.*

The whole school was under their sway. They were in their final year at the academy and among the best dancers in the entire institution—clean, muscular, full of a strength and bravado I'd never seen in American dancers. Watching them move on stage was less like seeing Louis XIV prance to a minuet and more like observing a well-drilled squad of elite marines jumping in midair from one helicopter to another.

Dance teachers gave them access to empty studios for practicing variations or playing the piano. Cafeteria staff let them stay late at tables, smiling and shaking their heads as the boys insisted they'd finish cleaning up.

When other students played rap and *discoteka* music loudly in their rooms, or left class to go drink vodka in the square off Frunzenskaia Street, Anton would shake his head and wave his hand in the air. "Come, Joy," he would say. "If you want to be a ballerina, you have to be cultured."

We'd pass by the drinking parties and visit art museums together, our student ID cards in hand, to convince the uniformed ticket sellers to give us discounts. We went to the Tretiakov Gallery and the Pushkin

Museum. We wandered the wood parquet floors, under thick stone arches. We stood in front of Rublev's panels of massive angels, letting the vibrant iron oxide, azurite blue, ochre, and gold of halos, archangel wings, and folded cinnabar robes sink into our retinas. We gazed upon the sly and beautiful portrait of Maria Lopukhina. We breathed in the piney morning light of Shishkin masterpieces: dew on forest branches, mist rising like exhalations from gnarled tree roots and wooded glens.

"These paintings and these poems tell us who we are," Anton said. "If you want to understand the Russian soul, if you want to express the Russian soul, this is where you start."

When I was with them, I forgot to be afraid.

CHAPTER 7

Cathedral of Dance

On a dark and frosty night in October, Anton linked his elbow with mine, and we left the green metal fence encircling the academy. We walked to a nearby metro station, then rode the black escalators, which smelled of burnt rubber, deep into the marble halls of Moscow's underground rail system. We sat in metal train cars that screamed through tunnels under the city northward to Teatral-naia Station.

When we rose again to the air aboveground, we saw what we had come to see. It sat pale and huge in the center of Moscow—a dusty square with a dry, bowl-shaped fountain, and rising behind it, a massive building, five stories tall, shrouded in billowing drapes.

This was the Bolshoi Theater—founded by an empress, as old as the United States of America. It had occupied a hallowed and tender spot in my brain for years. But the first time I saw it, it waited darkened and empty, shuttered to the public, sleeping under cloaks of construction fabric. Its lights were dimmed, its corridors covered in dust, its hallways spiked through with scaffolding.

Anton and I had come to see a performance by the ethereal Bolshoi dancers. But, in the fall of 2009, the entire nearly-two-hundred-person troupe had been evicted from the historic Bolshoi Theater for state-sponsored renovations. They performed in a building just next door, a place aptly named the New Stage.

We saw, in the cold evening dark of October, the ornate lampposts that blazed outside the New Stage, shining on crowds of people who streamed up stone stairs in winter boots and fur hats. Anton and I joined them, rising from the sidewalk and stepping through the theater's doors onto marble floors where women in heels and sparkling dresses handed their furs to coat attendants.

I had been desperate to see a Bolshoi performance. And the ballet to which we had secured tickets was rumored to have Natalia Osipova centered in a starring role.

Natalia Osipova was as responsible as anyone for me being in Moscow. She was—and still is—the lightest, most explosive, and most dynamic dancer I have ever seen or ever will see. Reviewers were in awe of her. They compared her to tensile iron alloy, a hurricane, a tsunami.[1] There was a documentary about her that I had watched over and over on YouTube. I had studied her jumps, listened to her words about warm-up routines and instructors. Osipova was everything I dreamed of being: a Kitri in wild and passionate abandon, exploding on stage; a dancer who took your breath away.

And somehow, by a stroke of luck, Anton and I had managed to obtain 100-ruble student discount tickets to her performance before all the seats in the New Stage Theater sold out.

I had worn my nicest clothes, brushed powder onto my eyelids, pressed gloss onto my lips. Anton had combed his hair back, worn his nicest dress shirt. We arrived at the theater like schoolkids on picture day, stepping into the auditorium, where the air was filled with the humming of low voices and the trilling, discordant sounds of orchestra members warming their trumpets and cellos. A chandelier the size of a hot-air balloon hung from the ceiling; its light gleamed on the gilded wall carvings. I started to search the seats for the faraway corner section of the theater, which was where our student tickets indicated we should sit, but Anton stopped me.

"No, no, no," he said, his hair raked into a gelled arch over his forehead. "We can do better than that."

He found, in the crowds of people scented with cologne, perfume, and cigarettes, a woman whose job it was to help guests find their places among the rows of sage-green theater seats.

"Ludmila!" He spoke to her like an old friend. She had a kind face, gray hair. They spoke to each other in familiar tones, saying things in Russian that I didn't understand. Then Ludmila guided us down a narrow back hallway, through a small door, and out to a pair of open seats close to the wide lip of the slanted, darkened stage.

"Much better," Anton said as we sank into our new seats and watched the lights dim, heard the theater hush.

The gold-and-herb-colored velvet curtain lifted, smooth and silent before us. A swell of a goblin sound rose from a glowing pit in the floor, quiet at first, then growing to a thundering crescendo. It filled the darkened theater with ethereal notes of music. We were so close we could see the tips of the violin bows and the shiny gold tops of the French horns.

I felt nearly ill with excitement by the time Natalia Osipova leapt on stage.

We were near enough to see the curls of hair on the nape of her neck, and the film of tulle left in her wake as she floated in a diagonal cut across the stage.

She was magnificent.

Her wrist turned in the air like a ribbon on the end of a wand, and her *grand jetes* left her suspended in time and place, hovering over the stage like a splash of water in an arc over a fountain, her arms stretched outward like wings. The way she moved was a sort of enchantment that made it seem possible to stop breathing, tilt your head, and glide into the air like an effervescent puff of smoke.

A lump rose in my throat as I watched. I was reminded of the church services of my childhood—the tiny, white-steepled building in Santa Monica where a pastor had called us to repent, to rend the stubborn hardness of our hearts and make ourselves tender before God.

I remembered how the music from those childhood worship services had filled my chest with emotion until I rose, compelled, weeping, and walked down the aisle to kneel at the altar, opening my heart, showing the humility of my intentions by lowering my body.

"I am a sinner," I had prayed in silence. "I want to go to heaven when I die. I want to be saved."

Those moments in Lighthouse Church had felt performative, dramatic, cathartic. Perhaps this mattered to God. Perhaps he wanted a certain movement of the body to prove that I was serious about following him. Perhaps he used music as a way to soften hearts so that we opened in vulnerability to him when he knocked. But whenever I answered the calls my pastor gave, I would leave the altar feeling grateful and loved, like God had reached down from heaven to place his hand on me.

This transcendence, this swelling of emotion that I felt in the sanctuary of my childhood church, returned when I sat in the darkened hall of the New Stage and watched Natalia Osipova glide across the raised floor. She was like something from another world, her feet moving in bright skips—more wheels than legs. She bent and twisted, her leg lifting to tap her ankle to her wrist over her head, then floating out parallel, like the pointed end of a spear. I couldn't stop staring at her. She was lit from within, a saint of the arts, working out her salvation in a cathedral of dance.

My body remembered, as I watched, the *plies*, *adagios*, and combinations that Arkhipova had given me to practice. What I would have given to move in the way that Osipova was moving. What I would have given to absorb an entire orchestra of sound into my body and express hours of mythical story with arcs of my spine, turns of my chin, and weightless, levitating bounds into the air.

After Osipova's performance ended, I was a changed person. I left the theater with Anton and the throngs of other theatergoers. But I couldn't forget what I'd seen. My chest still ached; my eyes still filled with tears when I thought about Osipova moving on stage.

Weeks later, there was a night, at the Bolshoi Academy, when I watched the graduating seniors put on a performance. The dancers I saw there were so far ahead of me, so much more talented and precise in their expression, that I was filled with longing and desperation.

I decided, in that moment, to conduct my own altar call. I waited in the wings of the school auditorium until all the dancers, all the audience members, all the students and teachers had left. The lights were turned off, and the dim, pink-cushioned rows of seats were empty.

Then I walked onto the quiet, abandoned stage. I dropped to my knees, humbled my body in the most Pentecostal display of repentance and desperation I could conjure. I touched my face to the dusty floor of the stage.

"Please, God," I said in a whisper. "These Russian dancers are so beautiful. They're stars. I wish I could be like them. Please make me into a dancer like Katia and Tania. Like Natalia Osipova."

It was dramatic and performative—something I felt even then. But it was something I hoped God might listen to. My family had always prayed about broken bones, growing tumors. These were the sorts of things that God had supernatural power over, they believed. If God could heal the body, perhaps he could turn it into a miracle like Natalia Osipova.

"I dedicate this to you," I told God, "I can't do this by myself, but you've done miracles in the past, and you'll continue."

Would it work? Would these theatrics, these good-luck charms offered in the right name, the name of God and of his son, Jesus, be heard? I was hopeful then. But I wasn't sure.

I threw myself into the Bolshoi Academy's classes.

In character lessons, we learned to put our hands on our hips, jut our chins in the air, throw our shoulders back, and fling our bodies into traditional Russian folk moves that felt wild, furious, alive. The boys stomped and squatted and kicked their legs out in front of them, threw their arms in the air. The girls clapped and bent, arms crooked at our waists.

In partnering lessons, we practiced promenades, lifts, turns, and jumps with our sweaty-haired, thick-eyebrowed boy classmates. They offered their hands to us, spanned our waists during turns, and lifted us high in the air during jumps.

In acting class, we infused our movements with feeling and meaning. We dipped into our internal wells of sadness, anger, and delight, and we painted these emotions on our faces, held our arms in ways that invited the audience to wonder about the longing and pain of our characters.

But Arkhipova's class was my favorite.

She was incredible. She stood at the front of our classroom, watching us from below her heavy bangs and purple-mascaraed lashes. Her T-shirts hung from her shoulders like windsocks as she pointed her toes and demonstrated steps for us. We longed to understand the secrets she knew about balancing on pointe or launching into fouettés, about capturing the gaze of an audience and then holding them spellbound for hours of wordless drama. These were the hidden codes she had inherited like crown jewels from Ludmila Bogomolova,[2] whose career was launched in the shadow of WWII, who had learned to dance from Maria Kozhukhova[3]—a performer of Aurora for audiences in the days when Lenin ruled Russia. And before them, Claudia Kulicheskaia, Lev Ivanov, Jean-Antoine Nicolas: lines of artists who survived the revolution, danced for czars, who had moved from Europe to Russia at the request and benevolence of emperors and empresses.[4]

Arkhipova's balletic knowledge reached back to before the dawn of ballet as an art form in Russia.

And, for reasons I still didn't understand, Arkhipova wanted me in her class. She treated my future on the stage as inevitable. It sometimes felt like joining a Russian school was a joke I'd played on everyone—like I'd said something outrageous, everyone somehow believed me, and here I was, making a fool of myself.

But Arkhipova wasn't fooling around. She pushed me in class to find deeper *plies*, longer and more expressive lines, more capacity in my lungs. Like a puppet master, she could, with a few words, a nod of her head, or a tiny hand motion, pull new elevations of dance from me. She stood at the front of the room, watched me struggle through a combination, then said, "Pull up here," or "Open your shoulders like this," and it would magically work, as if she'd been given a wand from past generations of dancers and could flick it at me to cover me with fairy dust.

This middle-aged, round-cheeked goddess of Russian ballet for some reason believed in me, and her belief launched me farther and faster than

I could have imagined. By November, she was pushing me to perform in actual stage productions.

She could see the anguish I was in about my slow progress, my crippling self-doubt. But she stood between me and despair. When I turned my anxiety inward, when I fretted about the shape of my body, my weight on the scale, my inability to master the perfection of turnout, she pushed away the darkness of my thoughts with her words.

"No, there's nothing wrong with you," she said, drawing her shoulders back in a gesture of grace for me to mimic. "Take a deep breath. Relax. Be confident in yourself. Try it again, and it will come."

She had a vision for me that I couldn't understand, but was desperate to trust. She saw me in the spotlight: groomed, shaped, devoted, improved. She spoke constantly about the dancers, the giants of the past I should be watching, studying, emulating.

"Think about Ulanova's Juliet," she would say as I sweated and melted in rehearsals. "You need to be fearless, but also romantic. You want the audience to feel your performance in the goose bumps on their arms!"

Arkhipova understood the achingly beautiful soul of Russian ballet, and she tried, in her steady, determined way, to make sure I imbibed it.

But I couldn't help worrying I wouldn't really fit the mold. I was American. I didn't even have the right paperwork to live and work in Russia once my student visa ended after graduation.

Arkhipova had plans for that too.

"You'll need to marry a Russian man," she said, waving her hand vaguely at the boys in black tights and white T-shirts who wore too much cologne as they practiced *soubresauts* in neighboring classrooms.

"Pick one out. You could marry Fedia. Or Tolik," she suggested.

She was completely serious. This was how things were done in Russia. You devoted yourself to become the best, yes. But when bureaucracy stymied your goals, you found a way around it.

Arkhipova was full steam ahead into the future. And I was grateful to have someone who seemed to have glimpsed the imminent and was assured about where I was going.

I tried my hardest to believe she was right.

Chapter 8

Dream

In January, there came a moment when it seemed possible I might occupy the dream that Arkhipova had created for me.

It was a dark night in the freezer-bottom depths of January. All of Moscow had been plunged in a deep, white chill that coated the sidewalks with ice, turned the air at underground grates into billowing, iridescent clouds, and froze the insides of our nostrils when we emerged from buildings to make our way to the theater.

I was so nervous, it felt as if a crack had opened in my chest. I could feel it stealing my breath as I pushed out the doors of the metro station and moved up the icy, crowded sidewalks on Tverskaia Street. My shoulders shook as I put my mittened hand on the back-door employee entrance to the New Stage.

This was the same theater where I'd seen Natalia Osipova dance just months before, a place I'd come for student performances in the fall. It still didn't seem possible that I could arrive here to perform. Nonetheless, there I was, pulling open the door normally reserved for employees, feeling the warmth of the air in the theater's basement, like an exhalation from the belly of something alive.

I was here to perform at the Bolshoi Theater's New Stage. Actual tickets had been sold to the public for this—a gala concert. And the cast list was filled with Russian ballet celebrities: Nikolai Tsiskaridze, Angelina Vorontsova, Ivan Vasiliev. Only a select few students from the academy had been chosen to join. The only reason I was here was because

Arkhipova had set me here, like someone plucking a wilted cabbage out of a box, then displaying it on a top shelf for everyone to see.

But my foot, as I stepped into the theater's underground hallways, was in agony. The fractured heel had slowly been getting worse as I rehearsed over and over in Academy studios with Arkhipova. I had been limping for days, and it was painful to put any weight on the injured area. I couldn't do barre; I could barely walk.

But there was no way I was backing out of my chance to perform at the Bolshoi's New Stage. I dragged myself along the theater's dingy underground corridor to the dressing rooms. After lowering myself into a chair, I slowly inched my snow boots off with gentle tugs, like someone carefully pulling an elderly person's arm out of a sleeve. What I saw inside was a swollen limb—pale and angry in the glare of the dressing room lights.

But there was no time to waste. I pulled tights up my calves and thighs, smeared rouge on my cheeks, squirmed into a glittering leotard and skirt. I hobbled upstairs to the stage, trying to keep weight off my right foot.

Please, God, don't let me fail. Please let me perform well. Please help me be calm and blameless. Deliver me. Don't let my feet slip.

The theater wings were in chaos. Dancers in costume rubbed their pointe shoes in resin. They turned loops on the wide expanse of open stage behind the lowered curtain. Reporters with microphones clicked around in high heels and sheath dresses. They were attached by cords to videographers with tripods who focused their lenses on the ballet champions, the primas and celebrities who were warming up in their costumes. Ivan Vasiliev was there, bounding through the air like some kind of astronaut to whom earth's gravity didn't apply. When he strode behind the curtain, warm and brilliant, he actually stepped on my (non-injured) toe in passing. I was so thrilled that I immediately posted about it on Facebook, together with a blurry photo of him marking out his steps.

I was giddy to breathe the same air as these ballet gods. I saw them greet my teacher, Arkhipova, with hugs and gratitude, like Olympians paying homage to the potentate who had led them to their current mountaintop of fame and talent.

But Arkhipova was focused on me. And after she was embraced by the kings and queens of the Russian ballet world, she came to find me, her newest protégé. She could tell with one look at my face that I was hurting.

"Your foot?" she asked.

I nodded.

"Okay," she told me. "Let's get you something for the pain."

There was no question that I would perform.

The pain relief spray administered to my foot did not quench the agony.

But when the theater seats filled with people, and the orchestra pit filled with sound, and the time came for me to perform, I stood upright. I clenched the muscles at my core and gripped the hand of Vanya, my partner.

Don't mess this up, I told myself. *This is your chance.*

What was a few minutes of torment if it got me onto the Bolshoi's New Stage in front of theater directors and TV cameras and all the leaders at my school?

I turned my face to the stage. It was a wide plane in front of me, blinding with lights, filled with muscle, tulle, and eerie faces plastered in makeup. I felt the pads of my fingers digging into Vanya's arm, his face focused and grotesque up close, caked with rouge and eyeliner.

You can do this. You can do this. You can do this.

My foot hovered limp and pulsing over the floor. I heard the opening notes of a full orchestra and the still, held breaths of hundreds of Muscovites.

Now.

We broke out from behind the curtains to the sound of cascading harps, the musical equivalent of softly falling flakes of snow.

I felt the surface of the stage in electric jolts of pain in my kneecaps and the back of my neck.

Somehow, with no awareness of how it was happening, tears appeared on my cheeks, shimmering above the smile chiseled onto my face.

I'm not positive I breathed for the first thirty seconds on stage.

There's no recording of that performance that I've found. I'm not sure how it looked to the audience. There were opalescent shades of pink and blue, rustles of tulle as I dipped and spun, careful notes of an orchestra playing music composed in the 1800s.

What I know for certain is how each moment felt from the inside. It was like dancing on nails, a smile carved onto my face. There was a moment—a sliver in time I can still feel in the back of my molars—when I arched into an arabesque and rolled down onto my foot. I felt a pop of tendon and bone that seemed louder than a trombone and seared so intensely I could taste it, like metal in my mouth, bile in my throat.

I knew immediately: something in my foot had snapped.

Each movement that followed was pain unlike anything I've experienced before. Lava? Impalement? Amputation? Burning? I don't know what to tell you except that I kept dancing.

I finished my first appearance on the Bolshoi's New Stage on the rim of consciousness, the edges of my lipsticked mouth turned up, tears running down my face, sparkling lavender in the stage lights.

Things moved quickly after that. As the music ended and the audience clapped, I collapsed behind the curtain, and Vanya lowered me to the floor. In minutes, a nurse was on me. A bag of ice landed on my foot, hands peeled off my shoes, prodded gently at my heel, my toes, the top of my foot.

I was shaking and crying, the face of Arkhipova over me, wrinkled in concern—calm but urgent.

"You did well, Joy. It's okay now, it's okay," she soothed, taking my hand in hers.

I was wrapped in a coat and taken from the theater to a hospital, where I sat, shaking, next to a doctor.

There were X-rays, the rustle of stiff sheets atop a hard, plastic hospital bed.

The diagnosis was straightforward and grim: broken.

"The bone has splintered," the doctor said. "If you do not address this, you might never dance again."

In the dark days of October, when I felt lonely and desperate and filled with a nameless, constant anxiety, a classmate in the Academy dorms told me she'd found an English-speaking church nearby.

"International Christian Fellowship," she'd said. "They meet on Sundays in a theater on *Arbat* Street."

The next Sunday I woke early, packed a Bible into my purse, and followed her to *Smolenskaia* metro station, then walked to the doors of a performance hall in the heart of Moscow.

It was cold enough by then to turn our fingers and knuckles raw, the ends of our noses pink. But inside the theater was warm and filled with loud and friendly American voices. We sat in a row of chairs, and I watched as men in button-down shirts and women in cowl-neck sweaters prayed into microphones on stage and led worship songs about bowing to a God bigger than anything in creation.

During a pause in the music, a man instructed us to turn and greet our neighbors. The hall was filled with expats: English teachers, oil executives, missionaries, journalists. There were a lot of Texas accents, some from California and Oklahoma, others from Ireland or England.

"Welcome," they said. "We're so glad you're here."

"You should meet the Lokkes," someone told me. "They host youth group meetings at their house after church."

It felt, as I shook their hands, and widened my face in a bright American smile, like I had found a piece of the home and family I'd left behind.

After the service was over, the Lokkes invited me to their house for a youth group meeting. They lived within walking distance of the *Arbat* Street theater in a majestic stone apartment building that overlooked the *Moskva* River. It was filled with smooth wooden floors, expansive American sofas, and enough rooms to dedicate one space just to exercise equipment.

"Come use it any time," Lori Lokke said. She was loud, and her eyes were sparkling and kind. The way she spoke was so friendly, it felt goofy. There was an extra cartoon-like gulp to her voice, like she was a character playing an exuberant mom in a Disney movie.

Her husband, Paul Lokke, wore collared shirts and big smiles and worked as a manager at an oil company. He was quieter than Lori, but kind and perpetually cheerful. He asked us how our weeks were going, helped us hang up our coats by the door, and sometimes led the Bible study sessions.

Their daughter, Amanda, was fifteen—the same age as I was. She had serious blue eyes, white-blonde hair, and an intensity to her that didn't stop her from laughing when we played card games or made huge batches of tacos in her mom's kitchen.

The Lokke family welcomed me with open arms. Their apartment felt like a home I hadn't realized I'd been missing, and visiting them for a few hours on Sundays to eat lunch and talk about Bible verses was a tiny break from the fury and relentlessness of the Academy. We didn't talk about technique or repertoire. We didn't stretch or practice verbs of motion. We ate cookies and laughed and played icebreaker games. Sometimes we watched a movie.

The Lokkes were always there for me when I was having a dark day.

But I didn't know how dark my days would eventually get.

In January, a Russian surgeon laid me flat on a white table and fed me, like an object dropped down a gaping white throat, into an MRI machine.

Afterward, he showed me a glowing blue-and-white image of the inside of my foot.

"I know exactly what's wrong with you," the doctor said, pointing to a tiny, bright dot on the screen. "You see that? That's a bone chip. That bottom part of your heel has come completely off. And I know exactly how to fix it. You need surgery."

I called Mom.

"I broke my foot, Mom," I said. "The doctor says it's serious and that I need an operation to keep dancing."

Mom has always been good in a medical emergency. She had many technical questions that I couldn't answer. She wanted to know about X-rays, bone scans, MRIs, CT scans, spirals, obliques, transverse, or comminuted fractures. I didn't know what to say. I'd barely understood what the doctor had said in Russian myself.

"I think you should come home, Joy," she said. "Let's get you a plane ticket. Let's get you in to some doctors here."

"This surgeon is really good," I said. "He designed the operation that fixed Artem Ovcharenko. He knows how to help dancers. He's the only person in the world who can do this operation."

"Joy." Mom's voice was quiet.

"He doesn't need to do a bone graft. He can just remove the chip. It's an incredible surgery. It got Ovcharenko back on his feet in just a few weeks. This is it, Mom."

Mom sighed. "Joy we have some bad news."

I heard Dad's voice on the line.

"Hey sweetheart," Dad said. His voice was quiet too.

"You need to come home," Mom said.

Dad cleared his throat, "Things aren't going well for us business-wise," he said.

"We don't have any money. We're going to lose the house," Mom interjected. "They're going to foreclose."

"We'll support you no matter what," Dad said. "Let's get you home and get you taken care of."

"We'll buy you a plane ticket back," Mom said. "But we can't pay for this Moscow surgery. Even if we could, we can't pay your tuition for the rest of the semester. You need to come home."

I couldn't believe what I was hearing.

"If you buy that plane ticket, you'll be wasting your money," I said. "I'm not coming back."

I hung up the phone.

I stopped talking to my parents. I stopped calling them, answering the phone, replying to emails.

I'd never done anything like this in my life. My parents had always talked about umbrellas of authority and how safety happened when you respected people in charge and respected God and honored your parents. It felt wrong to disobey them. But it also felt wrong to leave Russia.

Things had changed for my parents over the last few years while I'd been living in Washington, D.C., and then Moscow. The financial crisis had torn through Dad's bank account and capsized all the investors he'd been relying on. Mom had gone back to school and gotten her medical license to practice in Texas. She'd cut her long hair short, sent all my siblings to public school, started working at a hospital again.

When I'd visited them at Christmas, things had been more subdued than usual. Mom seemed more stressed than I'd expected. But Dad was the same as ever. His Facebook posts were filled with pictures of all the things he was proud of: videos of my ballet performances, pictures of my brother signing with Dartmouth to play football. He spoke of the big things we were all going to do, lapsed into bright hypotheticals, avoided the tension that wound its way around the room.

"We'll support you, Joy," Dad always said when we talked. "We're behind you all the way."

But things were worse than I'd realized.

In Moscow, after I finished talking to my parents, I felt scared and angry.

I checked out of the hospital and moved back to the dorm rooms.

My classmates came to see me. They sat down at the edge of my bed to stare at my injured foot and listen to me talk about my parents.

"It's awful," they said. "This is a tragedy."

Some of them said a decision to leave would mean the end of my career.

"If you leave here, you're done," they said. "You'll just be the girl who was talented but got injured."

Arkhipova came and sat on the end of my bed too. She thought the surgeon who'd fixed Ovcharenko was the right choice.

"Don't go," Arkhipova advised. "If you leave Moscow, you won't come back. You'll be done."

Even the school director, Leonova, had heard what was happening. She stood grimly at the edge of my door, her lipsticked mouth pressed into a line.

"We need to find a way to pay for this," she said. "Maybe I could contribute something. You need to get this surgery."

I was used to kindness and understanding from my classmates, but it felt a little shocking to see all my strict and unyielding teachers bent over my bed, their eyes filled with concern.

I agreed with all of them. But I didn't have the money.

I wrapped my foot in bandages, hobbled down the Academy stairs to a taxi, and drove to visit ICF. My friends there had been praying for me, sending me emails and text messages. But I wanted to ask for prayer in person. Maybe someone could lay hands on me or anoint me with holy oil or something. These were the tools that people at my church in Santa Monica had always said led to miracles. Maybe if I prayed hard enough, with the right amount of people, I'd get answers.

I sat through the worship songs, listening to lyrics about how powerful God was, how loving. And I couldn't help it—I started crying. I believed it, of course—that God was omnipotent and made out of love. But I wanted more than words in a song. I wanted a miracle.

After the service was over, Mr. Lokke came up to me.

"How are you, Joy?" He looked concerned.

I smiled and shrugged, wiped a tear off my cheek.

"I don't know what to tell my parents," I said.

"Listen, Joy," he said. "I don't really want anyone to know about this—it should just be something between you, Mrs. Lokke, and me, but we feel like God has put it on our hearts to help you."

I listened quietly.

"We'd like to pay for your surgery," he said.

I was stunned.

"Why don't you come live with us for a while? We'll drive you to your surgery, and you can recover at our place for some time after."

It was the miracle I needed. Within a few days, I was in the hospital, swaddled in a robe, my foot engorged, distended, and resting on an ice pack.

The Lokkes got on the phone with my parents to talk about money and medical care.

"This clinic is the best in Moscow," they assured Mom. "We go there for care ourselves. She's in good hands."

They helped me write a letter to my parents.

"Don't try to argue with them," Mr. Lokke advised. "Just explain your thinking and be respectful."

It took me close to ten tries to write the letter, but eventually I did it.

"I need to stay here," I wrote. "If the Lord has everything under control, then he's got me, and if it's in the Lord's will, then he'll open a door."

After that, Mom was different.

"Okay, Joy," she wrote back. "I can see that the Lord is moving in your life."

She gave her blessing, and I went ahead with the surgery.

The day of the operation, I lay down on a hospital bed and waited as a nurse wheeled me into the surgery theater. I watched the masked face of the doctor put a clear, plastic anesthesia cup over my nose and mouth. As I drifted to the edge of consciousness, I swear to you, I heard music.

"Just relax, Joy," the doctor said.

But as I blinked into blackness, I slipped into the most vivid and compelling drug-induced dream I've ever had. I was back on the Bolshoi stage, lights shining in my face, orchestra tuning their instruments.

"We're going to need you to keep dancing," a surgeon said in this delusion, walking onto the stage in head-to-toe scrubs.

"You keep performing," he added, scalpel in hand. "We'll operate while you dance."

"It will be okay!" my teacher encouraged from the wings.

It was a hard performance, in this dream that I still remember. It felt like running up a hill that kept getting longer and steeper while holding my foot steady for the surgeon's knife to cut. I strained and stilled, leapt and held, turned and bent and halted. But when the dance was over, I took a bow and saw, applauding from the theater seats, my family and all my old teachers from Austin and Santa Monica and Washington, D.C.

My heart swelled as I dipped into a curtsy—my foot miraculously good as new.

"She proved us all wrong," I heard one of my former teachers say as they clapped. "Look at her now."

CHAPTER 9

Return

This year is going to be different.

That's what I told myself, as I sat, strapped to a seat in the spine of a plane that fell from the stratosphere over Russia.

It was 2010, I was sixteen years old, and I had returned for another year of Bolshoi Ballet Academy training. But this time I was ready. The oozing sutures and inflamed tissues of my foot had mostly healed. I had cemented myself in Arkhipova's heart as her star student, able to rise from injury and star in difficult summer performances. My Russian had turned into something effortless—I could understand the voice of the pilot speaking from the cabin sound system, the phone conversations of fellow passengers, the signs in bolded Cyrillic at the airport.

This year is going to be great.

I let this confidence fill my thoughts as I stood in the cigarette- and cologne-scented line at passport control. I knew exactly where to collect my bags, and just how to switch my SIM card to see the little MTS service bars blink into life on my screen. I recognized the names of roads outside the airport, the lines of cars gliding up to the curb to whisk passengers away to the boil of Moscow traffic.

I'm ready. I belong here.

More importantly, Moscow, in a way I'd never before experienced, was ready for me. As I stood outside the glass doors of the airport with my suitcases, a black Mercedes sedan with tinted windows rolled to a stop beside me.

"Djoy?" A Russian driver bounded out the left side of the car. He lifted my bags into his trunk, then held the back door open for me. He had been sent there with orders to find me.

"*Spasibo!*" I thanked him in what I was sure was accent-less Russian.

We filtered smoothly into Moscow traffic, and I couldn't help smiling to myself. The car was quiet and smelled of leather. It was completely unlike the onion- and body-odor-scented metro tunnels and rowdy touring buses I'd been riding on all last year with my classmates. It felt as if I had returned to a city that wanted me.

Mom had spent weeks preparing me for this new Moscow into which I'd been invited.

"Make sure you say thank you, and leave everything cleaner than you found it," she'd said. "Don't take anything for granted. Pat may be a friend of your grandparents', but this is an incredibly generous thing she's doing."

I knew Mom was right. Pat was the reason I had a personal escort in an expensive car waiting for me at the airport. Pat was the reason I wouldn't be returning to the sewer-scented Academy dormitories. Pat was the reason we were driving down a narrow street lined with leafy trees, pastel-colored stone buildings, designer shops, and jewelry stores in central Moscow. Pat was the reason I was able to afford a second year of tuition at the Academy. Pat was the reason I was there at all.

"There's the Bolshoi Theater." The driver nodded out the window at the familiar limestone facade—still closed for renovations.

"You're a ballerina, right?" He looked at me in the rearview mirror, then out again at the huge Bolshoi fountain that splashed water into a stone pool, rimmed with pigeons.

"From Pat's house, you'll be able to walk to the best theater in the world in less than five minutes."

I smiled back at him.

This year is going to be different, and it's going to be better.

Pat stood at the open door to her third-floor apartment in slippers, her dyed red-blonde hair in a frizzy triangle around her head.

"Come in, come in!" she said, wrinkling her lips in a smile.

I clacked my suitcase over the transom to the smooth parquet of her entryway.

"Welcome!" She gave me a hug, her voice raspy from decades of cigarettes.

"Thank you so much for having me." I bent over to hug her, smiling in what I hoped she saw as gratitude.

The apartment behind her was magnificent: a columned entry, arched ceilings, soft lighting, and damask-upholstered furniture. The walls were so thick, they swallowed the sounds of Moscow.

"Here, you can hang your jacket in the closet," she said, sliding open a door to reveal a heavy row of fur coats so numerous, I couldn't see where they ended.

"Your room is this way." She stepped farther into her apartment and swung a door open to reveal a single bed and a wall filled with polished wood cabinets, bookshelves, and a desk with a chair.

"Make yourself at home," she said. "You're probably tired after your flight and want to unpack. We'll go out to dinner later."

She left, clicking the door closed behind her.

I stared at the wallpaper and the glossy window that opened to a yellow stone courtyard.

All this for me?

I couldn't believe the luxury. No hanging my wet laundry in a damp dormitory *sushilka* drying room. No stolen warm-up clothes or hoarded toilet paper. No used tampons and vomit on the floor of a communal bathroom. No *discoteka* music at one o'clock in the morning. I zipped open my suitcase and started draping my clothes over hangers.

I heard Mom's voice in my mind.

"Imagine you're at a crime scene," she'd said. "Clean up after yourself like someone might disinfect after a murder."

I arranged my shoes in a row by the door, placed my toiletries in a bag at a 90-degree angle on the desk, set my Bible on one of the shelves next to my journal.

Pat was someone I had met that summer in New York when my grandmother invited her over for a visit. She was a venture capitalist who'd spent years backing startup Russian companies in the chaotic 1990s after the fall of the Soviet Union. In some ways, she reminded me of my grandparents: her wrinkled skin, the pink blush on her cheeks, her pearl earrings and East Coast accent. She'd been good friends with my grandfather before he died. They'd served on the board of the Natural History Museum in New York, and they'd swapped stories about Moscow: her about venture capital in the gangster Russian 1990s, Grandpa about friendships with genius Soviet scientists. Both of them had refused to let Russia intimidate them.

In other ways, at that first meeting, Pat had reminded me of Dad. She mentioned, cigarette in hand, wild stories of business deals she'd knit together when she'd moved to Russia from New York. She was casual about the adventures she'd lived in a post-Soviet country where it was never clear what was and wasn't illegal. But her pale eyes lit up when I sat in my grandmother's apartment and talked about my dreams—of becoming a ballerina, of dancing at the Bolshoi Theater.

"It's good that you're ambitious. Don't doubt yourself, just make sure you work hard," she had rasped, tapping ash into a tray on my grandmother's table.

She and my grandmother had exchanged glances as my grandmother poured tea.

"I've always liked artists and actresses," Pat had said. "My roommate in college studied at Juilliard."

She'd paused, then asked, "How would you like to be my roommate?"

Pat Cloherty did not beat around the bush.

"I've got a nice apartment in Moscow—it's just a few blocks away from the Bolshoi," she'd said. "It's getting lonely. I'd like to have a roommate. Why don't you move in?"

I knew this was the year things would be better, not only because I had a fancy new place to live, but because I had a teacher at the Academy—Arkhipova—who loved me and to whom I'd proven myself.

Most of my friends—Anton, Artem, Trofim, and Katya—had all graduated and left the Academy for jobs at prestigious theaters around Moscow. I knew I would miss them, but I also knew I wouldn't be lonely this year. A new group of friends had joined the Academy—a trio of talent from America.

They were the first people I looked for when I showed up at the Academy later that week: Gabe Stone Shayer, Mario Labrador, and Masha Beck. I'd met them in dance classes in New York, and now they were in Moscow. They jumped on me with hugs when I saw them.

"I'm in Leonova's class," Masha said.

"And we're with Kuznetsov," Gabe and Mario said.

"Lucky you," I let them know. "Both of those teachers are legends. Leonova leads the school, and everyone knows Kuznetsov's boys are the best. If you're in his class, you're going to become great dancers."

Secretly, though, I knew I was the one who'd won the lottery. Arkhipova was the sort of teacher who saw the best in everyone. She was magic about turning students into the types of dancers they were meant to be. More importantly, she believed in me. This year, after all the progress I'd made, I knew she was going to launch me into new heights of success.

When I set foot on the green carpet of the Academy's second-floor hallway, I couldn't wait to see her. I wanted to tell her about my summer, to show her how much my fouetté turns had improved.

Most of my classmates were already waiting outside our studio when I arrived. They were spread out on the floor, stretching, their legs over their ears. We were like lions, I sometimes thought—awake and gloriously fast in the studio, but lounging, blinking in the sunlight, draped on the carpets and radiators in between rehearsals.

"*Privet!*" I called out a cheerful hello, then sat beside them on the floor, bending and pulling the muscles in my arms.

"How was your summer?" I asked Stasia. Then in a whisper, nodding at a new girl nearby, "Who's that?"

This was someone I had never met before. She was beautiful, with dark hair twisted in a knot on her head and impeccably turned-out hips that flattened her legs into ruler-perfected parallel lines when she pliéd, bending her knees.

"That's Nastia," Stasia whispered back. "From Belarus."

"Have you seen Arkhipova yet?" I asked.

But Stasia just stared at me.

"Didn't you know?" she said. "Arkhipova quit the school."

"Her husband got sick," another classmate offered. "She left to take care of him."

"We have a new teacher," Stasia said. "Elena Alexandrovna Bobrova."

Bobrova walked down the hallway toward us. She was thin with icy blue eyes, short-cropped hair and a delicate circle of jewelry around her neck. She walked quickly and nodded a greeting to us as she passed to unlock the door to the studio.

We all jumped to our feet.

"Hello, Elena Alexandrovna," we said in chorus.

She nodded at all of us as we filed past, clutching our dance bags.

I was bewildered.

Arkhipova quit? Oh my God. Is her husband okay? Will she come back soon? Is Bobrova our teacher for good now?

I lined up at the barre with my classmates and made sure to set my hand in the middle. It was the top spot that Arkhipova had let me stay all last year, the spot where I wanted to belong.

I didn't know much about Bobrova. She'd spent decades at the Bolshoi Theater dancing queen roles in all the classics: *Sleeping Beauty*, *Swan Lake*, *La Bayadere*. Her daughter had followed in her footsteps and was dancing at the Bolshoi now.

She stood quiet and grim at the front of the room while we arranged ourselves, then glanced at the pianist in the corner.

We began, at her instruction, to plié in neat, synchronized triangles as the pianist plunked out bars of music. Bobrova watched us closely, her arms folded, her eyebrows arched, her mouth set. When we moved to floor-sweeping tendus, she marched over to where I was standing at the barre, lifted my hand off the balustrade, and led me away from the center position. Then she nodded her head at Nastia, the new girl, who slid into the vacancy, the top of the pyramid, the center of Bobrova's attention.

Bobrova's heels clicked as she walked back to the front of the room.

"Together now," she told us. "We need to move as one—a united corps."

I felt my cheeks grow red as I brushed my slippered toes out against the floor and then back into fifth. I stared at the back of Nastia's neck, the pins in her hair, the line of her beautifully extended spine.

We weren't even ten minutes into class, and I'd already been demoted. *Who is this new girl, and why does Bobrova love her?*

I watched her without trying to seem jealous. Nastia was striking. Her turnout was arrow-straight. The port de bras of her arms and shoulders was as solid as a metal crowbar, and her movements were clean and precise. I watched as her arms floated effortlessly beside her during barre, her ankles rising in sharp, straight pillars over her pointe shoes. During combinations, she floated through the movements with intricate footwork and clean, hyper-extended lines.

I could jump, I could do turns, but in comparison to Nastia, I was not clean.

Bobrova saw right through me—my sloppy snowplow feet, my shaky carriage, my off-kilter pelvis. I felt like a sludgy, un-baked cake someone was trying to hide under fancy icing.

"No, no, no! Don't sit in your hips!" Bobrova called out, her mouth in a thin and disappointed line. "Lift up from your vertebrae!"

Bobrova hates me.

This was the thought that flooded my brain for the entirety of September as I marked out steps in the wings of the Academy performance hall, while Nastia rehearsed center stage. It rattled around in my thoughts as I took the metro home after classes, or sat on the floor stretching in Pat's living room as she sipped her Johnnie Walker and read the latest Nora Roberts's paperback.

Why is Nastia the favorite? Maybe it's because her turnout is so good.

I could feel Bobrova's anger smoldering at me over the unacceptable angle of my knees and the uneven square of my pelvis over my legs. In the mirror I stared at the curve of my hips and the line of my thighs. It was all wrong.

Nastia, on the other hand, was amazing. Her turnout was impeccable, and she was as thin and prepubescent as a nine-year-old.

I tried not to let it rattle me. I turned my attention to acting classes and character dance and partnering. These were the classes where I got to see Gabe and Mario.

Mario, from California, was soft-spoken and tall with waves of floppy, dark hair and ramrod-straight posture. His teachers cast him in prince roles and liked to pair us—two dark-haired Americans with a flair for the dramatic—together. He was kind and talented, and, when we practiced our lifts and turns, I was never afraid he'd drop me.

Gabe, from Philadelphia, was confident and funny and an excellent dancer. He was as obsessed with ballet as I was and obstinately determined to succeed. But, unlike me, he was a lot more relaxed about it—able to joke and put things in perspective. He'd nearly turned down a Bolshoi Academy scholarship to go to the School of American Ballet. But he was here now, and we spent our time between classes stretching and gossiping.

Gabe liked to joke about the mystery meats in the cafeteria, the vodka parties in the dorms, and which girls were the most difficult to partner with in class. He and Mario both groaned about how sore their muscles were and how insane their instructor, Kuznetsov, was.

I always managed to add some anxiety to whatever conversation we were having.

"Nastia's getting all the attention and all the good roles in class," I worried out loud. "I'm terrible and Bobrova hates me and I'm not getting any better."

"You're not terrible," Mario shushed.

"Why don't you join our class?" Gabe joked. "Kuznetsov will yell at you, and you'll spend the rest of the day limping around."

I laughed at the suggestion and also at Gabe and Mario as they winced off the floor and dragged their sore legs to the next class.

But Bobrova had given all the prestigious school roles to Nastia, and I was floundering in her lessons. I was desperate. I didn't take long to think about it. I set off through the school hallways until I found Kuznetsov outside his studio.

"Ilya," I said. "Can I join your class?"

He looked at me through his wire-rimmed glasses and paused before answering. I'm not sure whether or not he believed I was serious.

"Sure," he said. "Come tomorrow. And don't be late."

CHAPTER 10

The Markings of a Ballerina

Outside the classroom, Ilya Kuznetsov was unassuming and mild-mannered. He walked around the Academy with a shaved head, wire-rimmed glasses on his face, and the occasional bow tie around his neck. He was short with the ramrod-straight spine and muscled arms of someone who'd dedicated decades of service to either ballet or the military. When I spoke to him backstage at rehearsals, or in the darkened aisles of tour buses and airplanes during our school trips, he was quiet; direct and cerebral; fluent in English; and filled with informed opinions on history, photography, film, art, and social media. He ran a YouTube channel with professional-quality videos of student performances and Academy rehearsals.

But inside the classroom, Kuznetsov transformed into a Napoleonic alter-ego. This is what I learned as I stood in his studio in a line of second-year boys. His eyes narrowed to slits behind oval-shaped lenses, and he grew intensely focused, deathly calm, and darkly sarcastic.

"Let us return to 1862. We will put ourselves through the physical exercises endured by Maria Taglioni," he said, referring to the athletic nineteenth-century ballerina who was the first woman to dance on pointe.

He was serene as he lined us up at the barre, all facing the same direction. But soon his voice filled with cold fury, and he stalked around the studio in a rage, intent on the angles and velocity of our limbs. He made us repeat simple leg or arm movements—shifting from first to second position over and over for thirty minutes straight until our muscles shook and we could no longer feel our fingers or toes.

He saw things differently than my other teachers, was engrossed by inner, invisible gears—synapses, sinews, connections, and tissues that affected each of our gestures. Like a watchmaker, he tinkered, listened, stared, fixed. He was obsessed with the floor and our connection to it.

"You have to go through the floor! Inside the floor!" he would shrill at us. "You need to go to the basement level two!"

He unearthed troves of old Russian ballet diaries and notebooks, studied them, and designed his lessons around things past generations had discovered. But he had no patience for our inabilities. He sat at the front of the studio clutching his knees with frustration, rocking his chair backward until it slammed against the mirrors when we failed to properly hear the music or attach our muscles to it. He was enraged with our errors and would leap to his feet and slap our legs or arms into the correct position.

"I absolutely can't understand it. Is this what you call work? I don't get it," he'd say, shaking his head, then add with sarcasm, "You can go home and write in your diary tonight, 'My teacher hit me in class today.' Boo-hoo!"

He demanded perfection and insisted the class continue nonstop, just like in exams. If someone made a mistake, he screeched the lesson to a halt and demanded we repeat the entire exercise routine from the very beginning.

He did not take things easy on me because I was a girl. Once, I did eight repetitions of something instead of seven. Kuznetsov didn't miss.

"Stop!" he shouted.

Everyone groaned. One boy looked like he wanted to cry.

"What was that, Joy?" Kuznetsov said.

"I'm sorry—I thought we were supposed to do eight," I whimpered.

"Back to pliés!" Kuznetsov said, making us repeat the last forty minutes of work.

At my second or third class with him, I began to grow dizzy. He'd held us at attention for nearly an hour, our muscles on fire, sweat rolling off our chins, mascara streaming down my face. My body had not yet adjusted to the pace he set, and my legs trembled. But somehow I kept going, watching my arms and legs push through the pain to perform. It was horrible. I fantasized about throwing up, so I'd have an excuse to leave. I wondered if it would be possible to faint or fall to the floor unconscious so I could catch my breath. But I couldn't make myself do it.

It's just as well, I thought. *Probably Kuznetsov would just slap me awake and make me keep going.*

He was relentless. When our legs shook and tears streamed down our faces, he just stared back at us.

"Why aren't you doing it? Did someone tell you you can't? Just do it," he'd say, as if the only problem we were experiencing was our belief in what our bodies could do.

Sometimes I'd let the fear and insecurity I felt inside show up on my face in a creased brow or tear-filled eyes.

"I can kick you out of my class anytime, Joy," Kuznetsov reminded me. "Don't show me with your face that you want to be here. Show me with your actions."

After weeks of pushing past the limit of my physical stamina in Kuznetsov's class, I started to feel I was getting stronger—my muscles were turning to a flexible steel, my lungs expanding to draw in more air. My ability to turn out at the hip had transformed. I'd been trying for years to imitate the tilted ankles and board-flat pelvises I saw from naturally turned-out ballerinas. But Kuznetsov showed me the secrets he'd learned from his teacher, Pestov; how to push my pinkie toes to the floor, engage the entire back line of my muscles, access the inner rotators of my hip, and lift my pelvic carriage and vertebrae.

"It will take you six months to be able to do this," he told me, "and you won't be able to understand the value of it for years. But wait and see. This is how it's done."

He was right. More than a decade later, this is still how I teach my students to move.

In class, Kuznetsov loved making fun of us.

"You Americans think you have freedom," he'd say. "Your classes are just warm-ups."

He gave all of us nicknames.

"Hey, Democracy!" he'd call to Gabe. "You're not putting your heels down. Stand in passé."

Gabe put his heels on the floor, and Kuznetsov walked up to him.

"Do you feel strong? Do you feel stable?" he breathed into Gabe's face.

"Yes," Gabe said. "I do."

Kuznetsov put his foot on Gabe's thigh.

"Do you still feel stable?" Kuznetsov asked.

"Yes?" Gabe said.

Kuznetsov kicked him in the leg, making him fly backward across the room, all the way to the barre.

"Why didn't you stay in passé?" he asked. "I didn't tell you to go out of passé."

We left his classes drenched in sweat, dizzy, and nauseous, and we'd wake in the morning like centenarians who'd just been through hip surgery. We were stiff and sore, our muscles painful to the touch. But Kuznetsov's lessons sank in. We learned the technicalities of proper ballet form, the motions our body needed to make to function as a fluid unit, and how to attach our muscles to notes of music. It was masochistic and painful, but Gabe, Mario, and I all felt proud of ourselves for enduring. When we'd pushed past our limits and sweated through one of Kuznetsov's new challenges, we felt triumphant and fulfilled.

"Oh my God," we'd pant to each other in the hallway after class. "I just did that."

I grew stronger in Kuznetsov's class, but it didn't seem to make a difference to Bobrova. She ran her classes like an assembly line, sorting us into rows, running us through exercises. She focused on form and technical ability. Whomever she thought was best got her undivided attention.

I could tell she was frustrated with us most of the time. We had no form, no energy, no precision. She sighed and scolded.

"You're terrible! Why must I keep repeating myself?" she'd say.

Her eye was always on the end goal. She wanted to send one of us to a famous theater where we'd headline classical ballets and draw crowds. Then our name would appear on her résumé, and she'd be able to say that she made us.

"Every once in a while there is a girl who is especially talented: a girl with step, with turnout, lightness of movement, plasticity, transparency, spirit, and soul," she would say, a faraway look in her eye. "These are the markings of a ballerina."

When she looked at us, trembling at the barre, I thought, she probably just saw a bunch of factory rejects: misshapen, crooked, rusty at the hinges. I missed Arkhipova—without her reassurance, I felt a deep current of doubt begin to eat away at something inside of me.

Am I making any progress? Am I going somewhere? Am I a real ballerina?

With Arkhipova, I'd been sure. But with Bobrova, I couldn't tell. She seemed to have eyes only for Nastia. Nastia was the girl she praised and smiled at. Nastia was the girl she convinced school leadership to cast in leading roles.

Gabe knew all my insecurities and worries. He could see the way my body stiffened when I was nervous. He watched me grow frustrated whenever I couldn't do something and repeat myself over and over, blinded with anxiety, trying to get it right. I'd get worked up and worn out, just cycling through the same exact mistake over and over. I'd position my arms, draw in my abdomen, push off with my leg, lift my knee, and swing into a turn. But the anxiety made me wobble, weaken, and fall.

"Okay, shut up," he'd say, clapping his hands together and shaking his head after watching me. "Just. *Stop.*"

He'd wait until I was still, watch me take a deep breath.

"Relax," he'd order, staring at me until he could see the tension leave my body.

"Okay. Good," he'd say. Then he'd try again, "Now do it."

Bobrova and Kuznetsov saw the same problem. And honestly, Arkhipova had seen it too.

"You're not on a TV show, you're not Sylvie Guillem," Kuznetsov told me. "No one is filming you. You don't have to overact. Calm down. You're like a gust of wind."

Bobrova said similar things.

"Stop lying!" she scolded me in class. "Don't fill yourself to make it happen. These movements need to come naturally, honestly. You're flying ahead of the music. You're too nervous. Calm down."

But I could not be calm. It was November, and Nastia was still at the top of the class pyramid.

If I couldn't get lead roles, I wouldn't be able to convince the school leaders and the theater directors who watched our performances that I was someone who belonged at the center of a Russian stage. If Bobrova didn't believe I was destined for the Bolshoi, no one else would either.

Maybe it's my body. Maybe I'm too fat.

This is where my mind went.

I looked at the curve of my hips in the mirror, the shape of my thighs.

"Bobrova looked at me like I'm fat," I told Gabe.

"Oh?" He laughed. "What kind of look was that? You can't read minds, Joy. What are you talking about? You're not fat at all."

But I didn't believe him. I saw in the mirror how much tinier Nastia was. And in October, when we lined up at the scale for our weigh-in, I saw a number I didn't like.

I'd heard girls retching in school bathrooms, I'd seen the piles of vomit in the shower, by the toilets. I saw students who restricted themselves to single slices of bread and tiny bites of sausage in the cafeteria.

Teachers in Russia were blunt about everything, unconcerned with hurt feelings and fairness and explicit about the shape and size of our bodies.

"For us in Russia, the aesthetic is the most important thing." They would wax poetic sometimes. "If you don't have that aesthetic to begin with, then we can't even look at what you've done."

I took what they said seriously, just like everything else. They never encouraged vomiting, but weight loss was definitely suggested. The school scheduled regular weigh-ins to make sure we weren't gaining too much. We lined up by the nurse's office, stepped onto the scale, watched Academy staff take note of the numbers revealed by the sliding metal frame along a precariously balanced horizontal beam. If the number was too high, if our muscles, bones, and organs pushed too heavily on the scale, we could get dismissed from the Academy.

This is just part of being a ballerina, I told myself. All the best ballerinas in school seemed to occasionally go through rashes of vomiting in the dorm bathrooms.

This is how it's done, I told myself.

I convinced myself that regular food was bad and started to go on weird diets. I'd eat only yogurt. Or I'd skip breakfast and only let myself eat dried pineapple and candied peanuts after rehearsal. In the evening, I'd consume half a chocolate Kinder bar with a partially filled glass of raspberry-flavored *kisel'*—a gelled Russian drink that paused the constant, gnawing ache in my stomach. It left me shaky and dizzy in my ballet classes, but the number on the scale was something I could control. Losing weight seemed like the answer to my problems.

One of my classmates told me about an online site with instructions for starving myself, ridding my body of food. I scrolled its pages at night when no one was looking. It suggested various techniques to trigger a gag reflex.

A few weeks after arriving in Russia for my second year of ballet classes, I locked myself in the bathroom when Pat was gone, stuck something down my throat, and vomited into the toilet.

It felt terrible and hurt my esophagus, and it made my mouth taste disgusting. But, as I put my hand on the flush and watched the mess of half-digested food swirl down the hole, I told myself that this was a rebuke to all the mistakes I had made. If I could be the person to punish myself before anyone else, maybe I could avoid their displeasure and earn their approval.

My whole life I had heard women criticize their bodies.

"Ugh, I'm so fat," they told themselves out loud, turning away from the mirror. "I'm ugly."

I watched *The Devil Wears Prada* together with my mom and sister and we went around the house afterward, crowing a version of Emily Blunt's line about eating a cube of cheese as soon as you feel like you're going to faint.

Mom was a doctor, so she was always straightforward when it came to medical things. She was insistent about the harms of eating disorders—especially bulimia. "If you have to pick one, pick anorexia," I'd heard her say, meant more as a warning than literal instruction. "It's better than bulimia."

Vomiting changed the way your salivary glands operated, according to Mom. It ruined the way your pancreas, gall bladder, and stomach lining functioned. You lost essential nutrients, changed the acid base of your body, damaged your liver, affected your kidneys. Bulimia ate away at your internal organs and your brain. It was dangerous. So was anorexia. But in combination? In combination, these things could corrode your body from the inside, Mom said. In combination, these eating disorders could kill you.

She was always careful to talk about my body in positive ways.

"Honey, you're beautiful," she would tell me. "You're healthy, you're muscular, you look wonderful."

But I was pretty sure Mom herself had an eating disorder. Maybe Grandma too. I had memories of both of them going through weird periods of time when they ate too little. They liked to criticize themselves out loud and seemed to suffer from a type of fear that weighed on them in ways I didn't fully understand.

Mom was big on self-control. "It's a fruit of the Spirit," she'd say. It was a phrase she drilled into us. "Practice self-control," she'd lecture my siblings when they got in fights, when they yelled at each other inside the house.

Restricting the number of calories I consumed felt like self-control. This is what I told myself.

This is what it takes to be a ballerina.

The science of eating disorders doesn't matter.

If I'm skinny enough, my dancing will improve, Bobrova will notice me, I will be given the roles on stage that I want.

These are the things I repeated to myself, the things I wanted to believe were true.

But there was a part of me that knew—what I was doing was pulling the pin on a terrible and dangerous grenade, setting in motion something disastrous I wouldn't be able to stop.

Chapter 11

Protégé

By December, I was a mess. My throat was sore, and my fouettés were shaky. My face swelled, and the bones of my hollowed-out body poked out from under my skin like tent poles. I trembled in class, dizzy and unfocused. During one rehearsal, I lost consciousness and slumped to the floor. My anxiety was like a fever inside my veins—it threw me off-balance in the studio and infected all my movements.

When I felt bad about a mistake in class, or a look a teacher gave me or when I saw that my name was missing from a cast list, I turned my misery inward. I denied myself food as punishment, stuck objects down my throat as penance.

It reminded me in some ways of church—of the prayers I'd learned as a child, and the sermons I'd heard. I knew I was unworthy, disgusting, rotting with sin. I'd heard, since I was little, of the need to prostrate myself at the feet of a savior, confess my foulness, be purged of imperfection.

I punished myself and begged for help.

Lord, I need you. Lord, I can't do it on my own. Lord, help me fix what you want me to fix, learn what you want me to learn. Help me.

In the last weeks of the year, like a queen handing down land and a title, the school director granted me a role in an Academy performance of the *Nutcracker*. I spent weeks rehearsing it in the studios.

But on the cold December night of my performance, as usual, I was a mess. Gabe saw me waiting in the wings, my face caked with stage makeup, my hair slicked back and pinned with little fake pink flowers. I bent and jumped and kicked my legs in the air, warming my muscles, stomping like a racehorse at the gate. Fear radiated off of me, pulsing and rabid.

I knew of no other way to perform. Terror was baked into my nervous system. It was a knot of yarn that snarled in my chest and made me frantic whenever I had to compete or appear in front of an audience.

How am I going to do this? What if I fail? What if I fall? What if I can't make it through?

Gabe paused and looked at me, frowning. I'm sure I looked like a wild animal caught in a cage: my eyes wide, my movements jerky and desperate.

I turned up the corners of my mouth at him. It wasn't exactly a smile, but he knew me.

"Don't be afraid of what people will think," he said. "Just try to have fun. You've got this."

I bent at my knees, at my waist, pumping the blood through my body. It wasn't like I hadn't heard this advice before.

He frowned again.

"Okay," he shook his head and grabbed me by the shoulders. "When you go out there, don't try to be like Natalia Osipova. Dance like Evgenia Obraztsova."

I could see immediately, in my mind's eye, what Gabe was talking about. Natalia Osipova was explosive. She was Kitri, Carmen, Esmerelda. She moved bright: like the scent of an orange peel personified; like a supernova in human form with ballet shoes tied to its feet. She was overwhelming.

But Obraztsova was different: soft, smooth, thoughtful, delicate. She was Juliet, *La Sylphide*, Giselle—moonlight and elegance, a ribbon of cake frosting poured from the sky that spiraled graciously to the patisserie counter in mindful arches and folds.

I was always trying to be like Osipova—to overpower the audience with my expression. But maybe Gabe was right. Maybe what I needed was to channel a ribbon, not a firework.

I took his advice. I went out on stage to Tchaikovsky's harps, violins, and woodwinds, and I thought about Obraztsova: her lingering turns, her artfully poised elbows, her articulate bows and prances. I thought about delicate porcelain and deep pools of water and softly falling flakes of snow.

It worked. Somehow the focus on something measured and calm worked to deepen my breathing, slow my reactions, draw out my movements, center me in the moment where I watched my wrists and hands articulate slowly in front of me, like something pulled in slow motion through water.

Gabe was ecstatic when I got off stage.

"Ohmigod-ohmigod-ohmigod! Yes! Yes! Yes!" He squeezed me in a hug, and jumped up and down when I came to a standstill behind the curtain. "That's it! You've got it!"

It felt like I had fit an ancient key into its lock.

So this is what it feels like to dance as art—not to prove myself, not to react to fear, not to hit everyone over the head with how hard I'm working.

"You don't need to yell with your dancing," Gabe said, beaming at me in pride. "You can do it softly."

My *Nutcracker* performance was a success. But my bulimia remained rampantly out of control. My skin had turned gray, my cheeks hollow, dark circles had grown like bruises under my eyes. I felt shaky and weak. But when I stepped on the scale in Pat's bathroom, I saw a number that was lower than it had ever been. It made me feel trapped, like someone who could not perform unless she did terrible things to herself behind closed doors.

But Bobrova seemed delighted. In class, she could not stop staring at me. She showered me with enthusiastic corrections about how to feel pirouettes with the inner part of my leg; how to position my shoulder blades like weapons sheathed down on either side of my spine. She paced the front of the room in her elegant cashmere sweaters, her hair in shimmering, hair-sprayed loops, and spoke quiet words of encouragement.

"Good, Joy. Beautiful. Well done," she said.

She began calling me, *Joyenka*, telling me I reminded her of her daughter—the one who was a success, the one she had coaxed to a place of honor in the Bolshoi Theater's ranks of dancers.

I couldn't tell exactly what was happening. Was it that I'd found a way to be calmer and more intentional in my movements? Was this the result of Gabe's coaching? Was it the relentless technical focus of Bobrova's expertise? Was the conditioning in Kuznetsov's studio changing my capacity for movement?

I had also, for several months, been seeking the help of a private ballet coach who rehearsed me in secret in the mornings before my classes began. This was a woman, Tatiana Talanova, stooped with age and soft gray hair who had been an instructor at the famed Mariinsky Theater for decades. Perhaps the covert hours I'd spent in her studio, learning turnout and pacing, had finally improved me.

Or was Bobrova noticing me because I was losing weight, my body eating itself from the inside out?

I couldn't, in my anxiety-driven stupor, tell which it was. All I knew was that Bobrova began putting my name on cast lists. I donned a gauzy periwinkle costume and danced in *La Fille Ma Gardee*. I attached a tiara to my slicked-down hair and performed *Awakening the Flora* to delicate musical notes. When Jill Biden made a diplomatic visit to Moscow, I was on stage at the Academy to show her the talents our teachers were capable of refining.

The school director, Marina Leonova, noticed me. She often presided over our rehearsals, standing in the dark cavern of the theater in her Chanel jackets and polished heels. She kept a microphone in her hand to make quiet corrections—redirecting the shining, sweating students who turned and lifted and bowed on stage in front of her.

"Higher, girls, please," she would say. Or sometimes, "No, Vanya, that's too soon."

She commented with decisiveness after my *Flora* performance, "Joy is very good."

It was said in the deathly calm way she had, a steady gaze in her eyes, a stern set to her mouth, her hair swirled into a stiff and majestic twist on the back of her head. She was a woman at the top of the Russian ballet world's vertical of power, a person invited to important functions, a person whose opinion was sought in theaters across the continent. What she wanted was reflected in cast lists and teacher salaries; in who had a job, who had an invitation to audition, and who had the spotlight turned on them.

When one of the leads for an upcoming school performance got an injury, Leonova turned to me.

"We have a ballerina here just waiting in the wings," she said. "Let Joy take Rita's place. She can dance in the upcoming performance."

It was decided. My name was added to the roster that mattered. A cross-Atlantic ticket was procured in my name.

I was so excited, I started to believe I had achieved the impossible: the ability to abuse my body with no consequences.

I was triumphant, walking to Tatiana's house for my early-morning coaching lesson. It was March, and the snow was piled in silty layers at the sides of the road like the inside of a creamy, gravel-flecked *medovik* cake at a Moscow bakery.

My flight to Washington, D.C., was hours away. I'd been sending notes to my parents about the performance. Dad was excited. He'd already gotten tickets and was planning to fly up from Austin to see me. Even Grandma Piel had plans to attend, flying in from New York.

My body felt ready—light and warm in my boots and coat as I trudged up the sidewalk, my feet turned out on the ridges of snow and ice that had been carved over the tops of pavement. The sun was out for longer these days, thinning the hard crusts of ice that froze again overnight, turning the paths at dawn into slippery rinks, dropping hundred-pound icicles from roof ledges to the sidewalks below.

Even my costume was ready and fitted, approved by Bobrova, waiting to be packed: a sparkling white bodice, glittering tiara, and stiff white tutu. It was clothing that made me look like a Swarovski daisy—an ice flower that had magically grown during the dark Russian winter and was ready to bloom under the lights of a wide-open stage.

At the door to Tatiana's sixth-floor apartment that rose high over the traffic-clogged knot of Gagarin Square, I rang the buzzer.

We'd developed a routine in the months I'd been secretly visiting her, paying for lessons with money Pat gave me. I came to her apartment in the quiet morning hours before my Academy classes began. It was the only way to keep her coaching a secret. I couldn't risk the bruised egos my teachers might feel if they or anyone else knew I was seeking outside help. All the public glory of any of my achievements had to go to Bobrova and Leonova.

When I was inside her narrow apartment ballet studio, the ribbons of my shoes laced around my ankles, Tatiana pressed a button to fill the room with soft music.

"Let's warm you up," she said.

She watched, her hair pulled into a stiff, gray bun, as I went through the bends and bows and folds and stretches it took to wake my muscles. Some days she started our lessons by speaking softly to me, like someone might calm a shivering dog. She tried to direct my attention to falling flakes of snow or the incandescent colors of a winter sunset, as if the ability to take in beauty might soothe the anxiety she saw building and vibrating like a blister behind my collarbone.

But in March, in the hours before I left for D.C., she turned immediately to the piece I'd been rehearsing.

"Good," she said, as she watched me, her sun-spotted hands adjusting the way my back arched or my leg extended.

She paused on my chassés—a sort of gliding step—and frowned at them, the wrinkles on her face deepening.

"Do it again, please," she said.

I bent my knees, slid my foot along the floor, curved my arms into a rounded barrel.

"No, no." She shook her head, kneeling to the ground and watching as I repeated the step—a bend at the knee, a gliding of my slippered toes on her wooden floor.

"Your hips should be still and straight—don't tilt them," she said. "Try it again, with your pelvis forward like this."

She pushed her hands into my side as I moved, prodding my hips into the correct shape. But then, as I lifted onto pointe, she nudged me into a new position, and I tripped, my satiny shoes sliding like a toppling tower of champagne glasses until I fell, landing on my side on the hard parquet.

The pain was sharp, and I felt it in the bones at the base of my spine, like a thin wooden rod had snapped somewhere deep in my body.

"Joy!" Tatiana looked distressed, her eyebrows drawn together. She offered her arm and helped me to my feet. "What happened? Are you okay?"

"I think so," I said, standing unsteadily on my feet. Something felt off. There was a clenching pain in my back—a spasm that made it hard to stand.

I bent my knees up and down, trying to locate the pain. Tatiana studied the movements of my hamstrings and calves, the motion of my pelvis. But as I moved, we could find nothing wrong with my hips or my spine.

"I think I'm okay," I said, unsure.

"Be very careful," Tatiana said as I changed into my warm socks and boots, zipped up my coat. "Go home, make sure you put ice on anything that's sore. Make sure you stretch before your next class."

I nodded, packed my dance shoes into my warm-up bag.

"Stay calm," she ordered.

It wasn't until later that morning that I understood.

There was a strange pain that settled in my shoulder and my side. It shot up my arm as I stood in the rocking underground metro car. I felt it as I rested my hand on the escalator that pulled me up to the daylight, spit me out through swinging wooden doors into a blast of cold air as I stepped onto Frunzenskaia Street.

The ache worsened when I arrived at school and pulled my arm out the sleeve of my coat.

Bobrova saw me wincing at the barre as I warmed up.

"Joy, what happened?" she asked. "Did you hurt yourself?"

She looked concerned. The pain was undeniable now: a dull throb that erupted like a stab to my shoulder and elbow when I moved my arm to stretch.

But I couldn't tell her what had really happened or where I'd been that morning.

"I fell on the ice," I said. "I slipped when I was coming out of the metro."

Bobrova stared at my forearm. It had grown swollen and puffy.

"You need to get that looked at," she said.

Bobrova herself took me to the doctor's office. She sat with me in the waiting room, hours before our plane was supposed to take off.

She was composed and quiet as we waited for the doctor. Her blue eyes were grave, her wrinkled cheeks glowing with a tinsel-y pink blush.

"You've made so much progress these last few months," she said, patting my non-injured arm. "I've begun to think of you like a daughter, you know?"

I basked in the affection of her words, in the way she sat nearby as the doctor gently prodded my arm, then laid it on the X-ray machine and covered my chest with a heavy lead apron. The attention I'd longed for from her had finally come, warm and promising.

"You're one of the best girls in my class," Bobrova said, her blue eyes gazing at me. "You're on my heart."

When the doctor came out to show us the black-and-white images of a fractured bone in my wrist, the painful, shattered result of months of secret self-harm and starvation, I had only one thought. As it turned out, Bobrova had the same thought.

"Let's get the bone set," we agreed. "Do whatever is necessary. We have a plane to catch."

I arrived in Washington, D.C., my arm crooked like a coat hanger, swaddled in a plaster cast.

But there was no question: I was going to dance my role. I'd worked too hard for too long to get here. And the performance was a big deal. It was a tradition in Washington, D.C., to gather the best students from the world's top ballet academies to display their talents at the Kennedy Center. It wasn't just the Bolshoi Ballet Academy. Rosters of students from schools in Denmark, Japan, and Argentina had all flown in to perform.

By some miracle, the Bolshoi had allowed me, an American, a leading role. I was there, in my home country's capital city, to represent the best of Russian dance instruction. It felt surreal. "Protégés," the event was called. And I was named in the program: a protégé of Russian training, a star apprentice of the Bolshoi school of ballet. I was not about to let a broken wrist ruin a moment that felt miraculous.

When we arrived at the hotel in D.C., I asked the kitchen staff if I could borrow one of their knives. Then, holding my arm still on the wood of my hotel room dresser, I hacked at the stiffened cast on my arm. I laughed at the ridiculousness and stupidity of what I was doing as the plaque of gauze and plaster came apart in chunks, as the steel blade chipped closer and closer to my flesh. After minutes of concentrated violence, I cut a crack wide enough to allow my arm to wriggle free.

The skin of my wrist, freed from the brace, was puffy and creased, tender to the touch. The shell of my discarded cast lay in pieces on the hotel room table, like the white crumbles of an insect's exoskeleton.

But on the night of the performance, it didn't matter. I fitted myself into the shiny white bodice of my costume, pulled on my petalled tutu and shellacked my hair to my head with layers of chemically scented hair spray.

Grandma and Dad were in the audience with Aunt Melissa and even my friend Emily from Santa Monica. They held roses in their hands, told me they were proud of me, promised to pray for me while I was on stage.

There were dance critics, journalists, art experts there in the red-cushioned chairs of the theater with them.

I was thrilled. I had flown back to my home country to represent Russia on stage. I was wearing a beautiful costume. I was dancing to Prokofiev.

Just focus on the footwork. No one will be looking at your arms.

Mario was beside me, and he was prepared. He knew exactly where on my injured arm to touch in order not to hurt me.

"You're ready," Bobrova told us.

I nodded, holding my broken limb loose at my side, ignoring the painful twinge in the wrist. The bone and muscles felt sore when I held still, and I was nauseous with pain if someone touched me in the wrong spot. But Mario knew what he was doing, and so, I thought, did I.

It hurt, but it was nothing compared to dancing on a broken foot.

"Let's go," I said, setting my shoulders back and rising onto pointe in my shoes.

Days later, there were articles published online by critics and journalists who'd sat in the audience to watch our performance. They wrote about the undiminished greatness of the Bolshoi Ballet Academy and the generations of talent it had gifted to the world. Its magnificence had extended to a new, young American who had disciplined herself to its traditions—a girl who was confident, ablaze with developing talent.[1]

One of the reviewers gushed over the beauty of my wrists and arms. My limbs were striking and lovely, the critic said. I was liquid and expressive, my arm and shoulder movements channeled melody like waves rippling over the sea.[2]

At first it made me laugh—the best part of my performance involved the one spot in my body that wasn't working correctly, the one joint overwhelmed with pain. But then I thought back to all the instructions I'd ever received from teachers over the years about my arms and wrists. They'd asked me for softness and grace. "Make your arms flutter," they'd said. "Shape them into wings. Turn your hands—your flesh and bones—into water to express the current of music."

And now that I'd literally snapped my wrist bones out of shape, I'd achieved the fluidity, range, and movement required.

What my teachers and the audience, what ballet itself wanted from me had nothing to do with what was possible, what was healthy, what made sense. What they wanted was something superhuman, something sublime.

If I had to weaken, shrink, and eventually break myself to give it to them, then break myself I would.

CHAPTER 12

The Historic Stage

Finally, the moment I had been waiting for arrived.

I saw it in the searchlights that flashed across the clouded, dark underbelly of Moscow's nighttime sky. It was October 2011; there had been years of lingering delay. But now the historic Bolshoi Theater was opening at last.

Moscow was abuzz with the excitement of it. The pond-sized fountain in Theater Square had dried and stilled, the stone pavement had been cleared of passersby and filled with TV cameras. A long, ruby-red carpet lay unfurled on the ground. And rising above it all was a five-story limestone theater, stripped of its dirty construction robes, gleaming white, illuminated with floodlights like a model on a runway.

I could see the searchlights out Pat's Bolshaia Dmitrovka Street windows. They panned the clouds like Batman signals in Gotham City. The theater was just blocks away, but obtaining tickets to its opening was impossible for mere mortal students like myself. Instead, I had planned a way to view the event: a watch party. Pat was out of town; her apartment was empty, and I had invited my friends Gabe and Masha to join me. They came through the door laughing, jubilant, and rosy-cheeked.

We pressed a button on Pat's ancient, dust-covered box TV and turned it to Channel One, where a camera crane soared off the ground in a wide shot of the newly renovated theater, crowned with a bronze statue of Apollo in a chariot, galloping skyward.

A news anchor wearing a black suit reported breathlessly on the guests in gowns and fur coats who walked the red carpet, climbed the stone steps to the theater, and found seats covered in red, sound-enhancing Italian fabric. We saw government ministers and gymnastics coaches milling about the room, the patriarch of the Russian Orthodox Church seated in splendor, his gold-and-white *koukoulion* headdress arrayed atop his brow.[1]

"That's Monica Belucci!" the TV anchor confirmed with breathless excitement as the camera zoomed in on a dark-haired Italian woman on the red carpet, dripping in diamonds, swathed in a strapless gown.[2]

Crews had been working around the clock for years to renovate the Imperial-era theater building. They had worked deep underground, installing steel and concrete pillars to keep the walls from collapsing into nearby metro tunnels and the ancient, subterranean Neglinnaya River.[3] They had repaneled and reconstructed an interior that Stalin, in a fit of paranoia decades before, had ordered reinforced with protective and sound-absorbent cement. They had painted the balconies in a medieval recipe of egg yolk and gold leaf.[4] They had doubled the theater's footprint.[5]

There was gossip about how far behind schedule the project had been—about various contractors who had embezzled construction funds to buy themselves fancy cars, *dacha* homes in the Moscow region, properties in Europe. Tickets to the reopening were rumored to have been hoarded by Moscow's ever-present mafia lords, sold for millions of rubles.

Masha, Gabe, and I had been to rehearsals and performances at the Bolshoi's smaller New Stage many times. But we'd given up hope of sneaking into the grand opening of the historic stage. Instead, we pointed at the screen of Pat's television when we saw the camera pan to people we knew or had heard of: Maya Plisetskaya, Mikhail Gorbachev, and Marina Leonova, our theater director.

"There she is!" we said, when we saw her seated, straight-backed in the center of the hall. She was surrounded by the most powerful people in Russia: parliamentarians, deputies, the executives of various oil companies.

We'd heard gossip about her too. We saw the Chanel suits she wore, the designer shoes and fancy manicures, the black Mercedes with a private driver that swept to the front of the Academy to drop her off every morning, pick her up in the evening. We'd sat in her office with its inlaid wood furniture and wondered about her power and connections.

Leonova had been kind to me. She'd given me a place at the school, on the stage, at the center of the Academy's spotlight. And I hadn't had to pay any bribes for this, nor were my parents people she wanted to impress. Who was I to know how the backside of Russia's ballet world worked? My job was to dance so well that it didn't matter who favored me or why. This was what I still, in my teenage American naiveté, told myself was possible.

We were mesmerized by the beauty of the historic stage we saw on the screen. This was a theater hall where czars and czarinas had sat, princes and princesses. We'd heard stories about the scenes of history its walls had witnessed: votes to found the Soviet Union; WWII bombs dropped through its ceiling; dancers who pliéd, knees bending at the barre through war, famine, and purges.

Now we saw, on the TV in front of us, the entirety of Russia's modern-day nobility, draped in jewels, crowded into a theater paid for by sludges of oil dredged up from subterranean Siberian deposits. This was a place where Russia had always chosen to declare its dominance and majesty. It was a display of prestige for the czars, then a weapon of cultural supremacy for Cold War generals, then a bastion of legitimacy for a new country trying to remind everyone how important it was. The Bolshoi Theater: temple to the arts, sanctuary of Russian power.

We watched President Medvedev take to the stage, small and serious, in a suit and bow tie. He stood in front of a curtain that glowed red and gold, the word *Russia* stitched into the fabric over his right shoulder.

"The Bolshoi is one of our greatest national brands," he said, speaking fondly of cultural treasures, country-uniting symbols.[6]

The renovation had taken six years and much more than the reported twenty-one billion rubles. But everyone in Russia seemed to agree: it had been worth it.

Gabe and Masha and I went to Pat's closets and pulled her fanciest things off their hangers. We wrapped fur coats over our shoulders, strung jewelry around our necks. We watched opera singers fill the theater on screen with sound, glittering rows of dancers stream the stage with movement, like fairies.[7] We imagined ourselves into what we saw on the TV.

What did it feel like to be a ballerina there? To stand on a two-hundred-year-old stage, be applauded by presidents and movie stars, to become a part of history?

This was something we all longed to understand. And within just a few weeks, I would take my first steps into finding out.

I had returned to finish my third and final year at the Bolshoi Academy, triumphant.

I was a senior—tall, graceful, muscled, smooth. I wore flowing scarves and beautiful makeup. I walked through the halls of the Academy like a veteran—among the most experienced girls in the school. I was respected, beloved, victorious. I was fluent in Russian. I had friends from all over the world, a fancy Moscow apartment to live in. My name had appeared in world-famous newspapers and magazines. My teacher, Bobrova, loved me. And the school director, Leonova, trusted me. I was not just a good dancer. I was a dancer who had endured.

That wasn't the case for everyone. Of the eighteen Russian girls who'd started at the school in a hand-chosen class of eight-year-olds, only four remained. The others had dropped out—gotten injured, suffered mental breakdowns, moved away, or just given up. Those who now stood at the third-year barre under Bobrova's eye had come to the Bolshoi Academy from various far-flung corners of Russia and Europe—from Finland, Croatia, Belarus.

And then there was me. My broken wrist had healed, and so had the starvation-induced stress fracture that had ruptured in the bones of my foot just weeks after performing in Washington, D.C. I had spent the summer in Austin resting under the watchful eye of my mother, swallowing the vitamins she prescribed, eliminating wheat and dairy from my diet at her suggestion to ease the recurrent cramps that gripped my abdomen. I had hidden from her the urges I still felt to make myself vomit in secret, behind closed doors.

By the time I returned to Moscow, I was rested, confident, clear-eyed. But the glow of my summer break did not last long.

By the end of October, I was exhausted. Mario and I had been granted the lead roles in *La Fille Ma Gardee*—a ballet from the 1700s. It was a classic, danced by generations of Russian dancers. And it was to be performed on the Bolshoi's New Stage. This wasn't the recently reopened historic stage with its red and gold interior, but it was right next door, connected to the historic stage by tunnels. It felt historic to me.

The fact that Leonova had given Mario and me the main roles seemed nothing short of miraculous. Probably, I thought, God had changed Leonova's heart. Like Pharaoh with Moses, he'd hardened her heart toward Nastia and softened it toward me. "Not by human strength, but by God's will," I told my friends at church.

But getting ready for the performance did actually require quite a bit of human strength. I started waking early in the mornings for cardio training—tracking my runs through a lamplit, predawn Moscow with a Nike app on my phone. Then I rushed to Tatiana's house for an hour of coaching and ran back to the metro to make it to the Academy in time for rehearsal.

My days stretched to twelve hours. It was dark when I laced ribbons around my ankles and dark when I finally sat down and peeled off my tights. The constant sweaty pressure of my bones on the flesh of my feet grew into red, inflamed sores on my toes that pulsed and bled into the pink satin of my shoes. I collapsed after rehearsals, sank immediately into sleep. I dreamed about the woodwinds of music and the corrections from my teachers: *Plié, heel down. Echarté—open side, behind ear, shoulders down. Lift your spine and stomach from your legs, reach out and up. Don't sit, don't push your neck out. Relax your upper body. Don't be behind yourself. Don't rush. Listen to the music. Know what comes next. Breathe.*

I was tired, but I was not complaining. I loved being at the center of an entire production, the focus of our directors' corrections. So did Mario. We felt like professionals, like real, grown-up ballet dancers.

We performed in November—the month of early sunsets, frosty air, low skies, and, all across Russia, the midday of the country's celebrated nine-month theater season.

Dad used Delta miles from a friend and flew in from Austin. He booked a room near Pat's apartment and waited for me in his suit in the darkened hall of the theater, his iPhone in hand to sneak videos. My friends from church were there too—I'd helped them buy 800-ruble tickets, found seats for them, and reserved a hidden place in the back for my coach, Tatiana.

Mario and I felt ready. We'd rehearsed for hours in front of Leonova on the Academy stage. Bobrova had reinvented my pirouettes. And Tatiana had encouraged me to relax my neck and arms, soften my head, calm myself, listen to the music, get rid of my spastic nerves, compose my hands, turn my fingers into feathers.

"No one is going to help you," she had said, her dark eyes drilling into mine. "You have to believe in yourself."

This was a test of whether or not I was a ballerina, she told me. "If you can last through the whole performance, you will prove yourself."

Backstage, Mario was calm in his blue vest, knee-length tights and white slippers.

"We've got this," he promised.

I pretended to be calm. I pulled my hair back into a tight bun, fixed my costume in place, bandaged the lesions on my feet. But the longer I waited behind the scenery, the harder my heart pounded.

Help me not to worry, Lord. Help me to dance well. Help me not to be afraid. Help me be confident. Help me turn out, lift my body over my legs, raise my arabesque, relax my neck.

When the orchestra released its first notes into the air, we leapt out on stage.

I tried to give it my all, to let the coaching, the preparation, the striving and pushing fly into the moment.

The first act was a blur, filled with mistakes. The stage lights from beyond the horizon of my mascara blinded me. We fumbled with the props. We got the scarves we were holding tangled in knots. The butter churn fell over twice.

But, by act two, I started to breathe into what was happening. I felt the music in my bloodstream, leaned into each flute trill, each violin note with perfectly timed steps, pauses, arching movements of my arms. In rehearsal, we'd broken the performance down into segments, worked out each turn, each jump. Now we knit everything together, and I felt my body go through movements under the hot glare of the lights in a way that felt smooth and surreal. It was the same way I'd felt when I was little, playing in our backyard in Santa Monica on the tree swing, the wind rushing through my hair, tilted back, lifted in the air, whooshing above the ground, a bird in flight.

Later, when I saw videos of our debut, even I was proud. Mario and I were beautiful. Our arms reached high into the air like wings, our legs extended behind us like windmill blades. Mario raised me over his head, a weightless banner, his hands spanning my waist, his mouth smiling at me as he brought me down, eyes locked on mine, tenderness and love in his eyebrows, his open mouth. He created, with his movements, the character Colas—steadfast, strong, devoted, completely in love. And I embodied Lise—playful, young, flirtatious, bright.

We took the audience along with us so that they laughed and clapped as the orchestra carried us from below, filling the theater with sound.

By the end of the performance, my muscles were on fire, my limbs shook, my shoes rubbed the skin of my feet into a painful rawness. But when the sage-green curtain closed in front of our faces, the audience let loose a thunderstorm of applause. They rose to their feet, clapping and cheering, the sound of their delight, a vibrating, roaring, rolling stampede that took on a life and rhythm of its own. Even after the curtains closed, they refused to stop, calling us to return again and again as we pranced back out in front, holding hands, our arms raised. They threw flowers at us, synchronized their clapping, shouted "Bravo!" over and over.

I was so exhausted that my arms trembled and my chest heaved. The sweat on my face had melted my stage makeup. But the roar of their approval was like the break of dawn after a long winter night. I had danced my first full-length ballet on one of Moscow's most storied stages. I felt deeply, incandescently alive.

This is what I've been working for. This is all I want to do, I thought. *I will do whatever it takes to do this every day for the rest of my life.*

CHAPTER 13

Soup

The things I wanted were impossible.

I wanted to be Russian, to graduate the Academy top of my class, then join the Bolshoi's *corps de ballet*. This was the reason I'd come to Russia. I wanted to be a history-maker, the first American woman to join the Bolshoi Ballet Theater.

But the Russian theater system wasn't designed for American dancers. I knew of no others from my country who had secured dancing contracts at the Bolshoi Theater. Yes, there was David Hallberg. He'd made history when the Bolshoi artistic director, Sergei Filin, begged him at a Moscow sushi restaurant to join the company on an elite contract.[1] But that was different. David Hallberg was a star. He'd been acquired after years of dance renown, his name written into newspapers, like he was a star player, traded to the Dallas Cowboys.

There was also Keenan Kampa, the girl from California who'd moved to St. Petersburg to study at the Vaganova School. She was another history-maker—the first American ever to join Russia's northern, mint-colored Mariinsky Theater.

But no one had ever done what I wanted to do. There had been no American—man or woman—who'd trained at the Bolshoi Ballet Academy, then gone on to a professional contract in the great Russian theater itself.

Part of the problem was I didn't have the right paperwork. The pink-and-yellow visa pasted to the inner leaf of my passport allowed for only academic activities in Russia. My school had arranged these documents for me, papers that made it possible for me to live in Moscow, take Russian classes. But after I graduated the Academy, my student visa would expire, and I would be forced to leave.

This was something Leonova, our school director, had already thought of. Midway through my senior year, she called me into her office. It was January and so cold in Moscow that the sparkling water I purchased in plastic bottles at kiosks on the street outside froze solid before I could bring them in. Despite the cold, Leonova was thinking of spring and of my fast-approaching graduation.

"What do you want?" she asked, sitting behind her massive desk, the wall at her back filled with placards, trophies, and photos of her most famous students.

"Do you want to find work in Europe? In the United States? Or do you want to stay here?" she wondered, her blonde hair twisted in a careful spiral behind her head.

"I want the Bolshoi," I said. There was no question in my mind.

Leonova was thoughtful, her pink-lipsticked mouth pursed.

"I mean, what do you think?" I said. "Do you think I can actually get hired at the Bolshoi?"

"Based on your dancing, yes," Leonova told me. "But we don't know about the visa situation. I don't think they'll hire a foreigner."

"What if I figure that out on my own?" I asked.

Leonova paused, her blue eyes staring into mine.

"How are you going to stay here?" she said slowly. "Are you going to get married?"

I had spent a lot of time thinking about a paper marriage. Many of my teachers, including Arkhipova, had spoken about it. This was how things had been done in their day, back in the Soviet Union. If foreigners wanted to stay behind the Iron Curtain, they married Russians. It was the only way to get the right paperwork.

I wasn't yet eighteen, but I would be by the time I graduated. Getting married young was something that didn't seem strange. At

Lighthouse, the church where I'd grown up, lots of girls had married young—at eighteen or nineteen. Arranging a paper marriage would be efficient—I wouldn't have to date or waste my time. I'd go straight to the altar, get what I needed, and continue my career.

I started talking about the idea with friends. Fedia, one of the boys who'd graduated a few years before me, was open to it. He was working as a soloist now at the Bolshoi.

"If you need help, I'll do it for you," he said.

Fedia seemed like a good option. We'd been friends for years; I trusted him and knew he'd respect my boundaries.

My friend, Anton, was also willing. I'd known him since that first Bolshoi Summer Intensive in New York when I was fifteen. I knew I'd be safe with him. Plus, he had a car.

"Are you serious about doing this?" he'd asked me at a party recently. "I know someone who's a lawyer—maybe they could help."

"I'm definitely serious," I said. "I need to figure this out by graduation."

There was also Oleg. We were in the same year at school. But I didn't know him as well. He was tall, blond, obsessed with Berlin. His parents had careers as professional clowns in a Moscow circus. He'd heard I was trying to arrange a paper marriage, so he called my cell phone.

"I might be able to help you," he'd said. "How old are you?"

"I'm seventeen," I said. "But I'll be eighteen in a few weeks."

"Okay, if you're serious, I'll think about it," he said. "Let's talk again after your birthday."

In March, I began to panic.

None of my paperwork mattered if I didn't graduate.

Final exams loomed ahead like a quickly approaching sign on the highway. This would be my last chance to prove myself, to catch the eye of a director or theater recruiter. The triumphs I'd had before: my *La Fille Ma Gardee* debut with Mario, the Kennedy Center performance that had been so widely praised, the YAGP prize I'd been awarded in

November had shown my teachers I was tough, I could work hard, I could endure. But none of that mattered unless an actual theater director wanted me and was willing not just to offer me a job, but to go through the bureaucratic hoops it took to keep me in the country.

I leaned into the challenge like a racer, standing on the pedals of her bicycle, thighs burning, pressing all of her weight and muscle into pushing, pushing, pushing ahead to the finish line. I felt the pressure and competition of others around me—their breath coming in puffs, the shrill whine of their tires—I sensed it like gooseflesh on my neck.

I couldn't let anyone pass me. I needed to stay sleek, strong, focused, and gripped to the inside of the track. I needed to cut off my competitors. I needed to be lean and razor sharp. I needed to be the best.

The pressure felt like a weight against my chest. It drove me forward, disturbed my sleep. In the dark, unconscious, I had nightmares that I'd gone insane and started stabbing people or that my teeth had fallen backward, lodged into my throat, choking me. Sometimes I dreamed I'd suddenly become married to a stranger, or that my mother was hunting me, trying to murder me. I gasped awake after each horror, sitting up in my bed to the dull yellow of a streetlight from the courtyard shining into my dark room.

It was just a dream, I'd tell myself. There would be a moment of relief as I breathed air into my lungs, realized I wasn't choking. My tongue felt my teeth still firmly in my mouth, and my hands clutched my neck and abdomen, found them empty of stab wounds, my fingers free of wedding bands. But as my breathing slowed and my throat swallowed, the dread would return, pressing onto my rib cage as I remembered: *exams are coming.*

In the mornings, when I woke, I was met with new horrors. March in Moscow was hideous. The chilly air outside smelled of spring and the bone-deep, dog-cold of mid-winter was gone. The snow melted in patches, like hair molting from a skull. It laid bare archeological layers of cigarette butts, dog poop, garbage, and rotting animal carcasses. Poetry by Boris Pasternak spoke of "Black Spring," when the white of winter snow gave way to darkened, melting ice and the mud and stink of winter's death.

There was a poem for everything in Russia. Even—or maybe especially—the things that were universally hated.

My classmates had grown vicious. We were competing for spots now—traveling to auditions, sneaking off to Leonova's office to beg for consultations and letters of recommendation. We sent videos of ourselves to theaters around Europe and Asia. And we focused on surviving exams. There were four of them we needed to complete: acting, ballet, duet, and character.

When we rehearsed our pieces in the Academy studios, we thought about the theater directors from the Stanislavsky, Mariinsky, and Bolshoi Theaters who might be seated in the audience, watching us. They would judge how well we portrayed characters, how precisely we executed pirouettes, how high our legs extended in arabesque. All of it mattered to our future job offers, to our salaries, and to how directors saw us: as *corps de ballet* dancers or soloist material.

Journalists had begun taking an interest in me. The *New York Times*, Reuters, and NBC had all published articles about me being the first American student set to graduate from the Academy. They wrote about my single-mindedness and grace, about how I was poised to make history.[2] I was flattered by the attention, and remembered the things Dad always said about needing to create a brand, needing to build a certain amount of "buzz," in order for people to know I was there, ready to work. It would create an eagerness to acquire me, to partner with me, he said.

But it also felt like a lot of pressure. In all my interviews, I talked about how much I loved Russia, how desperate I was to get into the Bolshoi. I wanted to be the first American ballerina to graduate from the Academy with a red diploma, and, after that, to announce to the world that I'd achieved my dream, that I was joining the Bolshoi Theater.

I worried I was setting myself up for disaster. Launching pride before a fall, as Mom would say. I had set my goals as high as they could possibly go.

What if I can't keep up? What if I can't do this? What if I fail?

The articles and TV news segments bothered my classmates.

"Who do you think you are?" some of them said. "You're delusional, thinking you're going to get into the Bolshoi. Nobody needs you. You're nothing."

They made fun of my accent, told jokes about things related to Russian culture they knew I wouldn't understand.

"Joy, you think you're Russian, but you're not," they said. "You're just pretending you understand."

Fine, I thought, as I stretched by myself on the floors of the Academy's hallways. *I can live without friends.*

I didn't want to, but I could. Dad had always told me it was lonely at the top.

This, I told myself, *is just what it's like when you're trying to be the best.*

The bulimia grew worse. It was terrible in the morning when I woke, lightheaded and exhausted. It was bad at night too, when my head hurt and my muscles ached. Sometimes I felt nauseous and dizzy from hunger. My period was irregular, my skin was dry, my throat was sore. I'd been getting sick more often—shivering with fevers and lying in bed. I feared my injuries would return, that my secret self-harm would be revealed in more brittle and broken bones—newly fractured heels, shattered wrists.

Sometimes I prayed about it: *Help me fight it, God. It's evil, it's vanity. Free me—help me break the bonds of bulimia.*

Part of me wanted the binging and purging to stop. It felt wrong, sinful, possibly demonic. Another part of me reasoned that this was what it took. Every ballet school I'd ever been a part of had been filled with bulimic and anorexic girls.

"You can't be a professional dancer without an eating disorder," I sometimes told my friends in a way that now horrifies me. "That's just the way it is."

I tried to eat as little as possible. But whenever there was food out at parties or youth group get-togethers, I couldn't resist. I'd eat cookies and pasta, fluffy bread, chips, bowls of chili over rice. Then I'd sneak home, turn on the water faucet, and throw up in the toilet.

Pat had begun to confront me about it.

"I heard you throwing up, Joy," she'd say. "It's dangerous to do that to yourself."

"Oh, no, no," I said, smiling. "I just have a stomach bug, I think. It will be better by tomorrow, I'm sure."

It made me angry to be confronted, and I found ways to not only hide what I was doing, but hide the reality of what was happening from my own eyes. I made excuses and shifted blame so I didn't have to think about it.

I don't talk about your smoking and drinking habits, I thought when Pat approached me, worry in her eyes.

I'd forgotten what it felt like not to be hungry. A satisfied stomach felt wrong, like I was heavy or out of control. I had superhuman proprioception: an enhanced ability to sense where my body was in space that allowed me to turn dozens of fouettés in a row, my shoulders connected to my hips, knees, ankles, and toes. It was insect-like the way I could balance my body on a razor's edge, gripping, turning—a wasp zipping through the air.

But this self-awareness did not extend to balancing the well-being of my inner thoughts.

Mario worried about me. He saw how my bones protruded from my skin, how I never ate. He heard the way I called myself a fat bear when I looked in the mirror, the way I spoke about eating disorders as if they were inevitable.

"I hate what you're doing to yourself," he said one day after rehearsal. We'd been tense and simmering for days. The tender *Romeo and Juliet* scene we were working on had turned violent and vengeful. Even our teachers had noticed, told us to figure it out.

"What are you talking about?" I said, prickly and angered.

"Everyone says you're anorexic, and you're always degrading yourself, saying mean things about yourself," he said. "Everyone's talking about how you've stopped eating. It's terrible."

"I'm not anorexic. I don't do that," I said. "If you have a problem with me, talk to me—not to everyone else."

"But look at you!" Mario said, sweeping his arm at my sharpened rib cage, the bones that jutted from my back like spikes on a thistle. "You're too thin. I'm worried about you. It's dangerous what you're doing."

I grew angry. *How dare he bring this into our rehearsal? We have work to do and only a few days to do it before our exam.*

"This is unprofessional," I said. "Don't bring this sort of stuff into the studio."

I started jabbing my legs back into my warmup clothes, raking my things into a bag.

"Is this why you've been distant lately?" I said. "Because you believe rumors other people are spreading about me?"

"Everyone's talking about it," Mario said. "You can't take compliments. You're too hard on yourself, and you're killing yourself."

"Mario, if you have a problem with me, talk to *me* about it, not other people," I said. "I have to go."

I pulled my bag on my shoulder and left the studio.

I refused to hear what he was saying. I blocked it with excuses and anger: *He doesn't know what he's talking about. He has no idea. He's so immature.*

Mario was the best dance partner I'd ever had. He was safe and kind, and all the pas de deux we worked on together turned into magic. Leonova had begun talking to theater directors about us like we were a pair: the American wonder kids who'd submitted themselves to Russian discipline and were about to graduate as fully Bolshoi-trained professionals.

But she was talking us up to people who weren't Bolshoi directors. Mario wasn't working on his Russian residency permit. He was relying on Leonova and some other theater company to get him the paperwork he needed. If I stuck with Mario, I'd have to give up the Bolshoi.

Slowly, I began pulling away.

You need to stay sharp; you need to be smart, I told myself. *It's lonely at the top.*

"I'm here to make you soup," Bobrova told me.

She stood outside the door to Pat's apartment in a woolen coat, her arms full of plastic bags.

"Elena Alexandrovna!" I said, feeling both embarrassed and grateful to see her. I opened the door wide to let her in, took the heavy plastic bags out of her hands, hung her coat in Pat's closet.

"You're getting too skinny," she said, looking me over. "You have three more exams to do and the graduation *Paquita* performance. You need to gain weight. Leonova won't let you dance if you don't gain weight."

She pulled a pair of house slippers from her purse, put them on her feet, and marched into the kitchen, trailing a faint scent of perfume behind her.

"Thank you so much for coming." I followed her. "You really don't have to do this."

But she was already making herself at home, pulling cabbage, carrots, and beets out of her bags, rummaging through Pat's cupboards for a metal pot.

"Here." She handed me a knife and a freshly rinsed head of cabbage. "Cut this into strips for me."

I couldn't help but love the attention she was showing me, even though I didn't want to seem like someone who needed help. My classmates would be furious if they knew what was happening.

"You have to dance *Paquita*," she said. "Ours is the first class that will get to dance on the historic Bolshoi stage. It's an extremely difficult ballet, and we don't have anyone else in the graduating class who can pull off the lead. We need to get you ready."

She put an onion under running water in the sink, then tore off its papery brown skin.

"I make this soup for Natalya sometimes," she said, mentioning her daughter, who was a dancer at the Bolshoi. "She also gets too skinny."

"This is so nice of you, but completely unnecessary," I said. "I have plenty of food, you don't have to come all the way over here to cook for me."

"I want to make sure you're actually eating," Bobrova said, watching me as she peeled the outside of a lumpy brown potato.

She started talking about when she'd been young and employed at the Bolshoi.

"I was there for twenty-two years. It didn't pay much, but I wasn't there for the money. I was there for the ideas, for the art. There's nowhere like the Bolshoi," she said. "That's why my husband, Vasily Stepanovich, is still there. We've served ballet our entire lives."

I thought it was funny and sweet how she called her husband by his name and patronymic—it was so old-fashioned and courtly.

She dumped raw cuts of chicken into boiling water, sprinkled the surface with salt.

"But that doesn't mean the Bolshoi is right for *you*," she said, stirring the pot.

We sat down at the table while the water simmered.

"I feel spiritually close to you, Joy," she said, looking me in the eye. "I think of you like my own daughter. And I know that you're a ballerina. You're lyrical, dramatic, emotional. You can be any kind of ballerina you want to be—Giselle, Juliet, Carmen. You're capable of a lot."

Bobrova handed me a garnet-colored, earth-scented beet to chop.

"You might do better in a smaller theater, a place where you have a chance to be a ballerina. The Bolshoi may just stick you in the *corps* with the other new graduates," she said.

"But I've always wanted the Bolshoi. That's what I've been working for," I said.

Bobrova shrugged, tossing chopped dill on top of the soup.

"The Bolshoi is the best theater. Every year the best students from the Academy go there. The competition is so high," she said. "If you go to the Bolshoi, they might not use you. That would really be a huge pity—all the work we've done will be lost. You belong in lead roles, at the center of the stage."

"But *you* chose the Bolshoi," I pointed out. "So did Vasily Stepanovich—he's still there, and so is your daughter."

"There's nothing like the Bolshoi," Bobrova said, a faraway look in her eyes. "The talent, the artistry. And it's not just the dancers—it's the musicians, the opera singers, the coaches, set design, costumes, the history. It's an amazing place for an artist."

"That's what I want!" I said.

"I spent my career there. They gave me a soloist position," she said. "But there were so many roles I wanted to dance and never got. I would have done better somewhere else."

She began ladling magenta-colored, dill-scented soup into a bowl.

"I don't have the right to make this decision for you," she said. "I don't really want you to go to the Bolshoi. But in the end, you have to decide for yourself."

She set the bowl in front of me. Steam curled over its porcelain edges. Soup has always been one of Russia's hallowed secrets to good health, united in trinity along with hot cups of tea and piles of buckwheat groats. I believed in Bobrova's care for me. I also believed she'd support me no matter which theater I chose.

"Make sure you eat," she said, handing me a spoon.

She watched as I sipped at the broth and nibbled on the cabbage and beets. Then she took a thermos out of her bag and poured the leftovers inside.

"Bring this with you to rehearsal tomorrow," she said, screwing the lid on tight, placing it on the counter. "I want to make sure you eat all of it. You're going to need it to get through exams."

CHAPTER 14

Department of Public Services

When the curtain fell on my last exam, someone screamed.

I'm not sure who it was—maybe Polina. Maybe Irina. But then all of us started screaming, clutching at each other's arms, folding double, hands on our knees to let our chests heave, tears fall from our eyes, shrieking like teakettles letting off steam.

It was over. The hours, days, nights, years we'd poured into learning to plié, to listen to our teachers, to condition our legs and lungs to carry us through 120-minute performances, to tuck in our ribs, lift our chests, spin in circles, soar over the stage. We had crossed the finish line.

The curtain lifted again, and we saw the lights in our Academy auditorium blaze to life. Every pink velvet seat was filled with people clapping: parents, teachers, theater directors, students. Even the school janitors and hall monitors had come to see us.

My classmates on stage were near hysterics. Timur was boinging around like an antelope. Mario was laughing, his eyebrows raised in disbelief. Zhenia, Lucia, and Yulia had their arms around each other, giggling. Someone came up and gave me a wilting bouquet of yellow tulips. Bobrova hugged me, her face awash in satisfied approval.

"Well done," she said. "I'm proud of you."

I felt like a dishrag that had been twisted and wrung out. I was exhausted, my belly hollow and concave, my eyes heavy and dazed.

All I could think was, *Is it enough? Did I do well enough? Did I get into the Bolshoi?*

A panel of teachers and theater directors consulted about our performance, then gathered us backstage to read us the grades they'd decided on.

It was so Russian, the way they did it—no preamble, no thought to hurt feelings or embarrassment. Leonova stood in front of us, a lustrous pair of pearls in her ears, her face a blank sheet as she calmly announced everyone's scores like a newscaster reading daily market gains.

This public announcement was how I knew I had done very, very well. I got straight 5s in every single one of my dance exams and a 5+ in ballet and duet. In fact, all six of us in Bobrova's class had done well.

Later, when I sat on the edge of a damask-upholstered chair in Leonova's office, I felt confident. Leonova knew I wanted to go to the Bolshoi. She knew I was a good dancer. She had assigned me lead roles in so many of the important class performances that year, including our graduation ballet, which would, for the first time in history, be performed on the newly renovated Bolshoi stage.

I had proven my commitment, my dedication, my obsessive desire. I had shown not only that I could carry the weight of an entire ballet on my back, but that I wanted to do so.

"You did very, very well, Joy," Leonova said. "The way you and Mario danced in classical and duet—you're just a miraculously beautiful pair, absolutely wonderful."

She was seated at her desk, guarded by a vase of fresh flowers.

"Thank you," I told her, preparing myself for good news. "I'm so grateful I had the chance to study here."

"I've heard from the director of the Mikhailovsky Theater in St. Petersburg," she said. "He's very interested in both of you, and he's prepared to offer you working permits and contracts."

"Oh!" I tried not to show my surprise. "St. Petersburg?"

"It's a very good company. They offer excellent salaries, and more importantly, they want to see both you and Mario in principal roles," she said.

My heart sank. "What about the Bolshoi?" I said. "I—I've always wanted the Bolshoi."

"It's not an option. They're not even considering you." Leonova raised her blonde brows, pursed her mouth. "You're one of the best dancers in your class, but you have an American passport. The Bolshoi can't do the visa paperwork for you. But at the Mikhailovsky, everything will be taken care of."

"But I—I've never even been to St. Petersburg," I said. It felt like Leonova had taken my dreams out of my hands, packed them in a cardboard box, and shipped them off to northern Russia without even asking.

"Of course you should visit," Leonova said, her seashell-pink fingernails resting on her desk. "But you should go with a theater that will give you principal roles. That's how you'll develop as a professional."

I could barely hear what she was saying. All I could think was, *What about the Bolshoi?* Everything I'd done for years had been leading me to the Bolshoi. It didn't matter where or what the Mikhailovsky was—as long as it wasn't the Bolshoi, I wouldn't consider it.

I left her office feeling numb.

Halfway down the hallway to the coatroom, I realized: I need to speak to Oleg.

We met up and left the school building, walked south to the Moscow River with its granite embankment. We saw Gorky Park over the water where the tree crowns were prickled with a haze of new spring green. Children shouted and ran on a playground nearby, babushkas sat on benches, swaddled in woolens.

Oleg was taller than me—blonde with a square jaw and sharp nose. He smoked and could often be found outside, cigarette in hand, wearing headphones. He liked to find bands that others didn't listen to and dress in ways he thought were unusual and cool.

He had dreams of doing contemporary dance, maybe choreography, in a place like Berlin.

"Are you still looking to get married?" he asked as we walked along the embankment, the scent of river water and car exhaust filling our noses.

"I need it to get into the Bolshoi," I said. "I need the paperwork to live here, and the only way to get that is to get married."

"I've given this a lot of thought, and I think I really want to help you," he said. "I want to get a U.S. passport, and I want to work in Germany eventually. I think we can help each other."

"I would love to be able to help you with that," I said.

"But it's complicated," he added, looking ahead as he spoke, at a bridge that spanned the brown, slow-moving river. "We can't just do this; we have to make it believable—for official reasons. But also, I don't want my friends thinking this is just random. I need to convince them that it's real. We have to at least pretend that we're together to make this believable."

"You mean, like go on dates and stuff?" I said.

"Yeah, hold hands, go on dates," Oleg said.

That was something I could live with. Oleg was never someone I had considered romantically. We hadn't been close during the three years we'd both attended the Academy. But I knew he had a point. I didn't want to get in trouble with immigration laws, and I needed this to happen.

"I can do that," I said.

"Okay," Oleg said, his blond-whiskered mouth widening to a smile. "I think we need to get started on paperwork."

Things moved quickly after that. We started scanning embassy and immigration websites in Russian and English, calling lawyers, texting plans back and forth. I bought a wedding magazine and started shopping for a white dress.

If I'm going to get married, I might as well have fun doing it.

We went together to the Department of Public Services, or ZAGS, to register.

Oleg stopped me outside the gray, civil office doors, his Adam's apple bobbing in his throat.

"I think we should hold hands to show them we're a couple," he said. "We need to convince them we're for real."

"Okay," I said, putting my hand in his.

It felt strange to grasp his palm, which was warmer and bigger than mine. We talked on the phone all day every day now about documents we needed to get signed, immigration law details we had learned, places we needed to be. We'd tried going on a few dates. Oleg was courteous—always opening doors for me. He wasn't into drinking, unlike a lot of boys at the Academy. He liked talking about art, music, films. He enjoyed disagreeing with people, voicing opinions that were unique. He was handsome and interesting. But he wasn't someone I would have chosen to date, much less marry.

It's just for the documents, I told myself as we walked hand in hand through the double doors of the ZAGS, looking for the office worker who could tell us how to register for a wedding license.

It's just like dancing a pas de deux. You don't need to be in love with someone to act *like you're in love with them.*

I felt the eyes of the civil worker following us from behind her desk, felt conscious of the places where Oleg's and my arms touched.

Do we look like we're a real couple? Does she realize we're faking it?

We gave her our passport numbers, our dates of birth.

"You're an American," she said, looking at the battered cover of my passport. "Where's your notarized status paper from the U.S. Embassy?"

What notarized status paper?

"We're working on it—it's not quite ready," I said, looking to Oleg for support.

She sighed.

"We can schedule the civil services thirty-two days from the date of registration, then you need to appear in person on the thirty-second day to get your marriage license." She began rattling off a list of rules and procedures.

"Wait, thirty-two business days from today?" I did the numbers in my head. "But that's the end of June—that's too late."

If we waited until the end of June, I'd miss my chance to audition for the Bolshoi.

"The only way we can get you in sooner is if you have a certificate of pregnancy," she said.

"A certificate of pregnancy?" I asked, my voice shaky, looking at Oleg, who stared back wide-eyed, "Okay, sure. We can get that."

We left the ZAGS feeling jittery and unsettled. I hated lying.

"I think I know someone who can get us the papers we need," Oleg said. "I'll talk to my parents about it—I'll figure it out."

"I didn't like that," I said. "I hate lying."

"Me too," Oleg said, visibly shivering. We found a bench to sit on.

"Let's not fake this," Oleg said. "I hate all this pretending, going on phony dates so people don't get suspicious. Let's try this relationship for real, like actually date."

I could still feel, as we sat in our jackets near the ZAGS, the nausea of trying to deceive a stranger about something that was such a big deal.

"I like you," Oleg said, his brown eyes softening. "I think you're really beautiful. And I've always wanted a family. I think we can do this. And the lawyer we talked to said we'd need to commit for at least five years to get a residency permit. Five years is a long time to try to fake a relationship. I think we should really try this."

Oleg is kind, I thought. *He's close to his parents, he's an Orthodox Christian. It'll be like an arranged marriage. We'll make a professional decision and then see if the relationship works.*

"I'm willing to try it," I said. "I don't want to keep lying to people."

"Okay!" Oleg's face broke into a wide smile. He reached for my hands. "Let's do this for real."

"Let's do this for real," I repeated, holding his palms in my hands, his gaze in my eyes.

He leaned over for a kiss, and I felt his blond whiskers tickle my lip and cheeks.

It's hard for me to tell you how the kiss felt. It was as if I was watching myself from far away, like I was observing a drama unfold from the darkened wings of a theater or the crowded front row before a stage.

I'd seen the way Russian men treated their girlfriends in public. The metro escalators were filled with couples who made out as they rode the stairs up from underground, their mouths pressed together, their hands in each other's back jeans pockets, riding up their jackets and shirts. People who were dating held hands, strolled Moscow's wide boulevards, and kissed on park benches. Boys liked to give their girlfriends flowers and new phones and carry their boxy, leather purses for them.

When Oleg began doing these things for me, it felt strange.

On the one hand, I liked the attention—the way he checked in on me, made sure I was doing well. He told me I was beautiful and talented and strong. He stroked my fingers when we held hands, and stood close to me on the metro in ways that felt possessive and protective.

But it also felt strange to be kissed. Sometimes I flinched when he leaned in. I tried to laugh it off, distract him, smile widely enough for him to not feel rejected. It felt the way I had when I'd first tried dancing on a slanted stage, like I was balancing on pointe, trying to hold the entire situation in a tolerable stasis that didn't upset anyone. It wasn't that I didn't think he was handsome; it was just that things were happening so quickly, and Oleg was so different from boys I'd had crushes on before.

There were a few people I trusted with the information of what Oleg and I were doing. I spoke openly to the lawyers we questioned, Oleg's family, my dance tutor, and my friend Katia, who was still dancing at the Bolshoi. These were people who understood how Russia worked, how tricky it was to get documents. They knew how important it was that I get into the Bolshoi, and they knew that I needed to do whatever it took.

But I didn't tell anyone else: not Mario, not my classmates, not my friends at church or even Bobrova. I hinted that I was considering getting a marriage for paperwork, but I didn't tell them how much I'd committed to it.

I tried broaching the subject with my parents, but they freaked out as soon as I mentioned it.

"Joy, you're talking about a sham marriage," Mom had said. "If you're a Christian, you should believe in the sanctity of marriage. Making a sham marriage is making a sham of yourself before God."

Her words scared me. But internally I pushed back on them. *It's so Spanish Inquisition of her*, I thought. *She just doesn't understand. She doesn't know how Russia works. She's too American.*

I started shutting her out. We spoke on the phone often—she and Dad were planning a trip to visit me at the end of May to see my graduation performance. I talked to them about my rehearsals, about the costume I was being fitted for, about the audition invitations and job offers I was getting from theaters: Kazan, Mariinsky, Mikhailovsky. But I stopped mentioning Oleg and the plans we were setting in motion to get married.

CHAPTER 15

Secret Wedding

When I wasn't running around Moscow trying to get marriage documents from musty-smelling Moscow registration offices, I was back in the Academy studios with Mario, taking morning ballet classes and getting ready for our graduation performance.

We had been given the principal roles, and we were dancing them on the Bolshoi's newly renovated historic stage—part of the first graduating class ever to have been given such an honor.

I felt giddy with excitement every time I woke in the morning. The sun was out for much longer now. It brightened Moscow's sky long before I awoke and painted the evening clouds pink and gold until almost 9 p.m. Winter was a distant traumatic memory; the nightmares that had haunted me for months about my exams had disappeared. And the competition that had strangled my relationships with my classmates had dissolved.

I spent my days looking forward to rehearsals. It felt like everything I had learned over the past three years at the Academy had been strung together like beads in an intricate necklace. I poured all of this knowledge into the hours I spent in rehearsal. I walked in long, purposeful strides up Bolshaia Dmitrovka Street, a circle-shaped tutu under my arm, past the pastel-colored buildings of central Moscow to the huge limestone facade of the Bolshoi. Sometimes Russian tourists—people from the regions far outside Moscow—stopped me to ask for directions.

"Are you a ballerina?" they questioned, shyly, when they saw the frilly tutu in my hands.

At first the question startled me. I was a student of ballet. But then I realized, actually, I had completed my final exams. I was auditioning for work, I was starring in an Academy dance production at the literal Bolshoi Theater, I was being asked by Russians for walking directions.

"Yes, I am," I told them. "I'm a ballerina."

I had an employee pass to the Bolshoi now. Temporary, yes, but an official pass, nonetheless. It got me through the basement entrance to the theater, past the security guards and metal detectors, my bulging black warmup bag in hand. It got me into the underground tunnels, hidden hallways, elevators, and stage sets of Russia's most famous theater.

If it were possible to fall in love with a building, I was head over heels with the newly renovated Bolshoi. Its stage was huge, arched over with a ceiling that gaped taller than Pat's entire apartment building. Its expansive floor was smooth, easy for my feet to grip and so steeply raked that dancing on it felt like bounding off a trampoline.

Mario and I giggled when we saw it—if we set a marble at the top of the stage and let it go, it probably would have tumbled into the orchestra pit. I took my bags off my shoulder and set them at my feet, then lay on the floor on my side. Mario joined me, and we rolled forward, down the stage, over and over like wheel spokes, laughing.

Sometimes, when I looked out at the empty red and gold seats of the auditorium, I felt a swell of gratitude in my chest.

Every performance, every rehearsal, every class and practice session and sacrifice and blistered foot and broken bone has led me to this moment.

I remembered what the people at Lighthouse Church had said about the Holy Spirit. I remembered what it felt like to stand in a worship service and ask the Holy Spirit to lead, to let my heart fill with emotion and let strange sounds come out of my mouth. "Speaking in tongues," our pastor had called it.

It was the closest I got to describing the feeling of awe that came over me when I stood at the lip of the Bolshoi stage and stared into its gleaming inner sanctuary, lit by the softened glow of balcony lamps. The blossoming of happiness in my chest was like the voice of the Trinity.

This is a miracle, I thought. *This is where I belong.*

If I had believed in fate like my Russian friends did, maybe that's what fate would have felt like. But for me, the only word that seemed to fit was divinity. The Bolshoi was God's will for me. It was the one thing of which I was completely certain.

Oleg and I were married on the last day of May.

Katia was the only friend I invited. She understood my love for the Bolshoi, my desperation to get in. I knew she'd be on my side.

I called her on a Tuesday, late in the month.

"I'm getting married in two days," I said. "Can you be my bridesmaid?"

"You're getting married? In two days?" She laughed. Then she realized I was serious.

"Joy, you're crazy," she said.

But on the Thursday of the ceremony, she showed up at the door to Pat's apartment early in the morning to help me paint makeup onto my face and weave a string of pearls into my hair.

I hadn't told my parents what was happening that day.

I'll tell them when they come to Moscow to visit. I'll just introduce them to Oleg, I thought.

But as Katia curled my hair and zipped up the back of my white, strapless dress, I wondered if Mom had been right about what she'd said—that I was tempting fate, disobeying God.

My thoughts felt like the dizzy end of a thirty-two-fouetté sequence. I saw them flash unfinished and panicked in front of my mind's eye like a circular blur of stage lights–darkness–stage lights–darkness.

I remembered God's judgment of Herod in the Bible—how an angel of the Lord had struck the king dead because he didn't immediately give glory to God.

But glorifying God has been the plan all along. I need to have a career, a platform that vaults me to a position in which people look up to me. That's how I give God glory.

Katia watched me as I checked and double-checked that I had all my documents, the ring, the workout clothes I'd change into to make it to ballet class after the ceremony. It was as if she saw that I wasn't fully paying attention to what was going on. I was just focusing on one detail after another, hurrying to make it on time, to get done what needed to get done.

A small crowd waited for us outside the Moscow registration office with plastic bags and bouquets of flowers in their hands. A trio of Oleg's friends were there, tall and awkward. His parents stood nearby, dressed in art-punk, head-to-toe black with leather boots and belts. Even his grandmother had come. She wore a soft gray dress and waddled forward when she saw me, to plant a kind, wet kiss on my cheek.

"Our bride is here!" she said, a smile crinkling at her eyes.

Oleg was pale and serious, dressed in a stiff black suit, a spiky white chrysanthemum in his lapel. He looked distracted and excited as he handed me a giant bundle of flowers, pulled me into a hug, kissed me on the lips.

I plastered a smile on my face, tottered on my spiked silver heels.

What am I doing?

There were dozens of other brides in oversized white dresses and grooms in black suits waiting in the civil registration office. It felt like we were on a conveyor belt in a factory for marriages, with the somber notes of Mendelssohn's wedding march playing over and over every time another couple ahead of us walked through the door to the ceremony room.

Our turn came quickly. Oleg held his elbow out, and I slid my arm through, my skin against the fabric of his suit coat. We stepped through the doors next to a pair of musicians who sprang into music like a preassembled jack-in-the-box.

The woman conducting the ceremony announced her lines in a singsong-y, official voice.

"We are pleased to welcome you and your guests on this important day to the Moscow Department of Public Services," she said.

I wonder how many times a day she has to say this, I thought.

The ceremony took something like sixty seconds. It was so quick and smooth, I barely understood what was happening. Oleg and I said our dazed yeses, agreed to take each other as husband and wife. We stepped forward to sign our marriage license, then back to slide rings on each other's fingers. The officiant handed us our passports and marriage license, then they opened the office doors and shooed us outside.

I was married.

I went through the motions like a stage performance: I blew air kisses on the sides of his parents' cheeks, received a smothered embrace from his grandmother, a concerned squeeze from Katia. I stood still for photos, my mouth opened in a smile for the camera. I froze for a lingering kiss from Oleg, the cellophane bouquets crinkling between us.

"Skip class today," he coaxed, his arm looped around my shoulder, his eyes smiling down into mine. "Let's go out to a restaurant with my family."

"I can't," I said, slipping away, grabbing the bag of warm-up gear Katia had been holding for me. "We have that Paquita variation to get through today."

I escaped to the changing room, pulled off my dress, and slipped my feet into jeans, my arms into a jacket.

I fled to the metro, rocketed on a train through underground tunnels, and rushed up the escalators to make it to the wooden floor of my ballet studio on time.

In the Academy classroom, I could see the other girls staring at the careful makeup on my face, the strings of pearls in my hair.

"You look so nice today," one girl said.

As I went through pliés at the barre, a shaft of morning sun caught the gold of the new band on my finger. It sparkled so brightly, Bobrova paused, her attention drawn to it.

After class she pulled me aside, took my fingers in her hand.

"What's this?" she said, pointing at the ring.

"I got married this morning," I said. "Right before class. I did what I needed to do."

She looked at me sharply, startled.

"I understand," she said. "I'll make a few calls. You'll need to get on the Bolshoi's audition list."

A few days later, I broke the news to my parents in person.

Oleg and I went to the hotel they had booked in Moscow's city center when they arrived from Texas to see my graduation performance. We strolled into the lobby together, our hands clasped, megawatt, stage-worthy smiles on our faces.

When my parents saw us, they froze. Mom's cheeks went gray. Dad turned tomato red—he looked like a balloon about to pop.

"Joy, what is this?" Mom asked in a careful voice.

"Mom, Dad, this is Oleg, my husband," I said, leaning into Oleg's shoulder, my hand in his, my smile like a blinking neon sign.

Oleg stepped forward to shake Dad's hand, but Dad turned away and stared at the floor, refusing to even look at him.

"I can't shake your hand," Dad said. "I'm so angry right now."

Mom's face changed from gray to white. She looked like she might throw up.

"Sweetie, what . . . what would make you do this?" she said, her voice shaking. "You've never done anything bad in your life. Why would you lie to us? What have you done?"

Seeing their reactions frightened me, like a toddler who falls off a slide and looks to its parents to see if they are upset.

"Oleg is a good person," I said, trying to make the fear that rose in my throat come out sounding like anger and certainty. "I love Oleg."

I wish I could erase from my memory the way my parents looked at me then.

"I've had problems with your other siblings, but never with you," Mom said. "You've made the biggest mistake out of all of them."

"You've strayed outside the path that God wants for your life," Dad said. "This is a disaster. You just watch and see. Everything's gonna fall apart because you've abandoned God's will."

Over the rest of the week they spent in Russia, they refused to speak to Oleg, or meet his parents. They begged me to reconsider, to talk to a lawyer, to find another way. At one point they locked me in their hotel room, said I couldn't leave until I agreed to get an annulment.

But I was in so deep, I couldn't hear them. Instead, I found ways to dismiss their concerns. I watched them walk around Moscow and then St. Petersburg, and they suddenly seemed old and out of touch. They needed me to translate things for them. They walked slowly with dope-y American smiles on their faces. They misunderstood things around them in clumsy, conspiratorial ways and kept making ignorant, embarrassing jokes. This was what I chose to focus on.

"You don't get it, you don't understand the sacrifices I've made to get here, what I've been living through in Russia," I told them when they pressured me to go back to the registration office and get my divorce papers.

"I'm in love," I told them. "This is what I want."

As I said it, there was a part of me that started to believe it. I was used to cutting myself into pieces and only showing certain angles of myself at certain times to certain people. That was what it took to make people happy. People didn't want to know the truth about me. My Academy teachers didn't want to know about my back-door lessons with Tatiana. Mario and my parents didn't want to know about the marriage I'd spent weeks arranging behind everyone's backs, and the perfectly good job contracts I was turning down at the Mikhailovsky. Oleg didn't want to know that I struggled to return his kisses. And absolutely no one wanted to know about the vomiting I did behind closed doors in Pat's bathroom.

They wanted to see a perfectly formed, flawless ballerina on stage: poised, beautiful, strong, sleek. They wanted a heroine story, a miracle they could take photos of and brag about to their friends.

Well, I thought. *This is what it takes to give that to them.*

The audition for the Bolshoi was a formality.

Bobrova's shaggy-haired, mustached husband, Vasily Stepanovich Vorokhobko, who was a coach in the theater, said it wasn't a big deal.

"Don't worry about it. If you're invited to audition, then that means you're in," he told me.

He and Bobrova got me into the Bolshoi's morning classes in well-lit, freshly remodeled practice rooms where armies of beautiful, muscled Russian dancers in lumpy sweatpants, headbands, and T-shirts bent and bowed, pliéd and tendued in rows.

Vorokhobko was right. After my audition, I was called into the office of Pronin, the sharp-faced assistant artistic director.

"We're so excited to welcome you!" he said, his face beaming. "Of course we're going to take you into our company."

He laid out the entire process: I'd start taking classes and rehearsing with the company. Then, over the course of the fall season, they'd try me out in a few tiny roles: maybe a *corps* piece in *Nutcracker*, or a solo in *Don Quixote*.

"We'll start piecing you into the repertoire," he said. "Congratulations and welcome to the Bolshoi."

CHAPTER 16

Behind the Red Velvet Curtain

I was officially a Bolshoi ballerina, and the theater to which I'd come was the most beautiful I had ever seen.

It rose, in towering limestone glory, out of the earth in central Moscow—a city-state of hallways, elevators, lobbies, tunnels, skyways and stairwells. I kept getting lost as I walked its paint-scented labyrinth of corridors—bumbling into dance studios, arriving at the wrong sides of stages.

Hundreds of staff members filled the building, bustling at their work. There were attics crowded with seamstresses who stitched tulle to costumes, technicians who fiddled with stage-set levers, cafeteria workers who brewed cups of tea and chopped vegetables, dancers and coaches who refined eighteenth-century steps to intricate ballets, and musicians, their fingers set to taut metal strings, who filled the theater back rooms with unearthly notes of music.

My friend Katia showed me around to the cafeteria rooms with the coziest seating, the shortcuts up stairwells to the main stage, the best ways to avoid waiting too long for an elevator. I'd been granted a seat in her dressing room: a hairspray-scented chamber filled with desks, mirrors, and lamps. This was where women in fur coats arrived to change into costumes, smear makeup on their faces, and sit, feet on the tables in front of them, while stylists in aprons twisted their hair into buns or secured wigs to their scalps.

These other women eyed me with flat and jaded expressions on their faces, like the new and tender meat that I was.

"Don't stand at the center of the barre in class," they advised. "You need to make room for the primas. If you don't get out of the way, you'll annoy them."

They gave hints about the choreography I struggled to learn in *corps* rehearsals.

"No, no, the turn is on your left foot, not your right. Do it like this," they'd suggest, demonstrating an elongated leg while standing, half-dressed, a cup of coffee cooling in their hand.

They filled the mini-fridge in our room with salami, cake, and champagne. When they returned, sweating, from performances, they popped the green-tinted bottles open, spilled foam onto the floor.

"To us!" they toasted as they filled ceramic coffee mugs with bubbling drinks and swallowed in gulps.

I felt weighed down by the glory of the institution to which I had come. I wanted to become worthy of its magnificence.

I spent as many of my waking hours at the Bolshoi as possible. In the mornings, I tried to be the first one to class, and I attempted to get to know the different teacher-coaches who guided their battalions of dancers onto the stage. There was Vorokhobko, Bobrova's husband, with his bushy mustache and rolled-up shirt sleeves. He was an expert on the theater's brash and timeless Grigorovich repertoire. Then there was Kondratieva, a diminutive former ballerina with short gray hair and thrusted chin who swallowed her words and mumbled in class, but managed to land dancer after dancer in leading roles. And, of course, there was Tsiskaridze, with his wild mane of black hair, who towered over everyone in class and ruled his hour of ballet instruction with sarcasm.

"The American special forces are here!" he called out, his eyebrow raised, his mouth a smirk, when I walked into the studio.

Tsiskaridze, like Vorokhobko, favored the Bolshoi's Soviet Grigorovich tradition with its athletic feats and classic repertoire: *Spartacus, Nutcracker, La Bayadere, Swan Lake.* He had performed all these pieces himself and knew the body movements required to achieve the dramatic style, which had captured audiences around the world since the United States had tried to out-cosmonaut and out-dance the Soviets in the 1960s.

He found plenty of things to fix with me.

"What is this? Chicken arms?" He'd joke when he saw my port de bras. "Ladies and gentlemen, we have an American chicken here with us today. A KFC ten-piece special!"

He teased, but was ruthless and inspired in classes, surrounded by students who trusted him to tell them the truth about their dancing, to lead them to performances on stage that were fierce, imaginative and inspiring.

Tsiskaridze was something of a celebrity in Russia: the rare person who wasn't afraid to give critical quotes to journalists.[1] He was often invited to talk shows and TV specials on Rossiia-K, the national channel that specialized in cultural documentaries and broadcasts. There were many stars in his class, including the blonde-haired, angel-faced Angelina Vorontsova, who'd graduated the Academy under the tutelage of my former teacher, Natalia Arkhipova. She was perfect and so expressive, it was like the sun shone when she took to the stage, smiling and effervescent. Pavel Dmitrichenko, her boyfriend, was there too. He was the head of the dancer's union and one of the most compelling *Ivan the Terrible* dancers I'd ever seen—megalomaniacal and insane in costume, but down-to-earth, tattooed and kind in person. All of them were magnetic. Watching them perform—their muscled legs and tree-branch arms and effervescent bounds in the air—gave me chills. I couldn't believe I was lucky enough to take classes at their side.

The Bolshoi stage had burned in my heart for nearly a decade and now that I belonged to it, now that I had drawn close to it like an insect approaching a flame in the night, I understood that my years of toil and desire had been properly aligned. I saw, from the crowded dark of the wings, that there was nothing in the world like a performance at the Bolshoi.

Rainbows of light fell from the dark, cumulus heights of the ceiling when we performed. Intricate swarms of ballerinas, shimmering in costume, coalesced in flight patterns—crisscrossing, bending, bowing, turning. The orchestra created sounds that reverberated in the wood, velvet, and flesh-filled auditorium, churning, crashing, storming like waves pounding the shore of a gold-encrusted cove.

I longed, desperately, to make myself into the type of artist who would be worthy of this stage. But life in the theater, I learned quickly, wasn't like the Academy. There were no graded assignments, no regimented schedules, no constant drive forward to the graduation finish line. At the Bolshoi, no one gave me marks for my class performances, and there was no red diploma waiting for me if I did well.

I didn't know where I was supposed to put all my pent-up energy. There were classes and rehearsals, but they seemed to be focused on other people: the principals and stars, the artists who had already been assigned roles in the troupe's expansive repertoire.

My main job seemed to be standing around in the scuffed-up, mountainous wings, waiting. There were plenty of other ballet dancers there with me, trying to learn repertoire from the sidelines. Some of them seemed ancient by comparison, their muscled bodies bending and craning through stretched-out leotards. These were women in their thirties— nearly twice my age—who occasionally brought children and pets with them to the theater. They seemed so settled in their careers that it was like they could dance blind. They chewed gum and checked their phones while marking out steps, then stuffed the devices into the bra shelves of their leotards when they had to do a particularly tricky combination.

I guess this is just how it is at first, I told myself. *I guess I just need to be patient.*

The pent-up energy boiling in my chest spooled itself out into anxiety directed at the life I'd trapped myself in outside the theater.

I had created a mess. I no longer spoke to my parents, and I had abandoned the beautiful, quiet room in Pat's house just behind the theater to live with my new husband. I had packed my things into bags and moved an hour and a half outside the city center to a three-room apartment that Oleg shared with his parents on the building's sixteenth floor.

"We're married, we're a family now," Oleg had said. "We should live together."

And I, who had insisted to my mother and father that I was in love, agreed. We moved into his tiny bedroom, just down the hall from his parents.

Oleg, this person I had married, was someone constantly by my side: when I slept at night, when I woke in the morning, when I rode a series of grimy train cars and buses into work in the morning.

We slept in his room, the room of a teenage boy, filled with workout equipment, a lumpy mattress, a flat-screen TV. There was a ballet barre screwed to the wall, shelves above his desk that held hair gel and books about ballet, guitars he stacked on an ironing board in the corner so I'd have room to stretch on the floor in the mornings.

I had never seriously dated anyone before, was still a virgin when I slipped Oleg's wedding ring on the finger of my right hand. The sudden leap into a full-on marriage with someone I barely knew was overwhelming. I was attracted to Oleg, but the abrupt dive into intimacy stepped over a line inside me that I hadn't even known existed.

After we'd slept together, I remembered the words I'd heard at churches growing up about the importance of refusing to let yourself become tainted by sexual thoughts or activity. For a short period of time after the wedding, I had kept alive a quiet voice inside me that whispered, *As long as you don't have sex, you can still get out of this.*

But after we started sleeping together, the possibility of reversing the marriage I'd created, dissolved.

It's too late now. You're all used up, a chewed-up piece of gum, a ripped piece of paper. You made your bed, and now you have to lie in it.

I began having unpleasant flashbacks. They screamed into my life like jump scares at the worst moments—riding on the metro, lying awake at night, stretching by myself in the theater hallways.

These were memories of things that had happened to me when I was a child, things I'd long tried to forget. I'd never told anyone about what had happened to me. A person had secretly hurt me in ways no child should ever be hurt. It had happened when we were living in Santa Monica. I had been too little to know the words to describe what it was, too ashamed to tell anyone, too worried it had all somehow been my fault. The only thing I knew, back then, was that I was frightened, guilty, desperate to leave my young body and disappear.

For most of my life, I had tried to hide what had happened. When people asked if I'd ever been abused, I said no. But after I got married, the memories kept resurfacing like ghosts leaking out of a dead-bolted, padlocked closet.

Even when I successfully repressed the memories, my body could not forget. I felt it when I locked myself in the bathroom and vomited into the toilet, desperate to rid myself of the shame that seemed to crawl beneath my skin. I felt it sometimes with Oleg, when we were alone and I was uncomfortable but didn't know how to voice my concerns—only how to pretend that everything was okay.

I couldn't talk to my parents about how I felt, what I remembered. They remained deeply, incandescently, unshakably angry at my decision to get married. They were convinced I had removed myself from the safety of God's will.

I walked around Moscow with the sound of their disappointed voices echoing in my head, the looks of disapproval on their faces, burned into my retinas. The amount of shame and anger I felt was like a mountain that had fallen on top of me. I couldn't see past it. But I also didn't want anyone to see that it weighed on me. People were not capable of handling any version of me that wasn't perfect.

I tried to make it seem as if the life I was living was everything I wanted. I constructed an elaborate system of layers and illusions. I posted cheerful updates on Facebook, wished my parents public happy birthdays online, took romantic photos with Oleg, nestled in his arms, my face turned to his chest.

I didn't think about how a staged performance always comes to an end: the curtain always falls, the audience always leaves, the lights always turn to dark.

I turned my shame inward, like a knife wielded on my own abdomen.

I binged on junk food purchased at convenience stores, piled my plate high at buffets. Then, after stuffing myself, I got up from the table and rushed to a toilet, where I threw it all up in private. Everything felt out of control, and the purging felt like self-flagellation, penance, exorcism.

The way I split myself was like light passing through a prism until it filled the room with fractal, disparate beams—tense, shimmering, ephemeral. I kept a pleasant and compliant look on my face when I sat in the dressing room of my new colleagues. I held Oleg's hand on the subway, I listened to corrections from my ballet coaches, I worked my muscles into a burnished, pliable iron. But there was a constant pit of anxiety in my stomach that felt like it was growing into something violent.

Oleg tried. He did the things he thought husbands should do. He opened doors for me, took my elbow when we walked on slippery spots on the sidewalk, purchased bouquets of flowers for me, an expensive designer wallet for a New Year's present. We adopted a fluffy white dog that scurried around our ankles, licked at our faces, snuggled on our laps.

He gave his opinion on the things that I did, shook his head when he heard the terrible things I said about myself.

"You're beautiful, Joy. Stop being so mean to yourself. You're not fat," he would say. "You have to love yourself."

Sometimes I noticed the kind words he said, but I never let them in as reality. I watched them drift by, unheeded, like an insect flying past a window.

There was a darkness to the things Oleg liked—at least it seemed so to me, a teenager who had never played video games, had never been allowed to watch TV; someone who had previously considered the *Terminator* a movie too scary to finish. But there was a gritty genius to things he admired, the art he worked on. He dreamed of moving to Berlin and becoming a choreographer.

"You should let me choreograph a ballet on you," he said.

I liked the idea. It seemed like a way to become an artist who inspired people, a muse upon whom others could build their creations.

We found empty studios at the Bolshoi and began practicing together.

Oleg was imaginative. The childhood he had spent with his family in the Russian circus and the years he'd given to the Bolshoi Academy endowed him with an arresting stage presence, a genius for showmanship, and a craving for the strange and disturbing. His choreography reminded me of a quirky, inspired circus act. He tied my arms together and had me roll around on the floor like someone in an insane asylum wearing a straitjacket, a life-sized puppet pulled upward on strings.

We practiced in pockets of time after and in-between rehearsals and classes—late at night, after full days spent taking class, and rehearsing.

On one of those nights, we stood in the pale-walled stillness of an empty Bolshoi rehearsal studio. Oleg was intent on driving toward the finish line. I could feel the exhaustion of a full day of work pressed deep into my bones. My stomach had been empty for so long, it no longer rumbled, just shrank in on itself, dry, thirsty, resigned.

"No, not like that!" Oleg said, focused on the line of my shoulders when I raised them. He stepped forward from the mirrors to where I sagged in the middle of the floor.

"You should raise your shoulders like this"—he demonstrated—"like they're tied to a rope on the floor."

He moved my limbs into the position he wanted.

"Okay, let's try it again from the beginning," he said, stepping back to the front of the room.

I was so tired, my head felt detached from my shoulders. My eyes blurred, unfocused, but I started the dance steps Oleg suggested from the start of the sequence. The movement made me feel dizzy and sick. I stumbled, my face drained of color.

"I'm tired," I said, pausing to bend over.

"We've almost got it. Just ten more minutes," Oleg said. "Let's start again. From the top."

I waited until the room stopped spinning around me. Then I repeated the motions he had choreographed. I bent my knees to the ground, my arms thrust behind me, wrists bound in black fabric. But I felt dizzy. The edges of my vision dimmed into shadow.

I stumbled past Oleg, out of the studio, into the hallway.

I fell into the nearest bathroom and collapsed on a toilet, the contents of my stomach rushed up my throat and out of my mouth in a giant, involuntary heave.

I vomited into the toilet over and over, my eyes tearing, my nose running, my stomach contracting. I couldn't get myself to stop, even though it felt like there was nothing left inside. I heaved over and over until I choked and struggled to breathe.

By the time the contractions ended, I was lying on the cold tile floor, nearly unconscious. The toilet was filled with green bile and dark red blood.

Oleg waited at the bathroom door for me, his eyes round and frightened.

"I'm not okay," I said. "I think I just threw up blood."

He sat me down on the floor, brought me a glass of water, helped me dress in my coat and boots.

I heard him calling his parents. "Pop, Joy is sick, we need to get her to a hospital," he said.

Then he lifted me up, put my arm over his shoulder, and shuffled me toward the theater exit.

"We have to go, we have to get you to the car," he said over and over.

Outside, I doubled over on the sidewalk and threw up again: more blood, more bile. It frightened me that it was involuntary, that I couldn't control it. It frightened me that the heaving gripped my rib cage like a vise, constricting my lungs, closing my throat. And when the liquid came up dark red again, tinged with blood, I knew.

Something is really wrong.

CHAPTER 17

The Nutcracker

There was a romanticism in Russia about going insane—some deeply subconscious understanding that madness was a normal, even necessary condition for sensitive and artistic people. It was everywhere you looked in Russian literature and art. Tolstoy's Anna Karenina threw herself beneath the roaring iron wheels of a train. Yury Zhivago, fictional poet, lost his mind in the brutality of a Moscow destroyed by revolution. Ivan the Terrible, his haunted face immortalized in a painting that hung on display at the Tretyakov Gallery, had murdered his own son.

These were historical and literary figures I had studied in my years at the Academy. Suffering for art was a tradition here. It was expected.

The Bible, I'd learned in church, had these traditions as well—like Daniel, who allowed himself to be thrown into a den of lions, and Stephen, whose eyes saw the glory of God only after he'd been dragged out of the city and stoned. And of course there was Jesus—raised to the right hand of God only after dying by crucifixion.

"Blessed are those who mourn," I'd read. "After you have suffered a little while . . . Christ will himself . . . establish you."

At the Bolshoi, suffering was enshrined in *La Traviata* with a heroine who sacrifices herself for love, dying with a beautiful, trembling aria in her throat. Or *Swan Lake*, where Odette, with a flying plunge, her arms outstretched, her back arched like a wing, drowns herself in a lake.

Sacrificing for dance, for art—even dying for it—made a certain sort of sense to me.

But suffering was only beautiful when Dostoyevsky wrote about it or when Olga Smirnova acted it out on stage. In real life, it was awful.

In the antiseptic Russian hospital room to which Oleg brought me, doctors and nurses poked needles into my skin, drew blood out of my arms and dripped bags of fluid into my veins. They shoved otoscopes and endoscopes into my mouth to peer down my throat and prodded at the organs in my abdomen.

The ways in which I'd starved myself were killing me. I was down to a dangerously low weight. My face was swollen, my hair was falling out in clumps, my skin turning yellow from liver failure. The lining in my esophagus and stomach had disintegrated; my muscles were wasting away. The vomiting I'd induced for years had changed the way my salivary glands, pancreas, and gall bladder operated. I couldn't, even in the hospital, stop gagging and dry heaving.

The nurses added medicine to my IV. They numbed my stomach and calmed the vomiting.

Oleg called my mother.

"Joy's really sick," he said. "We're worried about her."

Mom got hold of my lab results, then insisted on talking to me.

"Joy, your liver is damaged," she said, scanning the numbers she saw in my medical reports. "You've lost essential nutrients that your body needs. You've changed your acid base. If you screw that up too much, it will affect your kidneys."

I was afraid of what she told me, but I'd been doing my own online reading, spending time on terrible sites that explained how to be bulimic with lies that promised it was possible to regiment things so they didn't get out of hand.

"I'm fine, Mom," I told her. "Oleg is taking care of me."

"This is serious, Joy. You're dying. This disease is killing you," Mom said.

I wanted to hang up on her. The panic and concern in her voice, the questions she asked sounded like blame. So I pushed back hard.

"You're the one who's always told me to try harder, be better. I've never been good enough for you," I said. I told her about the anorexia that had started in Washington, D.C., when I was thirteen, the vomiting that had begun two years ago at the Bolshoi Academy.

"I love you, Joy," Mom said. "I don't care if you are at the Bolshoi, if you're a good dancer, if you're a dancer at all. I don't care what you do with your life. I just want you alive. And these labs are telling me you won't be alive for much longer."

Mom wanted to find me an in-patient clinic that specialized in eating disorders. She talked about daily cognitive behavioral therapy and psychiatric medication.

"You don't understand how it works, Mom. I just got this contract at the Bolshoi. I can't leave now."

"Honey, you don't understand how much God loves you," Mom said. "This eating disorder is from the pit of hell, from the devil. You don't need it; you can do what you want to do on your own, without throwing up."

"I can't go check into some eating disorder program," I said. "I'll lose my contract at the Bolshoi."

Dad got on the phone with her. "Your Bolshoi contract doesn't matter if you're dead," he said.

"I'll be fine," I said. "Oleg is taking care of me."

My parents were nine time zones away; they couldn't force me to do anything. But Mom got on the phone with Oleg's parents and talked through the injections they'd need to give me to keep me from vomiting, the vitamin supplements and omega 3 I needed in my diet. She laid out a nutrition regimen with forced feedings and water intake recorded every two hours.

They told me they were sorry for the terrible things they'd said to me that summer.

"Why don't you and Oleg visit us in Austin?" they suggested. "We adore Oleg, we adore his parents, we adore you. We have no more reservations about your marriage. We just want you alive."

Oleg drove me back to his family's apartment. I was under strict orders to rest until I could get my weight back up, forbidden from dancing. I curled up on the mattress in his bedroom, with a book in my hands, and stared out the window at the gray sky hanging low over canyons of cement Khrushchev-era apartment buildings. October rain pricked at the window, soaked the yellow and orange leaves that fell to the ground.

Oleg's mom, with her sharp, blonde haircut, laid out the medication I needed. She scrambled eggs in a pan in her kitchen and watched while I picked them, yellow and rubbery, off the plate.

"Joy, you need to eat all of it," she'd say, as I forced myself to swallow.

I just need to sleep in a normal, clean room and be left alone, I thought.

I missed the quiet of Pat's spacious apartment and my friends from church. I missed morning classes in the Bolshoi's vaulted studios. I missed standing in the wings near the stage, watching dancers in costume whirl across the floor, like silky, colorful kites, borne aloft by music rising in swells from the orchestra pit.

The vitamins from my mother and the supervised feeding from Oleg's mother helped me gain weight.

As soon as possible, I returned to theater classes. I wasn't in great condition—my hair was still falling out. I was weak, and my brain was still filled with hideous words and disgust that I heard every time I looked in the mirror.

But I had gained some weight. I was no longer throwing up involuntarily.

I found quiet corners to stretch, returned to the edges of rehearsals to mark out the steps made by first cast members.

I retreated sometimes, after there was nothing left to rehearse, to a tiny balcony high above the historic Bolshoi auditorium. It was a hidden place, nestled against the painted ceiling where I could look into the face of the glittering three-tiered chandelier and onto the tops of the heads of hundreds of Muscovites who filled the theater seats. The sounds of cellos and oboes and trumpets washed over me, and I heard, like a rock absorbing oceanic swells, the sonic waves of tenors and sopranos singing notes that prickled at the back of my spine.

I wanted, in these moments, to feel tears fall from my eyes and a release of something bound tight in my chest. But my face stayed dry, and my chest unmoved. I was numb, shrouded in something unnamable, cold, and dead.

I'm here at the Bolshoi, the most beautiful theater in the world. My dream has come true. Everything about this is wonderful.

This is what I told myself when I saw the swirls of cerulean and scarlet paint on the ceiling, the reams of crimson and gold fabric woven in Russian monasteries that swathed the auditorium,[1] the firefly dance of ballerinas on stage.

But I could not feel the beauty inside.

Bobrova's husband, Vasily Stepanovich Vorokhobko, took me under his wing. He saw how unwound I had become, how nervous and distraught. It's possible that he and Bobrova spoke about me when they went home at night: about how skittish I was, how hard on myself, how my anxiety and eagerness could sometimes push me ahead of the music.

My frustration was sharp. I wished, above all, to turn into a robot who could perform anything on command: gratitude, appreciation, exquisite arabesques and feats of balletic wonder.

Vorokhobko saw my desire and tried to turn it for good. He started taking me aside for rehearsals and watching me work, his sleeves rolled to his elbows, his eyebrows knit together under his shaggy haircut, counting "One-two-one-two-one-two," in a rough voice like a skinny, cigarette-addicted troll.

"Plié, plié, plié," he would say, waving his arms softly through the air like a conductor quieting an orchestra, commanding me to bend gracefully at the knees, my back ramrod-straight and upright. "Pliés are your relaxation. Pliés are a gift. Pliés will save your life."

When he saw me growing frustrated or nervous, he'd put his hand on my forehead and move his thumb in a cross shape, like an Orthodox priest granting a blessing to a parishioner.

"If you have problems with your pirouettes, plié! If you are too nervous, do another plié! Plié will save the world," he'd say, like some sort of mustachioed Russian Yoda.

What can you do with a desperate dancer who cannot listen to reason? Perhaps, Vorokhobko might have thought, you give her the stage that she wants and hope the reality of its brilliance will obliterate the lies she's been telling herself.

In December, my name appeared on the cast list for an upcoming *Nutcracker* performance. And it wasn't just a *corps* role, it was a soloist variation: the Spanish doll.

"Excellent," Vasily Stepanovich said when I told him. "We need to get you ready."

He started running me through what he called the "Women's Regimen."

We'd find an empty rehearsal studio, and he'd order me to *soutenu* across the floor in a diagonal line, then come back across in a series of piques, then return doing a diagonal from Giselle. Back and forth, back and forth with relentless turns, steps, and movements until I forgot to plan or think ahead. All I could do was focus solely on breathing and completing each motion as ordered.

"Let's go, let's go, let's go!" he'd shout, flicking the lights on and off while I turned fouettés. "You need to be solid! Spry! Ready for anything!"

My debut was set for the last day of the year, the tail end of *Nutcracker* season.

"This is important," Vorokhobko kept telling me. "Filin and the other directors will be watching. If you do well on this, they might give you other pieces, maybe start working you into other parts of the repertoire."

I was excited to perform for the first time, but as the day drew near, I was increasingly panicked. My health was still fragile. The foot I'd had surgery on in school was acting up. It had grown swollen, red, and painful. Then, three days before the performance, I came down with a fever and my heel flared into a pulsing, angry knob.

"It's okay to cancel—we'll just tell them you have your period and can't perform," Vorokhobko said. "You have to be 100 percent sure you won't fall on stage. That's the absolute worst thing you can do."

"No, I'll be fine, I'm positive," I told him.

And sure enough, the day of the performance, my fever subsided.

I pulled on the red, mushroom-shaped skirt that had been customized by a tailor in the Bolshoi's costume department. It fit my body perfectly and sparkled in the light.

I left my dressing table and found a Bolshoi hairdresser and makeup artist to help me.

"Who are you? You must be new," they said as they stuck rhinestones into my hair and smoothed blush onto my cheeks. "Good luck."

My heart pounded in my chest as I walked up the stairs to the black canyon sides of the Bolshoi stage. They were dark and crowded with dancers in costume, stage hands in jeans. I held the side of the wall and bent, kicked my leg high in the air to shake out the jitters.

Vorokhobko was there to watch me.

"Don't worry," he said. "I will be right back here, holding you in the palm of my hand while you dance."

He smiled at me under his mustache, calm and proud.

"Joy!" My partner found me. "Let's go!"

I was the first in a line of ballerinas dressed as dolls who were supposed to start out on stage. I stood at the edge of the curtain, felt their tutus pushing into my back, like water foaming against a dam. I was hidden in shadow, barely breathing.

What if I go out too soon? What if I miss my cue? What if I forget my steps and mess everyone else up?

My partner was nervous about me too. When the orchestra breathed in before our musical cue, he shouted at me.

"Go! Go! Go! Let's go!" he screamed.

I burst out from behind the curtain into the blue twilight created on stage. The set rose in shades of green behind me like the giant, spiked boughs of a Christmas tree. I crooked my elbows and lifted my knees, turned my face to the auditorium that was washed in gold and filled with people from floor to ceiling.

My body remembered the steps for me, turning and jumping, a wide smile cemented on my face, my red tutu bouncing around me like a silky, polka-dot accordion. There wasn't any time to be nervous—just to put one foot in front of the other, turn, nod, skip, bend. After the first variation, we ran around the back of the scenery, our pointe shoes clomping on the floor, to get ready for our next scene. I was giggling, on an adrenaline high, and then I was back on stage, my elbows remembering to move the way Vorokhobko taught me.

I finished the performance breathing hard, smiling.

Oh my God, you just did that.

Vorokhobko was there, tears in his eyes, to clap me on the back.

"I didn't doubt you for a moment," he said, his cheeks crinkled in smile. "Do you hear your colleagues clapping for you from the wings? This is how we've done it since Soviet times. If the company stands and applauds you, it's a very, very good sign."

"You believed in me, you worked with me, you made it happen," I told him.

I'd spent all of 2012 in a panic, but finally, on the last day of the year, things had paid off.

I left the theater to a city covered with snow, the night sky bursting with New Year's Eve fireworks. I met up with friends from school, and we walked through the streets, singing, drinking champagne, toasting the old year, welcoming the new one.

My dreams had come true, and my heart was filled with new resolutions. The next time I danced, I wanted the theater's artistic director, Sergei Filin, to watch me. He was the man who'd given me a job here, the man with shining brown hair who'd played the roles of princes at the Bolshoi for years, the man on whom everyone's careers depended. His voice, his eyes were the only ones that mattered.

Next year, I told myself, *Filin will watch me dance.*

Figure 1   Joy Womack practices a ballet move in her school uniform. Author's Collection

Figure 2   Joy Womack, age 15, stands in front of the Moscow State Academy of Choreography—sometimes known as the Bolshoi Ballet Academy—in 2009, just after her arrival in Russia. Author's Collection

Figure 3 Joy Womack stands with her grandmother, Eleanor Jackson Piel, after her performance in "Protégés III: The International Ballet Academy Festival" in 2011. She performed with a broken wrist. Author's Collection

Figure 4 Joy Womack stands in a Bolshoi Theater rehearsal studio. Author's Collection

Figure 5 Joy Womack prepares for a performance in her dressing room at the Bolshoi Ballet Theater in Moscow. Author's Collection

Figure 6 Joy Womack dances in front of the red velvet curtain on the Bolshoi Ballet Theater's historic main stage in 2012. Author's Collection

Figure 7 Joy Womack takes a bow in front of the red velvet curtain on the historic Bolshoi Ballet Theater's main stage in 2012. Author's Collection

Figure 8 Coauthors Joy Womack and Elizabeth Shockman seated at Moscow café, 2014. Courtesy of Deborah Hoehner

Figure 9 Joy Womack stands next to U.S. ambassador to Russia Michael McFaul following her debut performance at the State Kremlin Palace Theater in *The Nutcracker* in 2014. Author's Collection

Figure 10 Joy Womack sits on the floor of the State Kremlin Palace Theater's dance studio, receiving instruction from her coach, Zhanna Bogoroditskaia. Courtesy of Alexander Kabanov

Figure 11 Joy Womack warms up before her performance with the State Kremlin Palace Theater. Courtesy of Alexander Kabanov

Figure 12 Joy Womack stands on the balcony of her Moscow apartment, looking toward Christ the Savior Cathedral. Courtesy of Alexander Kabanov

Figure 13 Joy Womack performs the lead role of Kitri in the State Kremlin Palace Theater's production of *Don Quixote*. Courtesy of Alexander Kabanov

Figure 14 Joy Womack performs in *Swan Lake* with the State Kremlin Palace Theater's ballet troupe. Courtesy of Alexander Kabanov

Figure 15 Joy Womack performs in *Swan Lake* with the State Kremlin Palace Theater's ballet troupe. Courtesy of Alexander Kabanov

Figure 16 Joy Womack poses on Red Square in Moscow with her dad, Clay Womack. Author's Collection

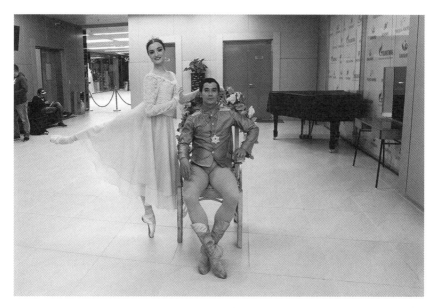

Figure 17 Joy Womack and her dance partner, Misha Martyniuk, backstage after performing for Russian president Vladimir Putin. Author's Collection

Figure 18 Joy Womack stands with her mother, Eleanor, at her wedding rehearsal dinner, 2021. Courtesy of Leslie Leis

Figure 19 Joy Womack and her husband, Andrew Clay, seated in a theater for the viewing of *Joy Womack: The White Swan* documentary. Author's Collection

CHAPTER 18

Acid Attack

Seventeen days after my *Nutcracker* performance, late on a January night, the gray sky over Moscow darkened to black. Snow filtered through the air above a parking lot at the center of the city.

Sergei Filin, artistic director of the Bolshoi, parked his Mercedes outside his apartment building and, just after 11 p.m., got out, his shoes pressing into the cold, white dust on the ground. Snowflakes caught on his famous mop of shining brown hair, on the clear, broad skin of his face. It was a face many ballerinas had fallen in love with, a face that could carry the heightened, dramatic emotions of a ballet on stage, a face that regularly appeared on TV. It was a face that had spoken words that launched my career at the Bolshoi.

He shut the door of his vehicle with a muffled *thud* and walked toward the hooded entrance of his apartment building.

He did not see how a man, his mouth and chin hidden behind a scarf, his forehead covered in a wooly hat, crept up behind him.

The man raised his voice, ominous and sarcastic, said he'd come with a greeting.

Filin turned and saw him, crouched in the shadows, his hand hidden behind his back.

He's holding a gun. I'm dead, Filin thought.

Maybe if it had been a gun, it would not have been so painful.

But it was not a gun. The man who stood before him held a glass jar filled with liquid. He flung it in a wide arc at Filin's surprised expression, then turned and ran.

Filin felt a splash onto his nose, his cheeks, his scalp, his eyes. It was like a blast of fire—the pain so horrific, he felt sure he was dying. He fell to the ground, blinded, in agony, and buried his head in the snow. He screamed for help, rolled on the cold pavement, blindly punched the number pad at the entrance to his apartment building and banged his fists on the door.

Help did not come. The burning did not stop.

It was not until he stumbled and crawled to the guarded entrance of the parking lot that he was noticed. By then he was shaking, going into shock, and his face was indescribable. It was so horrifically scorched that, when his wife came running at the security guard's call and saw how the skin was melting from his bones, she began to weep.[1]

The news of this attack on our artistic director, on the head of the Bolshoi Ballet Theater, flashed around the world in text messages, phone calls, news headlines, TV reports.

I learned about it in the gray morning light of a ballet studio in Estonia, where I was staying for a week to renew my Russian work visa.

"Joy, did you hear?" The Estonian theater director walked up to me. "Filin was attacked."

"What?" The words I'd heard didn't make sense.

"Your ballet director. The artistic director of the Bolshoi—Filin. He was attacked with acid," The director repeated, his eyebrows drawn together. He pointed to an article backlit on the screen of his phone.

I read the headline, then dropped my hand from the barre and reached for my own phone. It didn't make sense. Filin was young, beautiful, the recognizable representative of the Bolshoi. He was strict about people attending morning classes at the theater. He visited galas in tuxedos, sat in Moscow cafés with his assistants to review audition tapes.

Who would do such a thing?

I returned to Moscow and found that a static tension had settled over the corridors of the Bolshoi.

We had all seen the videos of Filin in his hospital room. They looked like a scene from a horror movie. His skull was completely entombed in a stiff, white cast, his eyes swollen shut. There were dark red stains on the gauze around his eyes that made it look as if he had been weeping blood. The only part of him that was recognizable were his hands, waving beautifully, descriptively in front of the camera as he spoke.

"He might be permanently blinded," people said.

"It's like a bad dream. I can't believe this is happening," girls said, shaking their heads after class. "I spent my childhood watching Filin. He's one of the most amazingly beautiful dancers I've ever seen."

Russian police detectives in button-down shirts walked the hallways of the theater. They pulled dancers one-by-one into separate offices. They wore grim expressions, and people whispered about the questions they asked, the lie detectors they kept behind closed doors.

At first, I'd thought, *A dancer, a person committed to beauty and art, would never commit this sort of crime. It has to be someone who isn't connected to the theater.*

But then I remembered things Filin had said in the weeks before the attack. He'd spoken about threats he'd received: anonymous people who called his phone, then hung up when he answered. Rude and angry messages that had appeared in his email account. A Facebook page that had been set up in his name and filled with terrible photos and words. A knife, stabbed into the tires of his car.

My phone rang and buzzed with calls and text messages from journalists who worked for the *New York Times*, Reuters, and *Time* magazine.

"Do you know who did it?" they asked. "Do you have any guesses? What do you know about Filin? About Iksanov? About Tsiskaridze?"

Sometimes I gave them quotes, but the truth was that I myself didn't know what was happening. The reporters who called me often knew things before I did.

Russian television couldn't get enough of it. They aired broadcasts in which they spoke about the dark side of the Bolshoi's history: shards of glass inserted in dancers' pointe shoes; needles laced, pointy-side-inward into costumes; cats and brooms thrown on stage to distract rivals; prostitution organized by Russian officials who traded access to dancers for money or political power.[2]

On one night there was an entire television show about the attack broadcast just fifty minutes before the curtain went up on a performance. We crowded in our tutus around the screen to watch people describe professional rivalries, blackmail, bribery, sexually compromising photos, and angry, vengeful love triangles. Then we hurried to the edge of the stage, waited for our musical cues, and leaped into the light.

The entire country was shocked by what had happened. They spoke about it on TV, around their kitchen tables, in wooden chairs over cardboard cups of coffee in city cafés.

Everyone I knew—friends from church, colleagues, former classmates—had opinions and theories. We were all dismayed, but the older generation of dancers, people who had become my teachers, who had dedicated their lives to ballet were especially aghast.

"If you want to figure out what's happening at the Bolshoi, you have to think about what's happening in Russia in general. You have to think about Magnitsky and Politkovskaya." This was the theory of my former Academy teacher Ilya Kuznetsov. Magnitsky was a lawyer who had died in jail after exposing corruption by Russian officials and Politkovskaya, a journalist and human rights advocate who'd been murdered in her apartment building—shot in the elevator—after reporting on Russian politics and leadership.

The acid attack on Filin, Kuznetsov thought, was just one in a long line of episodes that showed all the ways things in Russia had been going wrong since the Soviet Union collapsed. It was impossible to tell where the Bolshoi ended and Russia began. Was not the Bolshoi just the queenly crown Mother Russia wore on her head?

"When we were young, in Soviet times, we believed in a bright future. We were strong because we were united and worked together and had strong leadership," Kuznetsov said from behind his wire-rimmed glasses. "But then everything collapsed like a sandcastle."

Kuznetsov, who said these things while sitting at a high-top table in a Moscow Starbucks, knew his history. He knew about the Soviet-era purges that sent half the country to gulags. But he'd also lived through the collapse of his country, and, like many people of his generation, he wasn't sure the country that had emerged since was better.

"People stopped thinking about what could be good for Russia, for schools, for painters, for children, for ballet. Everyone just thinks about getting money, including at the Bolshoi," Kuznetsov said.

He and other teachers could remember what the theater had been like before the Soviet Union collapsed. The choreographer Grigorovich had been in charge, and everyone just had to do what he said, whether they liked it or not.

"People just danced," Kuznetsov said. "You didn't have to think about money because the government paid a lot. All the Grigorovich-era dancers were loaded down with cars, apartments, dachas, and everything. It was a great time."

Everyone who could remember the Soviet-era Bolshoi agreed with Kuznetsov. Things had been better then.

What the Bolshoi needed—what Russia needed—was an iron rule, they thought, a strong leader, an unbendable czar who sat at the top of the power structure and forced everyone to bend to his will.

CHAPTER 19

Dead End

By the middle of March, I was covered with bruises. They bloomed purple, yellow, and green in strange places across my body: my inner thigh, my collarbone, my shins, my back. It looked as if I had been taken to a dark Moscow alley and beaten.

The marks had come, all of them, from *The Rite of Spring*—a modernist piece at the Bolshoi in which I'd been cast. In rehearsals, I was dragged across the floor, pushed to the ground. Other dancers threw sand in my face, splashed me with water.

"You're thirsty! Dying for water," the director, a woman from Ekaterinburg, would tell us. "Taste each other! Barbecue each other! Make it sexual!"

It felt so absurd. Sometimes I'd catch the eye of another dancer, and we'd bite our lips and look away to avoid bursting into laughter.

I found myself growing annoyed.

Stop it, Joy, I had to remind myself. *You're acting like a brat. You should be grateful to have something to dance.*

But I had worked for weeks on a solo in *Sleeping Beauty*—the sort of classical piece for which I'd been trained—and, at the last minute, learned someone else had been given the role instead.

"It was Filin's wife," one of my dance coaches told me. "We worked really hard on it, and you danced it really well, but what can I do?"

I was crestfallen.

"But we put so much work into it!" I said.

"I know," my coach agreed. "This makes me sick, but there's nothing I can do about it."

I couldn't figure out how to get my salary from the Bolshoi. I'd been paid once in November—just over $1,200. But I couldn't understand how my contract worked. Every time I wanted to be paid, I needed to go to the assistant director's office to have a receipt signed. Then I needed to take that receipt to a cashier's office. But the director was never in his office, and the cashier's stand was always closed when I visited.

I'd begun using my dad's business credit card to pay for food and gas.

"It's fine," Dad told me. But I felt bad about it.

Pat, when she returned to Moscow, sometimes slipped me cash, but made me promise not to give any to Oleg.

The relationship into which Oleg and I had put ourselves was slowly disintegrating.

Oleg was fully committed, but I didn't want to be married, didn't want kids. I disliked living in his family's apartment, hated the energy I lost trying to make our togetherness into something I wanted. He'd lost his job at the Bolshoi after traveling to visit my family in Texas. Now he was desperately searching for another, while scrambling to pay for car repairs, groceries, phone bills, and the various bureaucratic papers, stamps, signatures, and seals that made our lives and careers possible.

In Russia, I was learning, there was always a way to pay for getting out of difficult situations. The more money you had, the easier and smoother your life became. But we had no money. We kept opening credit cards and moving rubles around. We had the equivalent of eight dollars on one card, ten on another.

The Womack answer for when things weren't working out had always been clear: try harder, do more. The idea was to embody a type of hurricane: keep moving, make yourself into a churning vortex that sucked up any opportunity in its path until it became a self-generating force that no one could ignore.

I tried to make myself into just such a vortex. I lined up teachers like cards in a game: Vorokhobko, Kondratieva, Tsiskaridze. I spoke to journalists when they called and said yes when Oleg found some sort of artistic documentary for us to film together.

I started visiting the Strelka athletics factory in the Moscow suburbs to search the overflowing shelves of stretchy fabric and dance gear for something that would cure the aches that persisted in my body when I danced. The factory was a strange place in a crumbling brick building set in a muddy parking lot. Its basement was filled with rows of industrial sewing machines and blank-faced, exhausted workers who hunched over, stitching and sweating.

When I walked inside, I climbed its peeling, linoleum stairs and perused the rows of shelving that spilled over with satiny, multicolored leotards. One day, the factory owner's assistant found me on the floor, trying new warm-up slippers on my feet.

"Hello," she said, a smile on her face. "You seem like someone Mr. Strelka would like to meet."

She brought me to the factory owner's office, which was filled with a massive desk and expensive furniture. Sergei Strelka, wearing a dark suit, his hair in a ponytail, stood up to greet me. He seemed like someone important, like someone able to make things happen.

"A Bolshoi ballerina is searching for some new dance gear, I hear." He smiled, motioned to a seat in front of his desk. He asked me about my work, the roles I wanted to dance, the type of pointe shoes I wanted to wear.

I told him what I was rehearsing and the theaters to which I'd been invited to do guest performances.

"How would you like to work together?" he asked, leaning forward in his seat, looking at me over the shining expanse of his desk. "We could get you to model some of our dance gear, design some leotards."

I'd heard of sponsorship deals, and this seemed like a good way to get my gear paid for and maybe earn some money to supplement what I was supposed to be getting from the Bolshoi.

"I'd love to do that," I said.

"Great! Why don't you come by next week to model our new warm-up coat? I'll have our driver pick you up." He smiled. "We make really wonderful dance gear—you'll see. We're going to change the ballet industry!"

I began posting photos of myself wearing Strelka dance wear on Facebook and Instagram. Oleg and I sketched ideas for new leotards and warm-up clothing and sent them to the Strelka design team. When Mr. Strelka invited me out to a dinner in central Moscow to talk about long-term business strategy, I got excited.

Maybe this is when I'll sign the sponsorship contract. Maybe Mr. Strelka will be able to open some doors for me.

I wore my nicest dress and one of Pat's fur coats to the meeting. Mr. Strelka sent his driver to deliver me to Nobu, a restaurant near the Bolshoi that served tiny plates of food in a dimly lit interior.

He was waiting for me at a table where a candle flickered and the sound of hushed conversation and quietly tinkling silverware on porcelain plates filled the air.

"Welcome!" he said, helping me out of my coat, pulling out a chair for me.

I held the smooth paper booklet of a menu in my fingertips, and Mr. Strelka grasped the transparent stem of a wineglass. He began asking me about where I saw myself in the future.

"Do you want a comfortable lifestyle?" he asked.

The question felt a little strange, but I talked about the travel I hoped to do, the promotions and roles I wanted to earn.

"I can't believe I get to dance in a company with people like Svetlana Zakharova and Evgenia Obraztsova. I'm trying to learn as much as I can from them," I said.

He nodded and smiled, then moved closer to me, snaked his arm around my shoulders. I felt a curl of dread and disgust at the back of my throat, and I shrugged out from under his arm, inched my chair away from him.

"How is your *wife* these days?" I asked pointedly.

But he didn't seem to get the point. He was smiling, drinking wine, flirting.

Okay, this is not *a business dinner*, I realized. But I wasn't sure what exactly to do. I didn't want to make him angry at me—angry men, I knew instinctively, were dangerous. Plus, if he was offended, he might not finalize the sponsorship deal he'd been talking about. I wasn't sure how to remain polite without encouraging him to think I was anything more than a business associate.

After we finished our entrées, he reached into a bag on the floor and pulled out an envelope, thick with cash, which he handed to me.

"Oh, is this our deal?" I asked, thinking of all the work I'd done for him over the past months—the designs I'd sent his team, the modeling I'd done for his factory's shoes and skirts and warm-up gear.

"Well, I'd actually like you to come back to my place tonight," he said. "We can talk more about our future there."

I put the envelope firmly back in his hand.

"No," I said.

The smile faded from his face. "Are you serious about that? Is that the decision you're making?"

"I thought this was about paying me for the work I've already done. I'm not interested in anything else," I said.

"Life is hard, relationships are complicated; we shouldn't have to suffer more than necessary." He shrugged, his voice coaxing.

I stood up from the table. "I'm not interested," I told him.

His face clouded over. "You're going to regret this," he said. "I'm not a person you want to make angry, and you are not a person who wants to have a bad reputation."

I turned and picked up Pat's heavy fur coat and the purse I'd set on the floor.

"I will completely make your name black," Strelka said, his face growing red. "You're going to remember this day and regret it."

I walked out of the restaurant.

When I stepped out into the cold, I was shaking with anger and disgust. I felt like running.

How did I not realize what this was?

I felt so stupid, like an idiot who'd wandered into oncoming traffic and been surprised by a car screeching its tires on the road before ramming into her.

What did you think that was going to be, Joy?

I walked home, cold and shaking in the diesel-scented Moscow air.

After the dinner with Mr. Strelka, I began looking at things in Moscow differently. At the theater, I noticed the flower bouquets that appeared in our dressing room, spiked with cards signed by members of the Russian parliament and oil executives. I saw the jewelry and fur coats that draped on the wrists and shoulders of some of my fellow dancers. They spoke about fancy dinners they attended after performances where they were served small cuts of raw fish, foaming sauces, glasses of tannic wine. They mentioned luxurious homes in Moscow's pine-forested countryside, which they visited on the weekends—places with marble floors and juniper-scented banyas. They hinted at multiple boyfriends who showered them with expensive gifts and money.

"I finally got enough to get a car," I overheard one girl say.

They spoke of it as something good, as a way they could manage to make various difficult parts of their life work.

"Did you hear about Aliona?" someone would say. "She just got a new apartment near Prospekt Mira. Now she doesn't have to travel so far to get to work."

I began to wonder—was this how dancers succeeded in Russia? Did it all come down to the rich Russian businessmen you dated, the politicians who took an interest in you?

I learned about the arrests in rehearsal.

It was something spoken about in whispers by fellow dancers who bent their heads together in the crowded wings of the theater. Pavel

Dmitrichenko—our colleague, our friend—had been apprehended in the night by Moscow police.

"They arrested Pasha yesterday," someone told me in a low tone. "They forced him to confess to the acid attack."

I went to my phone to look up the news. There was a video of Pavel standing behind the bars of a cage in a Moscow courtroom. I recognized him from the classes we'd taken together at Tsiskaridze's barre. But in the videos, he looked disheveled. His greasy hair hung in strands around his face, dark circles pressed into the pale skin under his eyes.

He squinted at the camera, weary and unfocused as he admitted that he had organized the attack on Filin.

But he said the attack had gone further than he'd intended. He was as surprised as anyone to learn about the acid. He'd had nothing to do with that part—he'd only wanted to intimidate the director, not physically and permanently harm him.

There were two other men arrested along with Pavel—the attacker and a driver—both supposedly hired to do the job.[1]

In one of the Bolshoi's cafeterias, I found friends who sat hushed, their heads together at a table. They whispered and picked at dill-covered salads.

"Did you see Pasha's eyes?" one of them said, using Dmitrichenko's nickname. "It looked like he hadn't slept all night."

"He looked terrible," everyone agreed. "Do you think they tortured him?"

We all knew Dmitrichenko. He was Orthodox, the head of the dancers' union. He was always sticking up for people, saying things that no one else was brave enough to say. He'd rehearsed with Vorokhobko for years, and we'd all seen his dancing—it was inspired. He was a true artist, and he'd been kind to all of us. We couldn't imagine him committing any sort of crime, much less one as violent as an acid attack.

"He looked like he'd been drugged," one of the girls next to me said, her tea growing cold on the table in front of her. "I bet they forced him to sign that confession."

"We should get some money together to help him out because this is awful," Alexandra said. "I have thirty thousand rubles I can give him."

"He's being accused. They're ruining his life—just as his career is starting to take off," another girl said.

"I heard they're putting together a petition in his defense. Nearly one hundred people have signed it," another dancer said.

She turned to me. "Joy, are you going to sign it?"

CHAPTER 20

Trial

In the black cave wings of the rehearsal stage, I stood and watched my colleagues turn, the pale muscle of their shoulders cut by leotard lines, their tutus spinning like enchanted dinner plates. A microphoned voice called out corrections.

"Softly, softly," the director said. "Talia, a bit higher, please."

I longed to be on stage with them. But it was the start of a new season at the Bolshoi—my second year—and I had not been cast in a single production. The Bolshoi *corps de ballet* teachers—those tasked with rehearsing the battalions of dancers in matching costumes who formed moving lines in the backgrounds of stage productions—didn't seem to like me.

Some said it was because I was American and hadn't spent my early childhood in Russian ballet studios.

"She's unable to do the movements the same as everyone else," teachers said. "She's talented, but everyone who comes to the Bolshoi has to go through the *corps de ballet*."

So I waited, unchosen, un-cast, on the sidelines.

Gennady Goviadin was a teacher who led our *corps* rehearsals, a microphone pressed to his mouth. He stood at the rails of practice stages in zippered fleeces, his round, red face watching, interrupting us with instructions. He joked, friendly and approachable, with the men and women of the *corps* who wore tights and T-shirts.

"I really want to understand," I told him during a pause in one of our rehearsals. "Why wasn't I cast in *Sleeping Beauty*? I worked really hard on it, but the role was given to someone else. Why? Is it something I did?"

Goviadin wheezed out a laugh that smelled faintly of vodka.

"Hey, I know you!" He smiled at me. "You're the American!"

I smiled back at him, standing wide in my pointe shoes, like I was ready to take a joke if he offered it.

"You worked on *Sleeping Beauty*, didn't you?" I said. "What do I need to do to get cast next time? Do I need to improve my dancing somewhere?"

"Don't you know the system around here?" Goviadin laughed. "It's pay to play!"

He shrugged and hurried off to fix something in the choreography, while I stood confused, watching him.

But I was persistent. The next day I found him again, standing on his heels by the piano.

"What do you mean 'pay to play'?" I asked. "Can you be more specific? How do I get cast in ballets? What do you want from me? What do I need to do?"

"Oh, you don't know about the price list?" He laughed, like I was an American hunting for some sort of scandal, and he was giving me what I wanted to hear. I couldn't tell if he was serious.

"Price list?" I smiled in case it was a joke.

"Don't you know about the director's dance foundation? You need to show that you can bring something in for us," he said. "Why else do you think you were hired?"

"Oh, you mean like sponsors?" I said.

"Yeah, sponsors," he said. "You're an American—don't you have people backing you? Show us it was a good decision to hire you."

He shook his head and went off to correct the way someone was holding their arms.

I felt confused, but what he said mostly made sense. Theaters around the world sought charitable donations and held fundraisers. Maybe that's what was happening at the Bolshoi.

Later that week, I spoke to Pat about it. She'd served on the boards of many foundations, and I thought she might be able to introduce me to people with an interest in the arts.

"I think they want me to find some American sponsors," I explained. Pat wrinkled her forehead.

"That's strange," she said. "This is the Bolshoi, not ABT. They just spent more than $680 million on a huge renovation. Don't they have oil companies to help them pay for things? Why would they need you to bring in money? How much are they talking about here?"

I went back to Goviadin, who stood in a cloud of vodka-scented air at the edge of the stage.

"I need a number," I told him. "Tell me how this works. What kind of sponsor do I need? How much money should it be?"

"Ten thousand dollars," he said. "With a ten-thousand-dollar donation to the foundation, you can dance a minor soloist role in *Don Quixote*."

Ten thousand dollars seemed like a lot. But then, I thought, maybe it wasn't a lot to the right donor.

Okay, I thought as I left rehearsal. *I know what to do. I'm the American. I have to bring American sponsors in.*

"Goviadin said I need to find some sponsors," I told Sveta as I sat on a stool in my dressing room, pulling pins out of my hair.

Sveta turned in her chair. She had been at the Bolshoi for nearly a decade. She was someone I confided in, someone who made time to watch me rehearse things.

"He said what?" she asked, her eyebrows raised, her shoulders straight and unbowed as she looked at me over the back of her cushioned chair.

"He said they need the sponsors to bring in like ten thousand dollars," I said, watching her eyes widen.

"Joy, that's outrageous!" she said, raking her brush in vicious strokes through her hair. "Don't you see? They're trying to get you to pay for roles."

"But it's fundraising—they want the money for the Bolshoi, for a foundation," I said. It hadn't occurred to me that this was something other than fundraising, but when Sveta said it, it sounded terrible.

"I've been here for fifteen years, and no one's ever asked me to bring in sponsors or money," Sveta said. "Why are they asking you?"

"Goviadin said it's because I'm an American. I think they want international sponsors," I said, hearing, as I spoke, how unbelievable my own words sounded.

"The theater never used to be like this." Sveta shook her head. "There was some corruption that started when Yanin was a director—fancy cars and pretty girls who would get special parts if Yanin liked them. But this is completely different."

I didn't know how to answer her.

"Look at the situation for what it is, Joy," Sveta said. "It's corruption."

In September, Sergei Filin returned to Moscow, fresh from Europe, where he had received twenty-two surgeries on his eyes and face. When he reappeared for a press conference among the chandelier-lit, red-cushioned chairs of the historic stage, we saw angry scars that blotched his jawline and marred his cheeks. He stood tall and straight in wide sunglasses as he told reporters and dancers that he was ready to take up, once again, the reins of the Bolshoi's directorial leadership.

I had read, in newspapers, that Filin's eyesight remained impaired, that his right eye was still mostly blind.

How will he be able to direct? I wondered.

Still, I was filled with hope. Filin was the one who had hired me. Now, surely, he would impose some sort of order on how things were run at the Bolshoi. He would resume control of casting decisions. He would grant me roles in upcoming performances.

I stood at the door outside his office, my heart filled with anxiety, and knocked. I wanted to know what I was doing wrong, what I needed to change in my dancing to be granted time on the stage.

"Come in, come in!" Filin opened the door.

His room was filled with framed photos of him in younger years, performing the classic Russian repertoire for which he'd become famous. Screens on the walls showed live footage of various rehearsals in progress. A portrait of Putin gazed down at us.

"I'm so happy you're back in Russia. We have been praying for your recovery," I said, sitting on an ornate wooden chair in front of his desk.

"Thank you, thank you." Filin nodded behind his orange-tinted glasses, closed the door to his office with a soft click. "Please, tell me how you are."

"If I'm honest, things aren't great," I said. "My name is not on any of the cast lists for upcoming ballets. Not even *corps de ballet* roles. I want to dance."

"Joy." Filin leaned back in his chair. "Naturally, you're not in the *corps de ballet* because, as I've been told, you don't want to participate."

"No, I go to every single rehearsal. I want to be on stage," I said. "I was on stage about seven times last season and only when other dancers got sick. Seven performances is really not very many."

"Hmm." Filin nodded, his voice conciliatory.

"And I can't understand what's happening with my contract—why don't I have a normal, permanent contract?"

Filin spoke of the difficulty of arranging contracts for someone like me, who hadn't yet acquired her Russian passport. He spoke of the system at the Bolshoi—that I needed to rehearse things with my teacher and prepare pieces for him to make decisions on.

"But I have been rehearsing. I've gotten lots of pieces ready, and still, no one is letting me on stage," I said. "You're a dancer—you know what it's like. I need to dance. What do I have to do? I can work harder."

"No, no." He shook his head, smiling, charming. "I know you're working hard."

He paused then, tilted his head.

"The time for being naive is over, Joy. You're not a student anymore. You've graduated. You're a married woman." He smiled. "In the theater, a person has to be a bit more sly, a bit shrewder. You have to think about what to do because the teachers don't want to work with you. You have to show them some sort of initiative."

What does that mean? Be shrewd? Show initiative? And why is he talking about me being married? What does that have to do with dancing?

Filin stood up, showed me to the door. "Thanks for stopping by."

I left his office feeling confused and slimy and bewildered, like I'd just touched something moist and felt the shiver in my spine.

I stood in the hall, staring at nothing. I felt angry and no closer to understanding what was wanted from me.

Was that a come-on? A request for a bribe?

I couldn't tell what was happening.

I danced a single time on stage. But then my name disappeared, once again, from the cast lists that were hung in the theater hallway, framed in glass.

In my dressing room, I slumped in my chair and stared at my friend Katia, who sat before a mirror, brushing mascara onto her lashes.

"I don't know what to do!" I said. "I can't even understand what Filin wants from me."

She put her mascara wand back into its tube and looked at me kindly. The makeup she used had slowly been changing. Designer foundation, eyeshadow and lipsticks in fancy metallic containers shimmered new and expensive on her dressing table. Last I'd heard, she'd been dating the head of the theater's finance department.

"Joy, why don't you want to just make friends with someone?" She looked at me with compassion. "It just takes one Mercedes Benz or something."

By now I didn't even blink at that sort of suggestion.

"I don't have that type of money!" I said. "I think people misunderstand when I say my dad is a businessman. It means something different in America than in Russia. He's not rich, and he's not in the mafia."

Katya sighed and began rubbing scented lotion on her hands.

"I remember worrying about this my first year at the theater," she said. "My coach told me to become friends with some Bolshoi donors. I did—and now I'm dancing. That's how it works."

Later, in the darkness of my dressing room, I hunched over my chair to speak to Sveta.

"I'd heard rumors about how things worked here before, but I never believed it until now," I told Sveta.

"This is what I've been telling you," she said, her elbow resting on her desk next to a bouquet of makeup brushes. "Filin only gives roles to *his* people."

"Why would he say I don't want to participate in *corps de ballet* stuff? I'm at every rehearsal," I said.

"You need to work on things, yes," Sveta said. "But it's not normal to exclude you from *corps* roles."

"I hate to say it, but this has given me a new perspective on Dmitrichenko," I said, lowering my voice to discuss a subject about which I knew Sveta was passionate. "He never wanted to throw acid at Filin. He just hired someone to have a conversation with Filin, to be like, 'Hey, you need to stop treating girls this way and taking money and cheating dancers out of their union stuff.'"

"You're not the only one who's seen corrupt things here," Sveta said. "I'm trying to get other people to say something. But everyone's scared. Especially after they fired Tsiskaridze."

She turned from her mirror to look at me.

"We all know Dmitrichenko is innocent. But if someone doesn't speak up, this trial is not going to end well," she said, arching a thin eyebrow in my direction.

Sveta was one of the people who had been trying to help Dmitrichenko. But I was afraid to sign the petition she and other dancers had started. Some people said those who signed the petition would be blacklisted, banned from the stage, unable to dance.

"You should speak out about what Filin told you," Sveta said. Part of me was convinced by the fury in her voice. Another part of me was frightened.

"I mean, I haven't actually had any direct dealings with Filin that were bad except for that conversation we had about needing to be shrewd," I backpedaled. "I mean, maybe he's right. Maybe I need to be more subtle."

Sveta shook her head and put down her makeup brush.

"Joy, you could be the person who helps us. We need something that shows Filin's character. Your story could do that," she said. "You could be the one who shows people what's actually happening behind the scenes here."

Her brown eyes grew bright and intense.

"Let me talk to a journalist I know," she said.

"I don't think I feel comfortable doing an interview," I said.

"I'll tell him your story, but I won't name any names," she said, her blonde hair falling over her ear as she leaned forward. "You'll just be one of a few people talking about the way things are here. Trust me, plenty of people feel the same way we do."

I hesitated, looking at her. I was eighteen and filled with a longing for someone to take me under their arm and tell me what to do. Maybe this was what telling the truth looked like. Maybe this was what justice looked like.

"You can use parts of my story," I said. "But don't use my name."

CHAPTER 21

Saltwater

I stood, shoulders hunched in my coat, my face turned to a cold wind that blew from the North Pole, across the White Sea, and onto the iced gravel shores of Arkhangelsk. The salty air was so fresh and so forceful, I could barely draw it into my lungs.

It was October. My friend Anton had called to invite me to join a cross-country ballet tour. I'd said yes. I needed to make money, I needed to dance, and neither of those things were happening at the Bolshoi.

We had flown north to just under the disk of the Arctic Circle, and we'd come to a theater with wooden floors that seemed transported from another era. It was filled with audiences who blew in from the bitter air in fur coats and red cheeks to watch us and applaud the *Swan Lake* excerpts we performed on stage.

Compared to Moscow, this northern port city filled with Soviet-era buildings was hushed. It swallowed noise, froze out confusion, swept away the scramble of thoughts that had crowded my mind for months. When I looked backward at the Bolshoi, it seemed filled with sticky, invisible webs that I didn't understand. I was constantly blundering into poisonous nests and tangles, offending people, annoying them.

But in Arkhangelsk, on tour with Anton, everything was simplified. All I had to do was dance, rehearse, dance, rehearse, travel, sleep, dance, rehearse.

"Saltwater cleanses more than any other water," Anton told me, his cheeks rubbed raw with the blast of exfoliating cold from the sea.

And it seemed to me, as I stood there beside him, that what he said was true.

Another journalist, a Russian man, had called me while I packed my bags, prepared to board my flight for the north.

"Are you Djoy Voh-mock?" he asked.

"Yes," I said. "Who is this?"

"My name is Dmitrii Evstifeev. I'm a reporter with the newspaper *Izvestia*," he said. "I got your phone number from your friend. She's a dancer at the Bolshoi."

Dmitrii asked about my interactions with Filin and Goviadin at the Bolshoi, about the hints they'd made of needing to pay money to appear on stage, of the strange language they used: "sponsors," "be shrewd," a "payment system."

"Is that true?" he kept asking.

"Yes, that's right, that's what happened," I kept telling him.

Later, when I thought back on the conversation, I realized I'd never confirmed that he wouldn't use my name in the article he was writing. But I wasn't worried. I'd made it clear to Sveta that I would only share my story anonymously. I wanted to help Dmitrichenko. I wanted to do what I could to speak out about how messed up things were at the Bolshoi. I wanted to tell the truth.

From Arkhangelsk, we flew to Vladivostok, on Russia's far eastern edge. We saw buildings that crumbled in the cold ocean air and watched sky-scraper-sized cargo ships roll into ports after steaming across the Pacific Ocean.

We took a train to Khabarovsk, crowded in a four-person sleeper car with rattling glasses of tea, plastic bags of snacks, and flimsy white slippers we used to pad back and forth to the sloshing hot water vat, where we refilled our cups with liquid that steamed and soaked our teabags.

I'd known Russia was vast, but to fly for ten hours and still not touch the end of it, to reach toward the Arctic Circle, then gaze upon the watery border of China and still be inside the Russian Federation was more than I could comprehend. In the train with my friends, I watched endless kilometers of brown, flat, grassy *taiga* flash past my window, the sky heavy and low. In some places, it felt like we were traveling back in time to dingy train-station toilets with no lids and no toilet paper; to wood-floored ballet studios, where, just like we'd seen in video footage from Soviet times, the splintered boards had to be sprinkled with water from a plastic watering can to keep our shoes from slipping.

I felt numb for most of the trip. I laughed and sat in trains and posed for the camera with friends on the tops of hills overlooking the sea, bitten by icy winds. I felt like something washed up on shore—like I'd been tossed and turned and battered by waves. I played, like a song on repeat in my head, conversations I'd had with Filin, with Oleg, with my Bolshoi colleagues, with my mom.

Are they telling me I can't dance? Are they taking advantage of me? Did I misunderstand what they said?

I felt as if I couldn't trust anyone. I'd started involuntarily coughing and struggling to inhale. I wondered if it was my subconscious trying to ring alarm bells, making it impossible for me to breathe.

My parents had paid for me to speak on Skype once a week with a Christian counselor, and Mom had started reading devotions aloud to me on the phone.

Help me not to worry about tomorrow, God. Help me to cast all my cares on you. Help me trust you to get me to where you want me to be.

Mom spoke often about divorcing Oleg, and I was starting to agree with her. I'd mostly moved back to Pat's house in the city center, but I still saw Oleg on weekends. I always felt relieved to leave his apartment, to jump out of the car when he dropped me off. When I imagined the future he described—having kids together, growing a family—I knew I didn't want it. But divorce was a sin, wasn't it?

Lord, tell me what to do, show me the path to take, I prayed when I had time alone to myself to stare out the window or lie in a hotel room at night.

But I couldn't hear anyone talking back.

There were moments, traveling with Anton, when I stood on stage in a tiara, the hand of my dance partner guiding me through a series of fouettés. I felt, in those seconds, alive and untouchable. I heard the orchestrated two-hundred-year-old music of Auber in my ears, and I felt safe, briefly ensconced in a stratosphere, removed from everything frightening and false.

Russia was too big to understand, too vast to define. Had I made a mistake in coming here? Or was I the luckiest person in the world to have arrived? I could not tell. But when I was on stage, I knew it was the only place I wanted to be.

In November, we traveled to Rostov on Don, a city set into the damp earth of Russia's southeast ankle, north of the Caucasus, where the Don flows into the Azov Sea. Like many places we'd visited on our tour, pulling into the Rostov train station felt like entering the past. The roads teemed with stray dogs, and the internet on my phone blinked in and out of service.

But no expense had been spared on the city's theater, which rose in modernist gleaming stone like the lifted lid of a grand white piano. Walking through the building's front doors into a foyer carpeted in deep red, illuminated by chandeliers, felt the way it always felt to enter a theater in Russia. It was as if you'd escaped the drab push and shove of daily life and arrived at some sort of temple to the arts. Ordinary people in their itchy dress pants and rumpled skirts could scrape the mud off their shoes at the door, find their velvet-upholstered seats, and, for an hour or two, be transported to some sort of third realm, their gloom pierced by a symphony of sound, their souls enraptured by people wearing clouds of tulle.

In the weeks I'd traveled with Anton and his dance troupe across Russia, my Moscow life had faded out of focus, like a train station disappearing in the fog behind a caboose.

But on the morning of November 13, Moscow came roaring back to meet me.

I arrived at the Rostov ballet studio at the back of the theater with the rest of my troupe, blinking and sleepy after a night in a local hotel.

My partner, Ivan, was there waiting for me in his sweatpants and warm-up gear, a concerned wrinkle on his forehead.

"Joy, did you see this news article about you in *Izvestia*?" he said, clicking a button on his phone and illuminating a headline that read in Russian: "American ballerina accuses the Bolshoi leadership of extortion."[1]

My heart paused beating in my chest as I saw a photograph of my face staring back at me from his screen.

Sveta and her journalist friend had not only published the story without giving me any warning, but they'd also used my name.

The article said I'd confirmed that Sergei Filin had asked me to pay ten thousand dollars for a role at the theater. It also said I'd been fired from the Bolshoi.

Reading the lines on Ivan's phone felt like getting punched in the stomach. They were sprinkled with quotes attributed to me that I knew had come from Sveta's mouth—about the Bolshoi being a terrifying place, that Filin himself had forbidden others from casting me, even in *corps de ballet* parts.[2] Some of the article was true, but some of it was flat-out false or it mixed up who had said what.

"Oh my God," I said. "This is terrible. I had no idea they would actually put my name in there."

I put my hand on the barre, my stomach nauseous.

Our performance was hours away, and I needed to warm up my body, rehearse a pas de deux.

I started to bend my knees in plié, to arch my ankles into relevé, but then I heard the angry hornet buzz of my phone. I dug in my pocket, pulled out the device, swiped my thumb across my screen to answer.

"Allo?" the voice on the other end said. "Is this Djoy Voh-mock?"

"Yes?" I said hesitantly.

"I'm a journalist from *Ria Novosti*. Can you tell me about extortion at the Bolshoi Theater? Is it true that Filin told you to pay ten thousand dollars for soloist roles?"

"I—I didn't say that." I was stunned, tripping over my words. "I mean, some of what's in the article is true, but I didn't say that. Those aren't my words."

Anton came and stood next to me at the barre.

"Who is that?" he mouthed.

I clicked the mute button over the journalist who continued talking and whispered, "A reporter. From *Ria Novosti*, I think."

He raised his brown eyebrows.

"Um, just a minute," I mumbled into the phone.

"You don't have to talk to them," Anton said.

"I'll—I'll call you back," I said, clicking the red button before the journalist on the other end could answer.

Anton and Ivan looked at each other.

"This is insane," I started to say, but then my phone buzzed in my hand again.

"Don't answer it," Anton said.

"I don't know what to do." I felt panicked. "I didn't know they'd publish it like this—with my picture and everything."

For the next several hours, my phone did not cease to ring. Journalists called from newspapers and TV stations in Russia, the United States, England, and around the world. Anton finally took my cell out of my hands and began answering it for me.

"No comment!" he barked into the speaker every time it buzzed.

By evening, as the light faded in the sky over the Don River, I sat alone in my dressing room, smudging my face with paint. My heart had dropped into the nauseous empty pit of my stomach, and the more my phone rang, the more frightened I felt.

I really screwed up, I thought, staring into my own stilled, pale face in the mirror.

Part of me had hoped to return to Moscow from Anton's tour, walk back into the Bolshoi, and figure things out. I'd seen theaters all across the country, and I knew there was no place like the Bolshoi, no dancers like the Bolshoi dancers. It was complicated, yes, but there was nowhere else I wanted to be.

It felt hard to focus on what I was doing—the thin metal pins that needed to be skewered into my hair, the string cords of my tutu that needed to be pulled tight around my waist.

What was I thinking? How could I have been so stupid? What am I going to do now?

From behind the closed door of my dressing room, I heard voices and a scuffling noise. Then a loud pounding on the door.

I jumped, dropping my hairpins on the floor.

"Djoy? Djoy Voh-mock?" a muffled voice called from the hallway. "We want to talk to you. We're from NTV!"

"Oh my god!" I stared at the door, frozen and trapped.

It seemed like there were several people in the hallway—maybe an entire television crew.

"Are you in there? Can we come in?" There was more banging on the door, and someone turned the handle, started to push it open. But then I heard Anton and Ivan out in the hallway, shouting and pushing back.

"No, no, she's not giving any interviews," they said, slamming the door to my dressing room shut behind them.

I leapt to my feet, unsure what to do, and leaned hard against the door to block the cameras and microphones from entering.

"Is it true what you said about Filin? Did he tell you to pay bribes to the Bolshoi?" someone shouted outside.

I'd always wanted to be in the spotlight, the center of attention, the one whose reputation drew people to theaters. But in that moment, there was nothing I wanted more than to disappear.

I returned to Moscow, where I saw that a storm had broken.

While I'd been traveling around Russia, my Bolshoi teachers and colleagues had been called into a crowded Moscow courtroom to testify about the things they had heard and seen in the theater—anything related to the attack that had been carried out on Filin.

These were people I'd seen in ballet class, whom I'd watched perform on the Bolshoi stage. They stood quiet and pale, in a dingy courthouse, answering questions from Russian lawyers. Most of them spoke kindly of Filin, but some, like Tsiskaridze, were there to defend Dmitrichenko.

Dmitrichenko listened to all of it, handcuffed, behind bars in the court. The men accused of being his accomplices stood beside him, large-shouldered, their faces furred over with beards and bushy eyebrows. Then Filin arrived, his head swaddled in gauze, to talk about the endless surgeries he'd endured and the pain in his face. He wept about losing his eyesight, struggling to see his children.[3]

He denied any sort of corruption or extramarital affairs with Bolshoi ballerinas and vowed he could not forgive Dmitrichenko.[4]

I cowered in Pat's apartment, and my heart pounded every time I heard a new update from the courtroom. *Will they mention me? Will they ask me to testify?*

I was afraid to leave the house. What would happen if I appeared on the cobblestones of Kamergersky Lane or Bolshaia Dmitrovka Street? I might encounter people from the theater who would scold me or move to the other side of the road to avoid me altogether.

Some of my friends and colleagues called me. One of them, a Bolshoi teacher, was filled with anger.

"What you did talking to that journalist was very, very bad," she said. She told me I'd put Filin in danger, I'd allowed myself to be used by people who wanted to soil Filin's name.

"You have to put out a statement, take back everything in that article," she said.

She gave quotes to journalists, saying I'd exaggerated my talents and struggled to memorize dance sequences. Other dancers took to Facebook to write about how terrible my pirouettes were, how I'd failed to conquer basic choreography.[5]

I heard, sometimes secondhand, the things people were saying about me. Some thought I was brave. Some thought I was stupid. Some thought I was lying. Others thought I was telling the truth and that I should talk to more newspapers. Some, including my parents, thought I should just give up on everything and move back to the United States.

Of one thing I was certain: I was no longer welcome or wanted at the Bolshoi.

I slunk back to the theater and met with a manager. They told me how to submit a resignation letter. Like everything in Russia, it involved a lot of paperwork, signatures, and seals. It took weeks to process.

It didn't matter that I'd tried to act with integrity. It didn't matter that I'd tried to tell the truth. I had destroyed the place I'd been given at the world's most beautiful theater.

Sometimes, even now, I feel regret. I look back at the words I spoke, the decisions I made, the conversations I had, and I see it all differently, through an older, more Russian lens. There were times back then when I wondered, with longing, if other girls had Russian mothers who whispered secrets to them about how to bide their time, how to play the game, how to gain favor, how to be shrewd. Maybe, if I had waited, like a fish hiding under a rock in a pond, for the uproar to pass, everything would have cleared, and I would have been able to dance the roles I wanted at the theater that had shimmered in my imagination since childhood.

But I didn't know how to play chess. And I wouldn't learn how until I moved to a new theater, even closer to the heart of the Russian game.

Early on a November morning, I slipped out of Pat's apartment, the straps of my heavy dance bag cutting into my shoulder. I crossed Bolshaia Dmitrovka Street and walked south toward Moscow's innermost ring road—the oval-shaped, eight-lane band that circled the Kremlin, Red Square, and a towering jumble of stone buildings that had stood in the Russian capital since the 1400s.

I ducked into a crowded tunnel under the street, and when I emerged on the other side, the redbrick walls of the Kremlin rose in front of me.

At its entrance, which bristled with metal detectors, I pulled my passport from my bag and gave it to a stone-faced Russian guard, who stood, bored and cranky in an olive-colored uniform.

"I'm going to the Kremlin Palace Theater," I told him.

He called someone on a radio, scanned the pages of my passport, then, in a monotone voice, told me to enter. The wide, crenelated stone passageway was empty as I climbed upward and passed beneath the medieval arch that led into the red-spired heart of Russia.

I tried to feel excited about where I was going and what I was doing, but the only emotions left in my chest were dread and shame. My name had been splashed across Russian news outlets. I had been ejected from its most famous theater. I had inadvertently created a reputation for myself that I was ashamed of. I wished, more than anything, not to be recognized. And I had a single-minded goal for being here.

I needed to beg for a job.

Oleg met me in the white marble halls of the theater. He'd been employed there for more than six months, performing and touring with the Kremlin ballet troupe. He took me through swinging glass doors, up stone steps, down marble-lined hallways to the theater's upper-floor ballet studio.

The room was empty when we arrived, its walls cut open with tall, clear windows that looked onto the white walls and sparkling gold domes of a Russian Orthodox church from the Middle Ages.

I began warming and stretching my muscles, piling my bags in as inconspicuous a pile as possible.

When other dancers arrived, I couldn't look them in the eye.

What do they think of me? That I'm stupid? That I'm arrogant? That it's dangerous to talk to me because I'll betray them?

I wanted to somehow crawl within myself or disappear. I felt—real or imagined—the judging stares of people who lined up at the barre next to me. I didn't want to be seen as a whistleblower. I wanted to be seen as someone who had an acrobatic overstretch and expansive wingspan on the dance floor.

I moved through the dance motions that my body had been playing on repeat morning after morning, season after season, year after year since childhood. My muscles knew what to do, even if my mind was tumbling around like a load of laundry in a washing machine.

A woman with pale blonde hair and sharp eyes—Zhanna Vladimirovna—paced the front of the room, calling out positions.

The Kremlin studio was narrow and crowded—especially compared to the opulent practice and rehearsal rooms at the Bolshoi. It was shaped in an awkward L, with barely enough room for dancers to battement without kicking each other in the face.

When the class was over, the other members of the troupe began shrugging into layers of sweaters and fleeces and leaving the room, their feet ensconced in puffy warm-up slippers. I left with them and made my way to the office of Andrei Borisovich Petrov.

Petrov was a gray-haired dancer who'd worked his way to the top position at the Kremlin Palace Ballet Theater. He'd been awarded a National Artist of Russia designation and now reported to a chain of command that ended at Vladimir Putin's presidential desk.

"Come in, come in," he said when I knocked softly at his office door.

I sat on a chair in front of his desk, the sweat still cooling on my skin.

"Thank you so much for allowing me to join class today," I said, trying to show my enthusiasm and gratitude.

He watched me, not unkindly, from the wheeled leather chair behind his desk, his wall hung with overlapping ballet posters, every surface in his office filled with framed awards and photographs of dancers.

I could see, spread in a fan on the table in front of him, a folder stuffed with articles that had been printed out from *Izvestia*, the *New York Times*, Interfax, the *Los Angeles Times*. All of them had my name on them.

"What are we going to do with you?" he said, shaking his head, as if we were both caught in the same troubling predicament.

I could feel in my chest the shame of what was printed on the leaflets under his eyes.

Never, never, never again am I ever going to complain about anything. I'm going to shut my mouth and never talk about news or politics or corruption ever again.

"My staff printed these out for me," he explained, shuffling through the papers one by one.

"I can see that you're a talented dancer," he added. "No one needs to tell me about that. I remember watching your Academy exams. You're very good. And our coach here, Zhanna Vladimirovna, tells me that you could potentially be a ballerina one day."

"Thank you so much," I said, thinking with silent gratitude about the woman with blonde hair who'd watched me arabesque in class.

He tapped his gnarled finger on the papers in front of him.

"But what can we do with you? Even if I take you, it's going to be a big fight," he said. "And how do I know you won't turn around and do the same thing to me that you did to Filin? How do I know you're not going to complain about me to a bunch of reporters?"

"I just want a job, I just want a chance to dance," I said. "I can tell you that I will be a good worker. I'll be the first one here in the morning and the last one here at night. All I want to do is work."

"Hmm." He leaned back in his chair. "If you want to work, we can give you work. I can promise you'll be busy."

"That's what I want. I just want to put my head down and dance," I said, hoping I didn't sound too desperate.

"We can give you a job here," he said, sweeping the pile of papers into a folder. "And the reason I'm going to fight for you is because I don't like the Bolshoi either. I worked there for years, and I know that everything you said in these articles is one hundred percent true."

I felt stunned. And then, unable to help myself, I broke into a smile.

He stood up, his eyes twinkling, to shake my hand.

"Well, Djoy Voh-mock," he said, a smile tugging at the corner of his mouth. "Welcome to the Kremlin."

CHAPTER 22

Diplomacy

I could not believe my good fortune. I had joined a theater inside the Kremlin. It felt like a plot twist in a Tom Cruise movie. This was the heart of the country, synonymous with the crown, the presidency, and the political leadership of all eleven of Russia's time zones.

It was also very pretty. I never got over it: the fifteen-foot-thick crenelated red walls, the green-roofed towers crowned by spinning Soviet stars that glowed red at night, the gold domes of cathedrals and bell towers that predated Columbus's first voyage across the Atlantic.

Sometimes I looked at its Christmas-colored spires, yellow palaces, and the medieval murals of Byzantine queens and archangels and thought, *Yeah. I can see why Russia has a hard time taking America seriously.*

But the ballet theater I'd been invited to was an upstart. It rose within the Kremlin's walls, gleaming and rectangular, like a giant stone and glass construction of LEGOs. It had been built in the communist era, fifty years before, as a modern addition to a red-stone fortress that had spiked into the cone tip of bluff above the Moskva and Neglinnaya Rivers since the 1300s.

When I landed there, I was bruised and frightened, running from an international scandal, desperate for work, holding in my hands the crumbles of an ill-considered marriage.

And Petrov, the theater's steel-haired captain, opened his theater's doors wide to welcome me. Shortly after I arrived, he granted me the dream I'd been longing for.

"Let's have you try dancing the lead in *Nutcracker*," he said.

Seeing my name at the top of a famous Russian ballet at a famous Russian theater felt like the opening blare of a train whistle and the loud unlocking of a whole railway of steel wheels. I was rusty from the months I'd spent on the sidelines of the Bolshoi, but now my race had been set, and I could see, at its end, the set-in-stone date of a performance.

This was the chance I'd wanted for years. But I knew that, if I didn't perform well, I would walk myself into yet another career dead-end.

Petrov, I'd heard, did not give second chances. He had a habit of scooping up ballerinas from other theaters and trying them out at the top of his cast list to see if he could talent-scout new stars. If dancers failed the tests he set, he let them drop to inconsequential *corps de ballet* roles, where they lived out the rest of their time at his theater in anonymous stagnation.

I had one opportunity to save my career. But the *Nutcracker* he was offering to me was the most difficult version of the famous ballet that I'd ever seen.

His choreography demanded light feet, fluent pirouettes, square hips, and expressive storytelling, and he wanted his dancers on stage as much as possible. His Masha, as the *Nutcracker*'s heroine was called in Russia, was not one who faded to the wings for frequent costume changes to catch her breath. He wanted his ballerina in the breathless, twirling, constantly-in-motion center spotlight, illuminating a complex and personal storyline for as much of the two-hour performance as possible.

And the stage inside the State Palace Theater, the canvas on which he set his creations, was unlike any I'd ever seen. For one thing, it was not designed for dancing. It had been constructed in the 1960s to host Communist Party assemblies.[1] Where the Bolshoi stage I'd grown to love was ornate and intimate—a tsarist-era crescent that drew its arms around the audience, the Kremlin auditorium was its opposite. It was wide, echoing, drafty, rectangular. It faced endless rows of cushioned blue seats and was perfect for showcasing row upon row of party delegates in front of oversized posters of Lenin. It was the *Star Wars* Galactic Death Star—aesthetically speaking—of performance halls.

Petrov used every inch of it. He composed sets that flexed and flowed and descended in layers to usher audiences into fantasy worlds of color, whimsy, and delight. He deleted intermissions and pauses between acts, pushed his *corps* into the background, left celestial chunks of distance and time for his prima ballerinas to fill with constant motion like tiny, sparkling *Sputnik* satellites, arcing across the darkened expanse of space. I wasn't sure I had the physical stamina to make myself big enough for what he envisioned.

But my stamina and abilities did not matter. The performance date was approaching, and I was scheduled to dance.

I can tell you unequivocally that, if not for the grace and patronage of the blonde-haired, blue-eyed Zhanna Vladimirovna Bogoroditskaia, I would not have made it through that first performance of the *Nutcracker*. I would not have survived at the Kremlin, and I would not be the dancer I am today.

Zhanna was a woman who stood with poise, draped in a wardrobe of art-house designer fashion, at the top of the Kremlin Ballet Theater's power structure. She was descended from ballet royalty, trained by Ekaterina Maximova, who was a student of the great Galina Ulanova—a dancer whose ethereal perfection was almost unbearable to watch. Ulanova was one of the most talented ballerinas of the twentieth century, a dancer who'd cast a spell on Prokofiev and caught the eye of the queen of England and the duke of Edinburgh.[2] She had inspired Soviet leaders to throw nearly every award in their arsenal at her feet.[3]

Now Ulanova's artistic granddaughter, for reasons I still don't entirely understand, had decided I was a dancer worth her time. She invited me onto the empty, black floor of the Kremlin rehearsal studio, stood with her back to the gleaming mirrors, called forth music from an ancient remote-controlled music player, and taught me how to dance.

"That's not quite it," she would say, interrupting me to demonstrate the precise articulation she wanted, moving with a slight limp from a career-ending dance injury to her hip.

She brought out and revealed to me the Petrov-interpreted canon of Russian repertoire and, like a surgeon conducting an organ transplant, infused it into my body.

This was what I had dreamed of—the sort of intimate coaching relationship I'd seen other Russian ballerinas rely on in order to grow. Zhanna had guidance on how I positioned my heels, the way my arms lingered in the air, the way I turned into a piqué. She counseled me on how to secure my hair in a bun before a performance, how to speak to my colleagues, how to navigate the endless twists of a prestigious, well-funded, and powerful Russian ballet company.

On the second day of February, I laced a pair of petal-pink shoes around my feet, parted my hair to the side, fastened a raspberry-colored bow above my bun, and penciled dark lines around my eyes.

The blue velvet seats of the Kremlin Palace Theater were filled with families: Moscow grandmothers in wool skirts, unsmiling Russian dads, seven-year-old girls who bounced in their chairs. In the front row was an entourage from the American embassy in Moscow, with Ambassador McFaul himself waiting pleasant-faced in a black suit and striped tie. Camera crews had set up at the sides of the theater to capture video of the American woman who had fled the Bolshoi and signed a contract to dance inside the walls of the Kremlin.

I stood backstage with my dance partner, who smelled of vodka. The rest of the troupe had running bets on whether or not he'd make it to performances and departing tour planes on time or whether he'd sleep past curtain rise and arrive to shows hungover. I'd drawn the lucky card today. He was steady on his feet. I, however, was nervous, my face washed in the blue lights meant to conjure darkened midwinter.

Zhanna stood nearby, her arms crossed, her blue eyes focused on the way my chest filled and deflated.

"Just keep your eyes open and watch the girl in front of you," she said quietly. "You have two legs—go out there and stand on them."

A bubble of something I might have called excitement was growing in the space behind my sternum. I firmly pushed it down.

Take this seriously—it's an honor, a huge responsibility. Zhanna and Petrov are counting on you—don't disappoint them.

I drew breath down my throat, into my chest, and, at the musical cue from the orchestra, fell out into the dusk of *The Nutcracker*.

The stage was a different place during performances. The auditorium was pitch black, the audience invisible and distant. As I skipped across the stage and turned circles with a doll in my hand, it was like I was performing alone on the edge of the atmosphere, staring into outer space.

I struggled to focus and to hit my stage cues, unsure whether the audience could see me and follow along, hoping I had enough stamina to last the entire two hours.

But, as I moved through my steps in the first act, I found a familiar place to which I sometimes went in my mind. It's a corner I've known since childhood, a private and imaginative spot I found while reading Nancy Drew novels, pretending to be a heroine who was calm, focused, and following her instincts, step by step. Here, in the quiet of my own thoughts, I could make the world into anything I wanted it to be, turn myself into anyone I wanted to be.

I let the lights that sparkled like falling snow transport me to a long-ago party, where skirts rustled, magic wooden toys came to life, and I was a young woman, rosy-cheeked and innocent, dancing around a candle-lit evergreen tree.

When I fell to my knees, weeping at the broken nutcracker in my hand, I felt in my shoulders and anguished face the broken feeling that remained in my chest from the things I'd done. I had disappointed my parents, distanced myself from Oleg, left the Bolshoi like a person jumping from a building she'd set on fire. I had abandoned the idea of myself as a good person, lost my innocence, just like the Masha Petrov wanted me to portray on stage. I let my pain and sadness show to the audience, but only I knew where it came from.

At the end of my performance, there was applause from the deep black hole of the auditorium. Backstage, a wide smile from Zhanna, a bristle of TV cameras with questions from journalists, and a handshake from the U.S. ambassador to Russia.

"What an honor for you to be working at this company," he said. "What you're doing here is important."

We turned, in unison, to the camera lenses pointed at us, my face streaked with sweat-melted makeup.

"I want to see you succeed here," McFaul said. "Art is the best kind of diplomacy. Nothing else bridges cultures quite like it."

I hadn't been thinking about diplomacy or bridging cultures or really anything beyond saving myself and the shambles of a career I'd almost destroyed. But I suddenly wondered if what he'd said was true. I was an American ballerina at the Kremlin Theater. Maybe the tiny successes I earned for myself, the small ways I created art, my mere presence behind the redbrick walls, were more important than I knew.

CHAPTER 23

Santa Barbara

Whatever I had done on the stage that day in February, it was what Petrov and Zhanna needed to see. My name began to appear on the Kremlin cast list pinned to solo and principal roles in *Esmerelda*, *Gamzatti*, *Giselle*, *1001 Nights*. Airline tickets were purchased in my name, and I was loaded onto buses and planes, flown and trucked with the rest of the Kremlin troupe to Spain and Kazan.

It didn't occur to me, in those first weeks, to be nervous or anxious about dancing. I was too awestruck at my good fortune, too unbelieving of my luck, too happy actually being on stage. I had been shoved out of the Bolshoi like a jumper pushed from a ledge. But somehow, miraculously, I'd fallen into the safety net of the Kremlin.

There is a distinct architecture to the career of a Russian ballerina. It's an arc that spans childhood to middle age like a bridge. When you are young, you devote yourself to rhythmic gymnastics or dance in a way that shapes your feet, legs, pelvis, arms, and spine into the necessary silhouettes. Then you apprentice yourself to one of several major dance schools: the Vaganova in St. Petersburg, the Bolshoi Academy in Moscow, or the Choreographic College in Perm. After that, you need a good theater to accept you into their *corps*, and you begin learning the backbone of Russian classical choreography: *Nutcracker*, *Corsaire*, *La Bayadere*, *Swan*

Lake, Sleeping Beauty. If you want to advance to soloist and prima roles, you do so slowly, with the help of a coach.

When Zhanna became my coach, I understood that I had set foot on the path that all Russia's greatest ballerinas before me had walked. She began, like a person lining up dominoes to knock over, laying the groundwork necessary to move me into the dancing career I so desperately wanted.

The other dancers at the Kremlin were not enthusiastic about my arrival. I was competition for roles that they relied on for extra rubles.

"No one here is your friend," Zhanna said, "but each one of them matters. You need to express your gratitude to them."

Zhanna had survived and made a name for herself in famous theaters after the fall of the Soviet Union. She pointed to my fellow dancers, the people who sewed costumes backstage, the musicians who played piano for our lessons, the clerks who stamped the endless piles of documents that living in Russia and working in the Kremlin required us to have.

"Don't be in a rush when you go ask for your tax form," she said. "You need to make people feel seen. Make them feel like they're part of your journey. Make them like you."

One day she brought me into the Kremlin studio to rehearse, then left abruptly, so I stood alone and confused in front of the mirrors.

When she returned, it was with another theater employee following her—a dark-haired man from the industrial city of Chelyabinsk, the Kremlin troupe's most talented and sought-after male dancer, Misha Martyniuk.

Misha headlined shows and showed up to classes on only the rare occasions when he felt like doing so. In the mornings, he screeched into the Kremlin's north parking lot just before rehearsals, a coveted official permit swinging from his overhead mirror. He'd stroll into the theater in a leather jacket and aviator sunglasses, his dark hair swept off his forehead and immediately start joking with the teachers, teasing the other dancers, and bounding in effortless leaps across the stage.

"Misha, can you come practice some pirouettes with my girl?" Zhanna said that day when she stopped him in the hallway.

Misha strode into the room, grabbed my hand, and spun me through a few turns. He was about ten years older than me and a much better dancer.

"Stand on your leg," he ordered, intensely focused as he twirled me around. Then, just as quickly as he'd come, he dropped my hand, made a joke to Zhanna, and left.

The next day, on the rectangular bulletin board where casting decisions were announced, I saw my name typed in Cyrillic, next to his. We had been assigned a "Diana and Actaeon" *pas de deux* together.

I wasn't sure why Misha agreed to dance with me. He had trained at the Perm Ballet School—one of Russia's top academies, with a reputation for unflinching discipline and military rigor. He was far more advanced than I was. Plus, all the other Kremlin teachers and dancers loved him.

Zhanna told me he had been partnering more experienced ballerinas and needed someone like me to keep his dancing youthful. What she told Misha was different.

"Help my girl out," she coaxed. "Throw a bone to the new kid."

In our rehearsals, I stood before Zhanna like an obedient sponge—earnest, compliant, waiting to soak up every droplet of wisdom she thought to offer. But Misha refused to be serious. He'd see me unfolded at the barre like an opened pamphlet, trying to overstretch my legs, and he'd walk over like Groucho Marx and start cheering.

"That's not enough! You can do more! More!" he'd say, crouching beside me, his eyes bugged out at my legs like a referee starting a countdown for a wrestler pinned to the mat. "Longer! Higher! Stretchier!"

Or he'd catch me concentrating on a tricky arabesque turn and start joking about the way one of my eyebrows rose higher than the other when I focused. He'd come poke his fingers into my forehead to make my brows move up and down.

"Kuku! Kuku!" he'd sing, like the lines above my eyes were Muppets performing a show tune. He became a sort of teasing older brother who poked fun at me, and helped me navigate the inner workings of the Kremlin.

I needed the help. I'd found a way to produce a miracle with my *Nutcracker* performance, but I was struggling to keep up with everything Zhanna and Petrov were throwing at me. My bad foot had begun to swell again; my toenails were bruised, cracking, peeling from my skin. Bulbous, painful corns grew between my toes. And I had continued, in the quiet at Pat's empty apartment, to restrict my eating and vomit up my meals. It felt both punishing and familiar: something flimsy and painful I threw in desperation at the things in my life that felt out of control, like a harness tossed at a wild-eyed horse.

I knew, by the time I'd finished my first Kremlin *Nutcracker* performance, that I did not want to be married. I resented the hours and days my relationship with Oleg required—the cooking, cleaning, waiting, talking, pretending. I didn't want to be a mother or a wife. All I wanted was to be a person my parents approved of and to devote myself to ballet at the feet of Zhanna, a coach who, like a blonde-haired Russian fairy godmother, was offering to make my dreams come true.

But I had chosen this marriage. I had fought my parents to get it. I had literally dug my own grave. And I knew, from the sermons I heard, the conversations I'd had with friends at my Moscow church, that getting a divorce was sinful.

"You need to work on your marriage. You need to try to reconcile," they said. "God hates divorce."

It's a hard thing to realize you want something that makes God hate you.

In church I sat in a cushioned chair in front of a preacher, silent, absorbing the knowledge that God disliked me. In the studio with Zhanna, I awaited instruction, desperate for her favor, agonizing over my mistakes. On the walks I took in Moscow under cold gray skies, I looked over the edges of bridges at the black and icy water oozing below and wondered what it would be like to step to the edge and throw myself over.

Repent. Pray. Be clean. Die to yourself. Ask God to save you.

The secret I held inside about the abuse that had happened to me when I was young had begun to press against my rib cage. Sometimes, when I spoke to my mother, I felt a volcanic anger and a burning desire to tell her what had happened. It caught in my throat and balanced, withheld, on the tip of my tongue. It felt like a continental shelf standing in the way of me and any sort of joy.

This weight was something I knew not everyone struggled with. I had friends who seemed to believe life could be enjoyed. Gabe was one of them—a person who always tried to laugh me out of my obsessive anxiety. Masha, who pranced through dark and musty Moscow tunnels, singing *Little Mermaid* theme songs at the top of her lungs, was another. And, of course, there was Anton, who walked with me in the snow and showed me a side of Russia that was deep and old and beautiful.

I saw the freedom and lightness with which they moved through the world and longed for it. These friends seemed to experience life as a ripe fruit—juicy, delicious, messy—something you bit into and tasted as nectar dripped down your chin. But I didn't know how to live that way, didn't know how to displace the weight I carried.

I tried to hide my struggles because I could tell they made people uncomfortable. No one wanted to be responsible for me; no one had the time to take care of me. Showing my needs was not possible. People were too busy, and they needed to be calmed by knowing I was okay. I needed to show them I was worth their time by being so successful, shining so brightly, they'd see and be dazzled and believe that I was worthy.

But in the months after I joined the Kremlin, I reached a breaking point. I wanted to be happy, I wanted to enjoy my life, I wanted to focus on dancing. And the only way I could see to start trying to do that was to stop pretending.

I told Oleg I didn't want to be in a relationship anymore.

I made myself stop caring whether or not I was a sinner. I did what I wanted to do.

Mom came to visit me in Moscow for a few days. We walked around the city, ate lunches at a vegetarian restaurant, stared at the medieval stone buildings of Red Square.

When I told her I wanted to get a divorce, she stopped what she was doing and turned around to look at me.

"Oh, Joy," she said, speechless with surprise for a moment, then, "Oh, honey, I'm so, so sorry."

I began talking about why I wanted to be done with the marriage, how miserable I'd been, how angry I was with her for the way she'd cut me out of her life.

She listened, then drew me into her arms with a hug.

"I'm so sorry for the way I hurt you," she said. "I flipped out. I was terrified of what you were doing. But it was all wrong—I was worried not just because of what would happen to you, but because of what your actions said about *me*. I tried to manipulate you and control you. It was wrong, and it hurt you, and I'm so sorry."

I almost couldn't believe what I was hearing. This was the apology I'd been waiting for. I started crying, and Mom hugged me.

"I got a divorce before I met your dad, you know," she said, her arms around my shoulder. We spent the next hour that way, next to each other, Mom talking about her past.

"In the end, you were right about Oleg," I told her. "I shouldn't have gotten married."

"I'm so sorry I pushed you away so hard," she said. "I should have been there for you. I should have been a source of refuge and nonjudgment for you. Will you forgive me?"

I said yes.

Later, I told her about the abuse.

Time seemed to stop for a moment, after I let her know what had happened. My words settled into the room like sediment that had slowly, finally, fallen to the bottom of the ocean.

Then Mom came over and hugged me, and I felt the mountain I'd been carrying on my shoulders finally shift, slightly, in a way that made it easier to see the light.

Mom stayed with me in Moscow for three days, and then she left. I wanted more of her.

After my divorce, after my conversations with Mom, things became easier in some ways. I retreated to the silence of my room in Pat's apartment. I slept in on my days off, and, when I woke, I was alone in the darkened predawn silence of my bed. In the evenings, I sprawled out on the floor of the living room to stretch and journal or draw and memorize vocabulary in French. I drank tea with my friend Masha in the kitchen. I joined a gym. On cold winter nights, when snow fell from the sky, I walked, a scarf around my face, to a Bikram yoga studio. There, on a vinyl floor with thirty other winter-pale Muscovites, I breathed. I bent and shaped myself into locust, camel, eagle, tree in a baking-hot room until I felt cleansed, released, boiled alive, reborn.

I began to remember what it was to feel human.

Zhanna and Misha were kind to me. They did not know the secret things I battled in my mind, but they could see the effects—the hyperventilation that caught at me before performances, the anxiety that caused me to stumble, the anger I directed inward when I failed.

"This is a waste of your time and energy," Zhanna said when she saw me agonizing over Oleg.

Zhanna herself had lived through one marriage and into another, and she saw no advantages to the ties I'd formed between myself and

Oleg, but she occasionally dropped hints about the benefits of becoming involved with men who were wealthy and well-connected. The leverage could be maximized for one's dance career, she said.

Misha saw how I worried about the drama my divorce would create in the theater backstage. But he laughed at the fears that haunted me, like someone who looks a monster in the face and pokes fun at it.

"Please." He shrugged. "All this relationship drama is just another *Santa Barbara*. Every theater has its *Santa Barbara*."

Misha, like every other Russian I knew, made constant references to an obscure American soap opera—*Santa Barbara*—that had aired throughout Russia after the fall of the Soviet Union.[1] I'd never met an American who'd seen it. But it lived large in the Russian imagination.

Still, the drama of my divorce felt continental in its immensity. My anxiety surfaced in debilitating waves from beneath my skin when Zhanna corrected me, when I stood too near Oleg in class, when I stared too closely at my body in the mirror, when I waited behind the curtain before performances. The terror that had infused my body since I was young would not leave easily. I danced the pieces Zhanna gave me to perform; I wore my feet to blistered, corn-riddled raw meat. I starved myself, weakened my bones and muscles and stamina with purging and binging.

But regardless of how difficult I found it to see past the mass of my own problems, there were other dramas, the size of actual continents, growing in immensity beyond the walls of my theater.

CHAPTER 24

A New Russia

Russia started to change.

At first, I barely had the capacity to notice. I was hyper-focused on my own life. But a drama, as violent and sinister as the stories we acted out on stage, had begun growing, like a storm on the horizon. I saw it building in intensity, scene by dramatic scene, on the screens of my laptop and phone: headlines and news stories about a rising anger, boiling in Ukraine.

At first, the videos showed thousands of Ukrainians flooding onto a square named Maidan in central Kiev, setting fires, waving blue and yellow flags, piling tires into precarious rubber towers. They said they wanted freedom from Russian influence, freedom from their Russia-loyal president, Victor Yanukovych.[1]

Then I read headlines that Yanukovych had fled Ukraine and taken refuge in Russia. I saw videos of Ukrainians crawling wide-eyed over the mansions and villas Yanukovych had abandoned.[2] He'd left behind pet ostriches and bears, boxing rings, tennis courts, gilded crystal chandeliers, and swarms of furious Ukrainians.[3]

The public protests and rejection of Yanukovych—the Maidan Uprising, as journalists had begun to call it—was an unacceptable turn of events for Russia. The response was swift. Weeks later, in the port city of Simferopol, where the Black Sea meets the shores of Ukraine's peninsular southern heel, Russian soldiers dressed in dark-green uniforms with masks on their faces stormed a Ukrainian naval building.[4]

They ejected the Ukrainian officers there at gunpoint. These Russian soldiers displayed no flags or military insignia on their uniforms, and Russian officials denied they were sent from the Kremlin.

Ukrainians, however, knew. The "little green men," as they called them, were part of an armed Russian invasion.[5]

Then, the storm returned to the Kremlin. While Zhanna coached me in the theater's glass-walled studio, Putin took to a podium in a baroque Kremlin palace just down the sidewalk. He announced, in a speech lasting more than an hour, that the peninsular Ukrainian region of Crimea was now officially part of Russia.[6]

If I had to pick a moment when Russia changed, this would probably be that moment.

In the weeks that followed, crowds of Russian men gathered in Red Square to celebrate, waving flags displaying Putin's grim, oversized face.[7] Giant billboards appeared around Moscow, filled with the bold tricolor of the Russian flag and the oversized, triumphant phrase, "Crimea is ours!" Shops sold T-shirts with Photoshopped images of Putin administering a karate kick to Obama's throat.[8] The voices on Russian television began shouting about the persecution of Russian people and the Motherland's duty, her God-given, historic right to annex the Black Sea port of Crimea.

Crimea was not just anywhere. This was the place Russians, for generations, had taken their vacations. It was like the Florida of the Soviet Union, a place brimming with nostalgic memories of sunshine, beaches, and Soviet resorts.[9] When Putin announced it was, once again, part of the country, many of the Russian people I knew shrugged their shoulders, as if to say, "Our Crimea is under threat—why wouldn't we take it back?"

There was something about the shouting and nationalism that surprised me. *"Crimea is ours"? Really?* It had the same energy as the crowds of male soccer fans I saw spilling out of Russian stadiums, red-faced, drunk, plastered in club colors, and screaming about how great their team was, setting fires, overturning cars. There were great swathes of Russians who were hungry for the alternate reality offered to them by Putin. The rhetoric about Russia seizing Crimea, "liberating" it from Ukraine, made them feel like it was possible to go back to being a superpower.

I watched what was happening but did not discuss it publicly. It didn't even occur to me—I'd had enough of adding my voice to newspapers. The last time I'd tried to comment on a news headline, I'd lost my job, been denounced by my friends, colleagues, and coaches. I'd become afraid to show my face in public.

I was not about to destroy the dream I was realizing by opening my mouth again. I wanted to keep my head down and work.

Petrov received orders to stage ballets in honor of the Motherland: dances that could be performed on Red Square, flags flapping in the breeze, Lenin's mausoleum and St. Basil's candy-colored domes in the background. The bosses wanted spectacles broadcast live on channels that reached across the country. They wanted art that would tell a story of Russian power and triumph.

This had always been the role of the State Kremlin Palace Ballet, the reason for its existence: to act out the glory of Russia in the medium that Russia knew best.

I was not invited. Petrov told me people who danced on Red Square to celebrate Russian imperialism needed to have red passports and Federal Security Service or FSB-approved security clearances. I simply wasn't qualified.

I was bitterly disappointed at being excluded. But Zhanna was unconcerned.

"Why would you want to go to that thing anyway?" she said. "It's just a mass performance. Save your energy."

There were other directives from higher up in the Kremlin. We sometimes received emails and text messages, informing us when important elections were taking place, where we were supposed to vote and for whom we should cast our ballots. There were notes regarding patriotic gala concerts, which, if we signed on to perform, offered bonuses and payouts. I received some of the messages but, as a noncitizen, was not actually able or expected to participate.

Instead, I watched the behavior of people around me change. There were times my American passport and accent worked in my favor. Guards at the Kremlin looked at the foreign name on my ID and said things like, "You're Miss America! I've seen you on the news!" with facial expressions as close to a smile as people guarding the entrance to the Kremlin on a cold morning could give.

Other times, my American-ness was a liability. I could always tell when the staff at the Kremlin had spent too long in front of the television, watching presenters on state channels deliver barbed anti-Western propagandistic monologues. One of the theater's musicians seemed to be a particular fan of political news. In the studio, she sometimes refused to play music for my rehearsal.

"You Americans think you're the best," she said with disdain, standing up from her chair to leave the room. "You think you just always get what you want."

Other times, grim-faced Kremlin Palace officials would pretend to be anti-American when important people, like my director, were in the room.

"What are we going to do with this American girl? She wants to travel again? Does she work for the Kremlin or no?" they'd say, loudly enough for everyone to hear. "Maybe she's actually working for the West instead of for us."

But then, behind closed doors, they became human again. They told me about their children who were studying at universities in the United States, asked questions about what it was like to live there.

Zhanna had instructions on how to navigate this. She wanted me to make myself a person to them, to express to them my constant appreciation. I carried gifts to their offices and spent extra time at their desks, asking about their families, answering questions about what it was like to be an American—something I was struggling to recall.

Sometimes I asked Zhanna about things I'd read in the *New York Times*—articles that mentioned Russian foreign policy or economic sanctions that had made prices in Moscow soar.

"What do you think?" I sometimes questioned. "Will it affect our work?"

"Joy, why are you asking these questions?" She would shake her head. "There's no need for you to think about this. Think about your work. Think about how to be more authentic in your Gamzatti variation."

She was insistent, and I believed her, that we were in art, not politics—as if, while dancing at the Kremlin, the two could be separated.

I'm an artist, I told myself. *I work at the Kremlin. I serve art.*

Pat encouraged me to think of myself as a diplomat in all situations. She herself had always spoken in positive ways about Russia. Often she mentioned the Russian Order of Friendship she'd been given personally by Putin.

"I have highly benefited from my career and my life in Russia," she always said. "I will not speak against it."

She had always been able to decipher the signs in Russia, like a weather forecaster who kept her eye on barometric pressure and patterns of moisture growing in darkness on satellite imagery. When the Soviet Union fell, she'd been ahead of history and rushed into Moscow to find business partners. She had always believed Russia had a grand future of freedom, democracy, and capitalism. For decades, she'd held tight to her faith that genius Russian entrepreneurs would innovate a new Russia into existence. But in 2014, after Crimea was seized, we sat on the floor of her living room, moving Scrabble tiles around her coffee table, and I listened as she spoke in ways that were sounding more and more pessimistic.

Things were not going well for Pat. Sanctions and partners and colleagues she'd nurtured had started to turn on her. It had become fashionable to be publicly anti-American. Some of the people she worked with had seen Russia's xenophobic shift in tone as an opportunity to try to claw assets and businesses out of her hands.

"I think it's time for me to leave Russia," she said one night, puffing on her cigarette and swirling an amber glass of Johnnie Walker in her hand. "I'm going to sell my companies at a profit and get out of town."

She seemed sad as she said this, her red hair a frizzy triangle around her head. But I wasn't surprised about her decision. I had become worried about her age and declining health. Plus, the rabid Russian nationalism we saw in the news was something she seemed to take personally. The country she'd loved and invested in for decades was disappearing.

"Leaving Russia for good, huh?" I smiled sadly. "What will Russia do without you? What will I do without you?"

Pat watched me over the tendrils of smoke that curled up from her cigarette.

"I'm planning to sell the apartment," she said.

"Oh!" I didn't know what to say. Her apartment had become a haven for me in Moscow. It was what made my continued employment at the Kremlin possible, my life in Russia possible.

"Don't worry, Joy," she said. "I know this is hard to hear. But don't worry. I'll take care of you."

"Pat, you don't owe me anything. It's not your job to find me a place to live," I said. "You've been so generous to me for so long."

She looked at me kindly. "I'm listing it in dollars," she said, tapping her cigarette on the ashtray. "It will probably sell quickly. But don't you worry. I know you want to stay in Moscow. I'll figure something out."

"You don't owe me a place to live, Pat," I said as I brought our dishes to the sink. I'd grown used to caring for her, watching to see what she needed like she was my grandmother whom I needed to wind down for bedtime.

But later, when I was alone in the room she had given me, I felt something like a water-heavy cloud settle in my chest. I remembered the nights we'd stayed up late, talking about history and politics and art. The laughter and tea I'd shared with friends in her kitchen, the way she had held me in her arms when things with Oleg had come to a bitter end.

Pat had created a refuge and a family for me in a strange and overwhelming city. She'd made me feel safe and human when I was frightened and ashamed. She had encouraged my dreams, and when I had struggled, she'd come alongside me, bright-eyed, smiling, like she knew a secret and was letting me in on it.

"Don't rush the journey," she'd always told me. "Struggling is one of the best things you can do. It will always teach you."

I'd looked to her for guidance. I'd come to rely on her steady belief in me, her generosity. I literally could not afford to live in the city that had come to feel like home without her.

If Pat was leaving, I wouldn't be able to stay.

What's more, if Pat, who had always had a sixth sense about Russia's future, was leaving, why would I *want* to stay?

Moscow softened in the summer. The trees broke out in glossy green, fountains splashed to life, and the sun rose around three in the morning, shone bright in the sky until nearly 10 p.m.

I felt reborn after the long winter, and, on a hot August day, as I ran across Volkhonka Street in central Moscow, I felt almost happy. It was easier than usual in that exact moment to push away the worries about the beloved home I would lose now that Pat had left Russia. Most of her things had been cleared out of the apartment, and the new buyers had already hired construction crews.

I pulled open the glass doors of an Italian restaurant where the smell of freshly baked pizza wafted in the air. I found a seat near a window with a view, across a stone square, of the oversized white and gold Christ the Savior Cathedral. I waited for the person Pat had told me to meet.

"Joy?" A tall woman with glossy red hair stood next to my table, her hand extended. I jumped up to shake it.

"Elena? It's so nice to meet you," I said.

She slid into the chair across from me, a sparkling pair of diamond and pearl earrings shimmering against her neck. I could see the Mercedes class S that had pulled up outside the restaurant to drop her off, the guards who stood carefully watching as she smiled at me from the other side of the table.

"Thank you for meeting me," she said.

I felt a little awestruck by her beautiful makeup and immaculate hair. She was like a czarina—tall, powerful, confident, gorgeous. This was a friend Pat had arranged for me to meet—a woman who'd grown a successful business in Russia, whose grandfather-in-law had been a powerful person in the Russian State Duma. She was the type of Muscovite I'd heard about and seen in the distance, but had never actually spoken to.

"So, tell me about your work at the Kremlin," she said.

I spoke about the roles for which I was preparing, the things I was learning from Zhanna.

"Pat told me all about your story, how brave you've had to be," she said. "I think it's wonderful. You are someone I'd like my daughter to resemble someday."

She brushed strands of carefully curled red hair out of her eyes as she started to speak about her family—the husband she'd lost, the courage she'd had to find to raise her children as a single mother, the family business she'd stepped into. I wasn't entirely clear what her business was, but I felt rude asking. Pat had told me it was something to do with real estate.

We nibbled on food that she ordered, while she told me how important she thought it was to support artists. At the end of the meal, she pointed out the window at the Moscow River glinting in the sun and the towers of historic buildings that rose on the opposite bank.

"Look across the river," she said. "I have a couple of apartments in that building there. We're not doing anything with them. Would you like to live there?"

I stared outside at one of the most beautiful neighborhoods in central Moscow—a place I'd passed many times. It was right in the city's glimmering, historic center.

I turned back to face her.

"Are you serious?" I said, my eyes round.

She pulled a set of keys out of her purse and handed them to me. "It's yours to live in if you want it."

"How much for rent do you want me to pay?" I asked.

"No rent." She smiled. "Why don't you go check it out?"

She wrote an address and phone number on a sheet of paper for me. "This is the number for Volodia. He can show you the apartment if you need any help getting in."

I was stupefied, kept saying things like "Oh my goodness!" and "Thank you!"

She stood up from the table and smiled at me. "It was so nice to meet you, Joy," she said. "Let's talk again soon."

Then she was gone, like a glittering, redheaded Russian queen, disappearing in the swing of a glass door and quiet slide of a retreating Mercedes.

I hurried out of the restaurant and across the ornately, curved iron of Patriarshy Bridge. I let myself in through the heavy doors of a tall sand-colored building and rode an elevator to the seventh floor.

When I unlocked the door to the address she'd given me, the first thing I saw was the view out the windows. It looked like a painting come to life. I stepped across the room, my mouth hanging open, and walked straight to the wall. The white sills were deep enough to sit in, and beyond them, shimmering in glass frames, Moscow spread out below me like a tapestry of shining gold domes, spiked towers, green-ruffled trees, and medieval red walls.

I moved in right away. Elena offered to pay for a renovation, but I was too afraid to ask for anything more. I couldn't believe her generosity. The apartment was simple and a bit dusty from months of sitting empty, but the location and the fact of its existence—all, entirely, for me—was unbelievable.

I used some money Pat had given me before leaving Moscow to buy a bed and mattress from Ikea, then paid a team of handymen to install a wall of mirrors and a long wooden barre in the living room.

Sometimes I wondered how long Elena's generosity would last. I didn't know her well, and I couldn't figure out if there was an expiration date on this space, or some invisible string attached to these rooms that I hadn't yet discerned. But soon, as I began falling asleep under the Kremlin lights that shone across the river, and waking to the sound of heavy bells that tolled in the cathedral down the street, I realized, *This is my new home.*

It felt like I'd entered a new Moscow. Zhanna was prepping me for increasingly difficult roles, Misha was finding more and more time to partner me in performances.

And somehow, impossibly, I belonged in this reality. In the mornings, I stretched by the barre and walked along the granite riverbank. I invited friends to gather around my new table. Photographers used my living room to shoot portraits, videographers came to get footage of my warm-up routine for a documentary, musician friends put together ad hoc concerts while standing in my apartment, my windows opened to fill the air high over the Moscow River with violin music.

Maybe things will be fine after all.

This was the thought I had, sitting in the deepened sills of my new living room, watching the sunset light the gleaming spires and domes of Moscow on fire. I had never felt so safe.

I made the right decision when I decided to stay in Moscow.

That was the thought I had at the time. And even now, when I look back at that golden summer and beautiful fall, sometimes I think about how it's possible to carve out a wonderful life for yourself, even when the world as you know it is ending.

CHAPTER 25

Murder on a Moscow Bridge

I felt safe in my new apartment and my job, but that did not mean that Moscow was safe for everyone.

There were people in Russia's capital who were against what the country's leaders were doing in Ukraine. I saw them on the news sometimes—opposition leaders who called Putin corrupt, a dictator who was destroying his own country. Some of my artist friends—young Muscovites who worked as photographers or entrepreneurs or ran their own design businesses—attended protests led by these leaders. They joined crowds of tens of thousands of people who thronged the icy streets to shout about how Putin was a thief and that they wanted a Russia without him. They signed petitions and were dragged out of protest lines by Moscow riot officers. Sometimes they spent a few hours or days in jail before being sent home with warnings about disturbing the peace.

"Soon it will be too late," these friends of mine said. "Soon, in this regime of Putin's, no one will be able to have a brand, create, or be an entrepreneur. No one will be free."

One of the opposition leaders my friends and other protesters rallied around was Boris Nemtsov. This was a politician whose name and face appeared often in the newspaper or online criticizing Putin and the military skirmishes that were growing in Eastern Ukraine. I'd read about these armed conflicts between pro-Russian separatists who, together with "volunteer" fighters from Russia, were increasing assaults, trying to claim more and more land from Ukraine. Sometimes the violence escalated to detonations in Ukrainian cities.[1] Then there was the passenger jet that lifted off from an Amsterdam airport, flew toward Malaysia, and was shot out of the sky by a Russian missile. Nemtsov was fully against this ongoing violence. He called the occupation of Crimea shameful, an international crime.[2] He organized demonstrations in Moscow, where people held signs reading "Leave Ukraine Alone" and shouted, in unison, "No to war!"[3]

I knew intimately that there was a cost to speaking out publicly against Russian authorities or against the decisions they made.

But still, I never expected the cost for someone like Nemtsov to be so high. I never expected he would be killed.

The events we read about on the news can take on a distant, cinematic pallor of unreality: gunmen shooting into crowds, bombs dropping onto cities, families drowning in boats on the Mediterranean Sea. When these events are far away, it's possible to tune them out—disable notifications, scroll past the headlines to avoid making yourself sick with the constant drumbeat of tragedy, suffering, injustice.

But when the news happens in your neighborhood, at your doorstep, right below the sill of your window, it's impossible to ignore.

When I stepped out of my apartment building on the morning of February 28, 2015, the reality of a changing Russia was right in front of my face.

I had been asleep when the assassination happened, but now, as I crossed the ice-slick street, I could see its aftermath in the distance under a low-hanging sky. Police officers had swarmed Bolshoi Moskvoretskii Bridge next to Red Square. They had parked their cars in a huddle, hung garlands of peppermint-striped tape to block off the sidewalk. They stood in the gray morning light, consulting over a body that had fallen, riddled with bullets, to the pavement, its unseeing eyes turned toward the sky where mist shrouded the domes of St. Basil's Cathedral.[4]

I turned away from the scene and hurried down the side of the embankment, tasting the damp cold and car exhaust that hung in the air. I was late for ballet class.

There was a feeling like nausea in my belly. I wasn't sure exactly where it had come from. There had been so many premieres in the past month: "Myrtha," *Magic Flute*, a new modern piece we were trying to choreograph. My knees were skinned and bruised. There were nights when my muscles shook uncontrollably and my legs buckled. When I couldn't stomach food. When I called Misha in a panic or begged a masseuse on *Tverskaia* Street to do something, anything to make the spasms stop.

Slowing down didn't occur to me. Zhanna was preparing me for a new solo role in *Sleeping Beauty*. And maybe, if that went well, something in *Swan Lake*. This was what I'd always wanted.

My bag was heavy and pounded against the sore muscles of my torso as I passed kiosks where vendors sold pirogi hand pies, underwear, and cell phone cases imprinted with pictures of Putin wearing a crown, his middle finger raised in contempt.

Out of the tunnel, across the street, I walked past bare trees to the Kremlin gate. I tried to appreciate the moment every time I arrived: the stone turrets, the stillness, the Archangel Cathedral domes that glinted and shone, even on gray days in February.

But on that morning, all I could think about was the murder and how close I'd been. How, if I'd happened just hours ago to glance out my apartment window at the right time, I might have seen the muzzle flash. I might have heard the shots fired into a man's head, chest, and stomach over the sound of cars driving through slush. I might have heard his girlfriend screaming beside him.[5]

The narrow, linoleum-floored dance studio was quiet when I arrived. I slipped off my boots, hung my coat on a hook, and lay, forehead to the floor, stretching the muscles in the backs of my legs. My colleagues arrived one by one. At this stage of winter, the dancers beside me were tired, pale after months of clouded winter skies. They bent and bowed, their bodies corded with muscle, like sallow stalagmites that had mushroomed off the floor of a cave.

I'd started to make friends with some of them, but most seemed uninterested or annoyed at my presence.

"Don't get attached, don't get close," Zhanna had told me. "You come here, you do your work, you go home. Make your alliances with people who are not in the theater."

Rehearsing always emptied my mind. I spent the next few hours under Zhanna's gaze, focusing my arms and legs and chest on her words. I shifted the gravitational pull of my body forward when I turned; I modified the way I came out of passé.

The concentration it took to meld my mind to the vision Zhanna had for each movement was all-consuming. But when I slowed to catch my breath, reality was there waiting for me.

Boris Nemtsov had been murdered under the very lamps of the Kremlin. He'd been shot down on one of the bridges I walked on to work, in the well-lit center of a city where I'd never before felt afraid to move around by myself, even during the long winter nights.

Later, after hours of rehearsal, after the sun had set behind an impenetrable bank of clouds, Zhanna offered to drop me off at my apartment on her way home.

It was dark by the time we left the theater, escaping the Kremlin gates in the cold and misty air, buckling ourselves into the quiet interior of her Audi. We drove across the river, where people had begun laying candles and flowers on the ice-encrusted pavement where Nemtsov had been shot.

"Did you hear about that guy who was killed on the bridge last night?" I asked as Zhanna drove, the streetlights reflecting off her glasses.

At first, she was quiet, the sound of her turn signal clicking like a metronome into the space between us. But then she spoke.

"Politics are for discussing at the kitchen table," she said. "They are never for discussing in public."

I swallowed into the silence as she turned onto the icy Sofiiskaia Embankment and rolled to a stop in front of my building.

I recognized what she had said: it was a Soviet response, something I had seen friends do in Moscow before. They lowered their voices when they shared controversial political opinions. Their eyes glanced upward to the ceiling, the walls, as if there were microphones embedded in the plaster.

I knew my history, and I knew there had been entire generations of Russians sent to the Gulag, betrayed by their neighbors or classmates or coworkers for disturbing the facade of united Soviet political opinion.

Zhanna had made a name and a career for herself dancing and teaching at a theater within the walls of the Kremlin. And she had created a perch for me there—a place of safety where I could learn and grow and perform. She felt like the mother I'd lost when I moved away from Texas, like the guardian who had vanished from my life when Pat left Moscow. Zhanna was the roof that kept me safe and dry when the storms of anti-Americanism, professional jealousy, and economic turmoil swept through the theater.

I took what she said seriously.

Later that night I got a call from Pat. She was worried for me, wanted to discuss Nemtsov.

"I can't believe it," she said. "This was right behind the Kremlin—it's blatant—someone meant to send a message. Russia is going backward into repression."

Pat had been living in the United States for nearly a year by then. Her rhetoric had grown increasingly anti-Putin. I wondered if she was being affected by the American news outlets she was listening to.

"I'm fine, I'm totally safe," I told her.

Don't let yourself have an opinion about Nemtsov, is what I told myself. Pat herself had always advised me not to let myself be polarized about Russian politics.

I can do this, I thought. *I can look away. I can keep my eyes on dance. I can be a diplomat. I can find the middle ground.*

CHAPTER 26

Stage Fright

I was afraid.

This was something Zhanna could see when we stood in studio together.

My steps faltered; my knees buckled. Sometimes my breathing grew shallow, and my chest heaved in and out like the hyperventilating of a terrified mouse, crouched in a corner, waiting for a predator to pounce.

On the bad days, neither Zhanna nor I could see the panic and my fear of failure for what it was.

"Yes, Joy," she'd say in studio, as she turned off the music, folded her arms, shook her head. "Using our brain today is not working, is it?"

"I need to be more grateful," I sometimes answered her, bent over double, my rib cage heaving. I was terrified of trying her patience, losing her devotion. I tried to beat the corrections she gave me into my brain, to be someone who only made mistakes once, and then filled in the craters of my inadequacy with extra work, extra perfection.

"I wish I could be a robot. I wish I could block everyone and everything out and just deliver," I'd tell her.

I searched for talismans that would calm the dread I felt inside my chest about going on stage. I called my dad the night before performances to ask him to pray for me. I stood in the wings and stared into my phone as an app promising to calm me filled the screen with videos of rain falling on leaves, wooden paddles raking through piles of sand with mesmerizing smoothness.

But still, I faltered in rehearsals, berated my every misstep, obsessed over the choreography. In the moments before performances, my knees shook, and I cried in the dressing room, terrified of the stage. I couldn't sleep the nights before performances or concentrate on anything other than the endless, revolving fear that spun like a whirlpool around my shoulders and chest.

When my insecurity was at its worst, my eating disorder would flare. It was always an attempt to establish control, to punish my body into obedience, as if I could manage the future by distilling the wild, chaotic present into a rigid, pinpoint question of whether or not there was food in my stomach.

Zhanna tried to help me.

"Just make it through the first ten minutes," she'd tell me. "You'll get rid of your nerves by the end of the first act, then be able to enjoy the rest of the ballet."

Even Petrov, the director, tried to help.

"I'm going to tell you a secret that will make you never, ever be nervous again," he said to me before one of my performances. "The people who are going to hate you will continue to hate you. It doesn't matter if you dance extremely well—that will actually make them hate you even more. So don't care about what they think. Just dance for all the rest of the people who love you because there are a lot of people who love you."

In the moments before I went on stage, Zhanna began standing in front of me, her hands over my temples, cupping my skull between her palms, like an abbess giving benediction to a novitiate.

"Guardian angels are watching over you," she said. "Everything will be okay. You can do this."

I left Moscow.

It was early December, and I sat exhausted in a mud-splattered tour bus that traveled long, potholed roads in Russia's south. I watched the Caucasus Mountains rise out of the curve of the earth, Krasnodar behind us, Essentuki, at the foot of the stratovolcanic Mount Elbrus, before us.

My academy friend, Anton, had asked me, once again, to join him on a ballet tour. It was easy to say yes. For one thing, I was desperate for money. The Kremlin hadn't updated its pay scales in years, and Moscow was reeling from economic sanctions. There had been one month, after injuring my foot and missing performances, when I'd made the ruble equivalent of only fifty dollars for the entire four weeks.

I'd started teaching private lessons at my home, online, at the U.S. Embassy. I'd opened a company with my dad to sell supplemental nutrition bars, marketed to dancers. But, still, I needed extra income.

Anton loaded us onto a bus that drove through the night to Dagestan, Kabardino-Balkaria, Chechnya, Sochi, Southern Ossetia, Ingushetia, Karachaevo-Cherkessia, Rostov-on-Don, Ryazan. Rain drizzled across our windows, dust coated the underbelly of our tour bus, police officers stopped us in the night to check our passports, question us, then wait, amused, until we handed over cash payments—exotic souvenirs like Brazilian reals or South African rands from our home countries. Bribing was a jocular game. The road police just expected it, and the gifts we handed over made them smile, laugh at our jokes, cheer us on.

The other dancers who sat with me on the bus were wonderful. They were young and talented and kind. We played cards, ate snacks, and tried to sleep on lumpy, reclined seats. Sometimes we stared out the window at grime-covered semis, bare tree branches, splintering wooden homes, and roadside kiosks selling apples, cabbage, honey, fish, pickles.

I could see the difference between the regions through which we were traveling and Moscow. The Russian republic of Dagestan was not where the Kremlin spent its oil rubles. But I felt privileged to be there, to see places I'd heard about only on the news, to stay in the strangely shaped hotel rooms with leopard-print upholstery, shiny wallpaper, and mauve-flowered carpets. I felt lucky to take classes in the echoing Soviet-era regional theaters that filled with audience members at night.

Every city and village we visited had a stage somewhere. Even if they didn't have reliable internet, there was always, at the center of some pot-holed square, a dusty theater with a graffitied bust of Lenin stuffed into a back closet, foyers decorated with Soviet-era frescoes of bountiful facto-ries rising out of the Russian countryside. The stages in these places were always guarded by dingy curtains that had survived from the 1970s and continued to rise and fall faithfully on dramas that transported audiences far away from the cold and crumbling infrastructure and hopelessness into a world that beckoned and delighted. The performances touched the soul, imparted a bittersweet longing that made it possible to continue feeling human, even when everything else looked impossible.

This was it, I realized—the Russian soul that I'd wanted so badly to understand since my first weeks in Moscow. It was a sort of desperation for beauty and life that drew Russians to fill their schools with literature- and art-education requirements, to stem their suffering with a passion for poetry, painting, photography, and music, to feel pride in the state and municipal tax dollars that went to pay for city theaters, musician and dancer salaries.

No one knows despair like Russia. But the ways in which I saw people absorb their fate depended, in some ways, on where on the map I looked. In Moscow, people drew near to power to find relief. In the regions, they turned to vodka. And in pockets everywhere, people romanticized their lives. They saved their rubles to purchase ballet tickets. They turned to the discipline of creating and performing art with dignity and talent and told the truth as they saw it: that suffering is inextricably, unavoidably linked to life, that creating and enjoying beauty is a necessary part of being human.

I felt privileged to see this tradition, to be part of it—to dance on these scattered Russian stages and express the art form that had been handed down to me. And it was in the easygoing circle of Anton's ragtag group of international dancers that I came to understand this. We had so little time to rest or rehearse. We drove through the night, parked in front of theaters, and rushed on stage to perform excerpts of classic Russian fan favorites we'd never practiced before. I didn't have time to be nervous, just to slap makeup on my face and jump in front of the audience, surrounded by friends, adored by spectators who were just grateful to be there.

The farther from Moscow I traveled, the more Zhanna's voice, and my own internal fears of judgment, faded from my head. If I messed up on a tattered stage in Ryazan after getting only two hours of sleep, who was going to judge me? Anton? Juan and Anya, who'd also gotten only three hours of sleep, their necks crooked on the arm of a bus seat? No one cared. I could just enjoy the moment for what it was, and watch Russia fly past me through the dirty glass of our tour bus.

We were there to dance. We goofed off backstage and made fun of the cranky train stewardesses who enforced rules they made up like grouchy medieval czars. We laughed at the strangeness of the hotels we stayed in and wondered at the emptiness of the cities we passed through. We took pictures with the sweet, shy convenience-store cashier who told us she'd never before met someone from outside of Russia. We breathed in the briny air of the Black Sea, let the music of waves crashing over pebbles fill our ears, immersed ourselves fully in the moment, oblivious and uncaring of what was behind or in front of us.

What am I so worried about? I started to wonder. *My dream has come true. I live in Russia. I'm a prima ballerina. I get to dance.*

CHAPTER 27

Art and Politics

Every person who wants to survive in Russia needs a "roof" to shelter them from the winds that blow, the powers that be. In Moscow, Zhanna was my roof, and I drank her instructions like lemonade. I never spoke ill of the Russian government or its leaders. I carried packages of chocolates with me to gray-suited palace theater bureaucrats, and I laid the bouquets I was given after performances at the feet of the people who sewed my costumes, painted my face in makeup, cleaned the floors of our dance studios.

I charmed them; I made them fall in love with me. I created a world in which I didn't have to fear people betraying me.

Zhanna showed me a path to walk at the top of a Russian theater that felt like the stories of girls at the center of dark Slavic fairy tales. These were fables that seemed to say, "Feed and honor and value the tiny mice, the birds, the magic dolls, the myriad people around you. This is how, in your hour of need, when given an impossible task, you will have an army of friends to help you. This is how you learn from and escape the forest witch."

"The Russian school of ballet is the best," I told anyone who would listen. "I love working at the Kremlin."

And I did. I loved Russian ballet. I loved working at the Kremlin.

Zhanna wasn't the only one who guided and shaped me. Misha Martyniuk understood the greasy machinery of the Russian ballet world as well as anyone I'd ever met. He knew exactly how to work the gears to get him where he wanted to go, which was mainly to theaters that paid excellent honorariums to guest performers.

We began smuggling ourselves out of Moscow and traveling to distant places like Irkutsk, Mirny, Sergut, Kazan. These were far-flung Russian towns famous for things like oversized power plants or for being home to the second-largest man-made hole in the world. They were always cold, always dark, always potholed, and always marked by beautiful theaters with loyal, passionate local fans.

We developed a shtick of a *Don Quixote* pas de deux that showed off our jumps and that we became so accustomed to, we could perform it in our sleep. We'd fly in a rattling plane with angry flight attendants to a random-ass city in Siberia, drive to the theater, change into our glittering black and red costumes, swipe on some stage makeup, and go out to perform the routines we knew by heart. We did it through blizzards and sleepless nights. There was even, with a different partner, a particularly memorable bout of food poisoning that had us pirouetting on stage, then running behind the curtains to yank each other's costumes off and sprint for the toilet.

There's nothing like a mid-performance bout of diarrhea to help you stop taking yourself so seriously.

I didn't have time to be nervous for these performances. I just ran on stage, moved through the choreography my body had memorized, took a bow, and left, some extra rubles in my pocket, Misha by my side, a smile on both our faces.

It made me feel like the Russian stage, vast and eternal, stretching from Europe to the cold Pacific, was as familiar as my living room: a place to which I finally, *finally*, belonged.

Petrov received an order to stage an unusual ballet.

It was May 2016, and he came, in his collared dress shirt, to the cramped and humid Kremlin studio to personally take us through the rehearsal.

The drama he'd chosen was something I'd never seen performed before—a ballet he'd choreographed decades ago for a Russian state visit to Thailand: *Katia and the Prince of Siam.*

Misha and I were given the lead roles, and Petrov watched us from tired eyes, sitting on a chair in front of the studio mirrors. He was intensely focused on every aspect of our run-through. He wanted to make sure we got our lifts just right, our arms raised at the correct angle, our positions properly marked in formation.

"Respected ladies and gentlemen, this is a very, very important performance," he told us, sternly. "A *very* important performance."

The next day, almost our entire troupe was loaded onto a plane and flown south from Moscow to Sochi. We landed at a wet, green airport at the edge of the Black Sea, where palm trees spiked into the misty air and rain pricked into puddles on the asphalt. We loaded onto a bus and drove far up into the Caucasus Mountains, where we couldn't tell if the wispy, gray clouds had lowered to touch the trees, or if the trees were breathing out lacy moisture that hung in the air like oxygenated tulle.

There were a few places I had started to associate with President Vladimir Putin: the red-walled Moscow Kremlin with its gilded palaces and ancient bell towers, certainly. Crimea, which he'd claimed, through military might, as his own. But the Black Sea resort town of Sochi and the athletic complex he'd ordered built there for the 2014 Olympics was a close third. So many oil-fueled rubles had been poured into this resort town: its stadiums and hotels and smooth black roads and five-star gyms. But the compound to which we'd been bussed was next level. Hundreds of white-walled, green-roofed buildings filled a leafy mountain valley on the banks of a stony river. Snow-covered peaks rose into the sky, glowing pink in the morning as the sun climbed over the Caucasuses.

It seemed more like a resort you'd find in Switzerland or Germany, not Russia. There were pools, treadmills, bubbling hot tubs, wooden lounge chairs, window views of furred green mountain slopes, waterfalls tumbling off cliff sides. I wished it was a place to which I could afford to travel on vacations. But being invited there to dance felt like its own privilege.

The security was like nothing I'd ever seen. Guards and FSB agents checked our passports and waved metal-detecting wands over our bodies. They shook their heads in rebuke when I took my camera out to film warm-ups and continually checked the badge I'd been issued to make sure my presence was allowed past various checkpoints.

We were shown to our beautiful rooms and the tiny dressing closet we'd have to share with dozens of performers from choir and folk dance groups who'd been bussed in from other parts of the country. We found ourselves gathered on a stage in our raggedy sweatpants and insulated slippers, looking like a bunch of kids in pajamas, surveying a room filled with banquet tables where lighting and sound experts crisscrossed a raised platform, adjusting switches and cords, volume and angles.

After our rehearsals, after we'd pulled on our tights, secured tiaras to our hair and fake eyelashes to our lids, we were crowded and shushed into a tiny backstage room.

"Don't push!" we hissed at each other. "You're going to smear my body paint!" "You're going to rumple my tutu!"

Petrov glared at us. "This is a momentous performance," he lectured. "You must dance your roles with mus-i-CAL-i-ty."

When the door was opened for us, we scampered to our places on a stage in a darkened room where the presidents, sultans, and prime ministers of Vietnam, Malaysia, Myanmar, Thailand, Singapore, Cambodia, Brunei, and the Lao People's Democratic Republic sat at a half-moon table, watching us with serious faces.[1]

I arabesqued, jumped into Misha's arms, was raised and lowered in the air, turned pirouettes, and watched the room flash past in a blur of blue and purple lights. Then, when I fluttered to a stop, lowered into the prop throne next to Misha that had been set up on stage, I looked out at the table in front of us. There I saw the actual living face of Vladimir Putin staring back at me. His hand held a spoon over a bowl of soup, his grim attention focused unbroken on the emotions and movements we'd performed on the platform in front of him.

That's him! The president of Russia, watching me!

After a crescendo of music, curtsies, bows, and polite applause, we were rushed out of the room.

Misha and I were in disbelief.

"It's not bad to watch the president watch you while he's eating soup," Misha said, shaking his head as if he were considering an underbaked slice of bread that was edible, but not notable. "Not a bad day of work, Joy. Not a bad day of work."

"We just performed for Putin!" I was giddy and proud. I couldn't believe my company had let me, an American, represent them on stage to the leaders of Southeast Asia, to the leader of Russia himself.

Petrov was beaming when he came back in the room to talk to us.

"What did they say? What did they think?" Zhanna wanted to know.

"They thanked us for the beauty, for the wonders of Russian ballet," he said, his face filled with contentment and pride. "Well done. Well done, everyone."

Later, Petrov pulled me aside.

"Putin asked me about you," he said, adding that the president had noticed my American name, transliterated in Cyrillic, on the program.

"I told him we were very proud of our American, our Russian American," Petrov said. "I told him, 'She's our dancer.'"

I had tried for years to fit in, to be Russian, and the fact that I had been noticed for my art by the leader of a country whose ballet disciplines I had devoted my life to, was perhaps the proudest I had ever been.

In that moment, I believed that our presence and focus and work on the stage in front of those world leaders was meaningful. We filled the air with music, parted the dramatic shadows with light that shone on our arms, necks, and wrists. We bent and flowed and arched with nuance, rhythm, and purpose. Surely this made a difference to the politicians who sat in a semicircle and watched us, sipping their soup and resting their minds from the push and tug of negotiations. Surely a musical display of art—our lingering hands, our traded glances, our sparkling costumes—helped them imagine a world defined by beauty and goodness, a world they themselves could have a role in creating with their trade agreements and political treaties. If we could lift their minds to a higher plane, a different way of seeing, maybe it would infuse the diplomatic bridges they were building with a sense of brotherly purpose and cooperation.

I still believe every diplomatic gathering should include art. Economic trade conference? Bring in the orchestra! Congressional committee meeting? Invite a few opera singers! Parliamentary debate? Send the parliamentarians through an art museum for a bit of contemplation before kicking things off. Art is supposed to tell a sort of truth, to inspire reflection on what it means to be a person, to make space for compassion, for seeing the world through someone else's eyes.

There's another way to look at this, of course. It is, I realize, possible to be greedy with art—to use it as a show of force and intimidation or to flaunt it in your enemy's face. Art can be a distraction and a means to drown out important voices that need to be heard. The Nazis stole and hoarded art. The Soviets used it for propaganda. Stalin himself famously loved dance and cinema and gave it a place of honor in Soviet life—and look what he did.

Had I, that day in Sochi, inspired world leaders toward bettering humanity? Or had I been used as a cultural weapon, a vanguard for an imperial agenda?

That day I wasn't asking those questions. I was high in the green mountains of Sochi. I was profoundly proud of the work I had done. I felt like I had been accepted as a ballerina, as a Russian, by a country that had defined what ballet meant.

CHAPTER 28

Waiting

It was 7:30 in the morning, dark, -10 degrees Celsius. I stood in a crowded parking lot, Moscow's November cold biting at my nose, creeping beneath my scarf, as I waited in line.

Is there any experience more Russian than waiting in line?

I had been awake for two and a half hours, traveled on metro trains, taxis, and my own frost-stung feet to get to this Godforsaken parking lot on Moscow's far southern border. When I arrived, I found that I was late. There were already 241 people in line ahead of me.

This was the barren wasteland of Russia's Federal Migration Service—the office I needed to beg, once again, to let me live in the country.

I had wanted to be Russian since the day I'd first stepped foot in Moscow. I'd gotten married to someone I barely knew for the privilege of living there. I had begun in my thinking, in my memories, to feel more Russian than American. But, still, I had not gained the passport or residency permit I needed to continue living there.

I had been to the Yuzhnoe Butovo migration office at least fifteen times. Each time I came, it was armed with a bag of meticulously gathered, stamped, and notarized non-expired medical, security, residency, family status, and citizenship documents. And each time I arrived, there were hundreds of people in line ahead of me.

It always took hours of waiting to receive a ticket that granted me the privilege of standing in another line, at the end of which I could hand my documents to a deeply bored and meticulous immigration official. I had thus far never been able to convince any of these officials to accept my paperwork. They always, inevitably, found that I had filled something in with the wrong color ink, written unacceptably in the margins of an official form, forgotten to bring along a third extra copy of a scanned visa page, or included an expired document. They'd point out the mistake, hand my papers back to me, and order me to start the entire, months-long process over again.

This is my way of telling you that the Russian Federal Migration Service was hell.

But by the fifteenth time I returned, I had a new secret weapon. I had convinced a Kremlin Palace Theater office manager to come with me.

This office manager—let's call him Vadim—was astonished at the hundreds of people, most of them from Uzbekistan or Tajikistan, who had made it to the migration center before us on a cold November morning. Probably they had spent the night there.

"It's not going to work to just stand in line," I had to tell Vadim. "You've got to push through to find whoever has the list and is keeping track of who's in what place."

He followed me wide-eyed as I elbowed my way past fellow applicants to whichever person had appointed themselves line president for the day.

"It's hard to be an immigrant," Vadim said, trailing behind me. "There's no way we can wait through this."

I didn't know what to tell him—this Kremlin official who knew less about Russia's migration system than I did. My friends all joked that I spent my days off standing outside the migration office. But this bewildered Kremlin theater manager couldn't imagine it. When we reached the crowded door to the center, he spoke up.

"We're from the State Kremlin Palace," he announced quietly to the officials inside.

Like most things in Russia, it's not what you know, it's who you know. As soon as those officers heard the word "Kremlin," they ushered us through their doors, to the well-heated office of a suddenly expedient clerk who glanced through my documents, asked me a few perfunctory questions, and signed off on my petition.

Just like that, after years of gathering documents, waiting in lines, begging for signatures and stamps, it was done.

Nine months later, I held the residency permit in my hand. It was blue and folded open like a passport. It meant I no longer had to apply for visas or worry about being able to stay in the country I loved, the country that felt more like home than any place I could remember.

I burst into tears. Russia was officially, as blessed by the Federal Migration Service and the Kremlin itself, a place where I belonged.

It was 2017 when I received my residency permit. By then I was twenty-four, I had lived in Russia for eight years, half of which I'd spent at the Kremlin Ballet Theater.

I had grown, under Zhanna's tutelage and my harebrained tours across Russia, into someone who was technically proficient, arresting on stage, able to do what was required, in performance after performance. I had traveled to China, Spain, Irkutsk, Bulgaria, Hong Kong, Korea, Siberia. I had danced in *Swan Lake*, *Sleeping Beauty*, *Nutcracker*, *Snow Maiden*. I was respected, sought after, a principal dancer.

I was also exhausted, and I had begun to feel like a circus animal, jumping through hoops, barking on command, performing tricks because I'd been trained to do so with barely enough pay to survive on.

Zhanna had transferred her three-dimensional encyclopedia of dance knowledge to my body and brain. In rehearsal after rehearsal, she had called forth the outlines of past performances: Plisetskaya's arms, Maximova's wrists, Ulanova's lingering glances. And she had successfully imprinted these generations of balletic mastery upon me.

I was grateful to Zhanna and proud of how far I'd come. But I had also started to long for change.

The Kremlin had begun to feel stifling. I felt burdened by the traditions I was expected to carry, sick of dancing under the inescapable judgment of dead Russian ballerinas. I wanted to try dancing new characters, different roles, fresh scenes. More importantly, I wanted to add my own interpretation and personality to the stories and emotions I was portraying. I wanted to be an artist, not a parrot. I knew Russia's poetry, literature, music, and choreography. I'd seen the industrial cities of Eastern Russia, the Caucasus Mountains, the inner heart of the Kremlin. I wanted Zhanna and Petrov to trust me to create my own interpretations. I wanted to cut myself open on stage and allow the audience to see who I was at my core—to tell the people who came to watch me what *I* knew, not just what Zhanna told me to do.

Many of my Russian friends could not understand my impatience. They were more practiced in receiving the things that life sent them. They did not strain at accepting their fates. They knew how to wait. "You have a place, why would you leave it?" they said.

Misha understood me, but his advice was practical and very Chelyabinsk: "Everyone has the same boogers, no matter where you go," he said. "You just have to pick the place where you like the boogers."

"Just be patient," Zhanna told me. "In two or three years, you will have everything you want."

When I look back now, I think she was right. If I had stayed at the Kremlin, I would have climbed, with Zhanna beside me, to the very top of the Russian ballet world.

But I wanted to grow in different ways, to step away from the relentless pace of Kremlin ballet tours and performances, to give myself the space and time for creativity. I wanted to make myself into an artist.

I wrote a long letter filled with gratitude and explanations. Then I went to a Russian department store and purchased something silverplated, expensive, and meaningful. I brought them both to Zhanna.

"There is nothing I could do that would ever be enough to thank you," I said. "You made me into the dancer I've always wanted to be."

"This is foolish, Joy," she said. "But I can see your mind is made up."

Zhanna had a hard time understanding, but Petrov wished me well, told me I was welcome back at the Kremlin whenever I wanted.

"I need to go," I told them both. "I need to try this on my own."

For months, I let ballet be my passport. I traveled to Australia, Thailand, Turkey for galas, guest performances, teaching stints. I took a vacation on a pink fishing boat in the South China Sea; I spent months at a South Korean Theater.

I practiced calming my body. I exercised the dictionary of Russian dance pedagogy Zhanna had passed down to me. I created a space for myself that allowed my brain to work, think, create, and feel in ways I'd never before allowed it to.

I missed Zhanna, but I learned, after I left the Kremlin, how to become my own mentor, how to add freedom and creativity to the Russian disciplines of ballet I'd been trained in. And, after less than a year of traveling, I was ready to come back to Russia. I missed home.

CHAPTER 29

Home

Home has always been complicated for me, and Russia has always been complicated for me—it's familiar, dear, unbearable, frustrating. And, in the months I spent away from it in 2018, I found that I missed it.

I don't know what home feels like to you, but to me, it's waking in an Ikea bed to the ringing of church bells from Christ the Savior Cathedral across the river. It's the dragon roar of trains in the deep, labyrinthine underground of the metro. It's the guttural, hard edges of a language that's gruff in public, kind in private. It's the porcelain of a teacup growing cold on winter nights when, removed from space and time, I crowd around a kitchen table with friends, talking for hours about concerts and art museums, excavating my soul for another person to hear.

When I returned to Moscow from my months of work and travel, I felt like kissing the dusty concrete pavement. It was summer, and the air over the Moskva River shimmered in a pink, smoggy haze on the morning runs I took around the city center. Swallows dipped and circled in the sky over the trees in Gorky Park and the gold domes of Christ the Savior Cathedral. My tiny, yellow-walled apartment waited for me, its windows open to breathe in the summer gusts that blew over the Kremlin from Moscow's north.

This was a place that had once been incomprehensible and frightening to me. Now it was a place I recognized and belonged to. I not only felt at ease there—I felt triumphant. I had, through toil, study, and patience, made Russia my own.

I returned to my beloved gym. I enrolled in a graduate program at the Russian Institute of Theater Art. I returned to the beautifully reno-vated Bolshoi Ballet Academy to see my teachers and take some classes. I texted all my friends to let them know that, whether it was for yoga studio visits, meals at Thai restaurants, concerts, ballet debuts, birthday parties, or strolls through the Pushkin Museum, I was back.

Things had changed in the months I'd been gone. Russia had spent billions on building and renovating airports, hotels, and transportation infrastructure for the World Cup.[1] Officials had given Moscow streets a makeover and, in cities around Russia, raised more than a dozen stadiums from the ground up. Moscow was sparkling with freshly installed granite pavement, colorful flower displays, fancy coffee shops, and streamlined electronic banking and government services. I could use an app to order takeout and car services. I could access any type of food I wanted. I could pay my taxes at an electronic kiosk. For the first time, I thought, *Russia is an easy place to live.*

I was so grateful to be there. I had finished my travels feeling strong and disciplined and thoughtful enough to begin imagining a new future. I threw myself into the classes and reading assignments required for my new theater degree. I took on dance students and found nannying and housework positions to pay my bills. I took gigs at theaters and joined Misha Martyniuk on ballet tours, flying to Switzerland, Italy, Siberia, Kazan, to dance at theaters hungry for beloved Russian classics. I made more money freelancing than at any paid troupe position I'd ever had.

I couldn't remember the last time I'd felt so happy. I had lived in Moscow before, but I had always been tied to the demands and timelines of a director, dependent on theater or school, or the political whims of my superiors, anxious about whether I'd be able to satisfy the demands of whoever was in charge.

But now, for the first time in my life, I was the one in charge. I decided whether or not to accept new students or nannying work. I made the call on whether or not to fly to Yoshkarola or Italy for performances.

I sat in music classes and visited art galleries and exercised with a personal trainer and listened to the calming, kind words of the Nike Run app instructor. I wasn't driven by fear anymore. I was driven by what I wanted.

When I dreamed about my future, I dreamed about living in Russia, performing on Russian stages, seeing my career followed and feted and supported by devoted Russian audiences.

Sometimes, I dreamed about the Bolshoi Theater.

I couldn't help myself. To this day, there is not a theater I love more than the Bolshoi. I love its limestone facade; its trampoline-sprung stage; its endless, high-ceilinged rehearsal rooms; its tulle-filled costume department; and the gorgeous, relentless, vibrating repertoire that fills its stage with heartbreak and song and beauty from September through June.

When I had free time in between my university studies and private lessons, I bought tickets to Bolshoi Theater performances. I sat in a red-cushioned seat with a rapt Moscow audience and watched these productions like the onset of a storm. First, the darkening of the auditorium lights, then the percussive pattering of instruments like raindrops, then the raising of the curtain like a blast of wind and the entrance on stage of something miraculous and fleeting, like a flash of lightning.

The Bolshoi was the best. It was where I wanted to be, and what I hadn't made public before returning to Moscow, was that I'd been given an invitation to return to ballet classes there.

Invitations to take class at new companies often lead to invitations to audition, which often lead to invitations to join a ballet troupe. And I desperately wanted to be invited to join the Bolshoi Theater troupe again.

In the years since I'd left, the old guard of Bolshoi leadership—Filin, Iksanov, Tsiskaridze—had all been dismissed from their positions. It was, I was hopeful, a different place. And I was a different person—I had learned how to keep my mouth shut. I'd learned how to make friends with crusty and cranky theater bureaucrats. I had made myself into someone who could cut paths safely through dangerous terrain. And I was a professional dancer. I'd performed leading roles in all the classical repertoire. I was strong and confident and in demand at theaters around the world. Friends who were less experienced and talented than I was were being admitted to the Bolshoi.

I knew I had a chance.

But there were others I needed to convince if I wanted to be offered a Bolshoi dance contract.

The newly appointed theater director, Makhar Vaziev, had taken the throne in Filin's former office and wore the title of Bolshoi ballet director. The hallway outside his office was often crowded with dancers in warm-up gear who waited like supplicants hoping for an audience with a monarch. I soon joined them, standing, my hands behind my back, in the corridor.

During our meetings, Vaziev sat in his cream leather chair in expensive, tailored shirts and waved his hand over stacks of papers with the elegant gestures of a lifelong ballet dancer.

"Why do you want to come back here?" he asked.

I told him of my infatuation with the Bolshoi—its beauty and grandeur—how I loved it more than any other place I'd ever danced.

"I've read the articles about you—the accusations you made about corruption," he would say, leaning back in his chair. "Is any of it true? Who asked you for the money? When? How? Is that person still here?"

He wanted to know what faction I'd been a part of during the year I'd been employed at the Bolshoi; what I thought of Tsiskaridze, who had been my teacher; where I had committed my loyalties. He wondered whether, if I was offered a new contract, I would publicly retract the statements I'd made to journalists about the Bolshoi in the past.

Every time I was called to his office, I came in, full of hope that we would discuss employment possibilities. But we never got around to contract details. Instead Vaziev discussed things like the clothing I wore in ballet class.

"You've signed up for class today, but you didn't wear the proper attire," he would say, in pauses from phone conversations. "You need to wear shorter skirts; I need to be able to see your legs. Come back another day. I don't take girls who wear skirts that are too long."

The way he spoke to other dancers was similar: in short, direct, irate sentences, as if politeness was a waste of his valuable time and the things he wanted should have been obvious. He treated us as if we were disobeying rules, defying him, deliberately trying to irritate him.

After months of delay, when no contract or job offer appeared, I began to doubt myself. My brain had always turned to self-criticism when it was unsure.

I'm probably too fat. If I were thinner, if my hips were as narrow as Katia's or my arms as tiny as Galia's, the Bolshoi would want me.

I returned to the eating disorder I'd always relied on to deal with difficult emotions, loss of control. Part of my brain told me, *This is not helping.*

But I didn't know what else to do. I'd drawn a connection in my brain from anxiety straight to self-harm. Punishment was still the action that felt most familiar and safe.

I stayed in that way of thinking for a few weeks—immersed in the slick and oily shame that clung to me like a suffocating film. I allowed myself to believe that my failures and deficiencies were the reasons I couldn't be accepted at the Bolshoi.

But there came a moment, as I stood in the hallway outside Vaziev's office with a bunch of other quiet and submissive dancers, when I thought, *This is embarrassing.*

And that was it. I stopped taking classes at the Bolshoi. I stopped trying to make myself into a person who would do whatever it took to be accepted there.

Looking back, I'm proud of myself at that moment.

But I still wasn't brave enough to choose the life I wanted just because I wanted it. Working as a freelancer in Moscow felt great, but I still craved official validation and acceptance. If I couldn't have the Bolshoi, I wanted to be chosen by another theater, another director who'd worked themselves into a position of authority in the upper echelons of the ballet hierarchy.

"No one is going to take a twenty-five-year-old freelancer seriously," my friends had been telling me. "You should spend more time working in a theater at this point in your career. You should give America a try."

A few weeks later, when I got a call from a director at Boston Ballet, asking me how quickly I could be available to move back to the United States, I felt validated and wanted. This director promised me a good contract and soloist roles at a respected American company.

I had never worked in a U.S. ballet troupe.

Maybe this is the next step in my career. Maybe this is what I need.

I accepted the offer, bought a plane ticket, packed my bags, and flew west.

Chapter 30

Culture Shock

I came to Boston in the sizzling asphalt heat of August 2019, when I was twenty-five years old. I carried with me an ulcer of anxiety about the nearing horizon of my career. There are go-years in ballet—one and a half decades, maybe two—when you get to dance. You give away your entire childhood, and, if you're lucky, you get to spend your twenties and thirties in painful, shining, out-of-breath performances. And then it's over, gone before you know it, and you have to find something else to do.

I'd often wondered if I was missing out by not giving American ballet companies a chance. I was American, after all. And life in America was good, right? It was a place Balanchine and Baryshnikov and Makarova had all chosen over Russia. It was a place that offered legitimacy and stability. And, in 2019, it was a place that offered me a job.

I have made a lot of terrible decisions, but it turns out that moving to America—the country of my birth, family, childhood, and citizenship—is up there among my worst.

At first, it seemed to me, to my parents, and to my new theater managers that setting up life in a major American metropolis would be easy. It was expected that I would feel at home in the chain-link fences, Dunkin' Donuts shops, parking ramps, and oversized garbage cans of a major American city. I was twenty-five years old. No one doubted that

I would know about things like car insurance and American cell phone plans.

But I had never lived in the United States as an adult before. I had never driven a car, never built up the mysterious and important bureaucratic necessity of a credit score. I didn't have a Netflix subscription, a library card, a driver's license, a 401(k), or a T-Mobile contract. I had never graduated from an American high school. My English had taken on an Eastern European accent. Boston was completely foreign.

Navigating international airports and conjugating verbs in multiple languages, I could do, no problem. Turning thirty-two fouettés in a row on a raked stage or dancing a classical ballet variation with a new partner and zero rehearsal time? Absolutely. But driving in an American city? Opening a U.S. bank account? This was completely new territory.

Every theater I'd worked at in the past had helped me find housing, and everywhere I'd traveled in the world had been filled with generous friends who opened their homes and their lives to me. I'd never rented my own apartment.

How hard could it be? Five hundred dollars a month for an apartment in Boston is plenty.

The morning after I landed at Logan International Airport, I went straight to the theater to get my assignments. For the first week, I lived in the guest room of a friend of a friend of friend. But then this host began to speak about the other guests they had coming, the space they needed that I was taking.

I found a place to sleep on another acquaintance's couch until that acquaintance began speaking about the cost of their mortgage and electricity bills and the need to contribute.

I moved from couch to couch, home to home, trying to make as little noise as possible in the living rooms of people on whom I felt I was trespassing. I kept my things in compact folds in my suitcase, avoided using the bathroom or kitchen at inconvenient times. I tried to shrink myself into an unnoticeable and un-irritating package, like a ghost whose presence was felt only at night, but who disappeared in the morning onto hours of bus rides, ballet classes, and rehearsals. I hid in libraries and public parks and empty rehearsal studios.

I had no place to cook regular meals or get enough rest. I watched the weight melt from my body, my clothing stretch and fall limp from my shoulders. I attended ballet classes and scanned online rental listings on my phone that I couldn't afford.

Why, I wondered, *is it so easy to become homeless in America?*

I called my parents for help.

"You're an adult," they said. "You need to figure this out on your own."

I asked my company for help—a raise, a temporary place to stay, an advance to help me make a security deposit, or a letter that would convince a landlord to let me move in.

But my new bosses had nothing to offer me.

"That's up to you," they said.

And late on an afternoon just three weeks after I'd left Russia, when a Boston Ballet director called me into their office and asked me to step on a scale, I saw, in the gray digital numbers in front of my face, that I had lost a dangerous amount of weight in only three weeks.

"Hmmm," the director said. "Let's get you to a doctor to do some bloodwork."

The bloodwork was conclusive. There was a dearth of electrolytes, vitamins, and minerals in my body. The ability of my kidneys to continue functioning was in peril.

"You have an eating disorder," the doctors told me.

"Yes, I do. It's a problem," I said. "But what I really need is a place to live. I'm just stressed and tired, and I need a place where I can keep groceries and cook for myself and sleep."

"Your kidneys are going to fail," they said.

They admitted me to the hospital, dressed me in a scratchy white gown, and stuck needles into my veins to pump my body with fluids.

Nurses brought me trays of lukewarm, plastic-wrapped hospital food and composed meticulous lists of what I ate.

After two weeks, I was admitted to an in-patient clinic filled with girls who spoke about wanting to kill themselves, who cut their food into minuscule pieces and threw it under the table. They were injected with needles, attached to IVs. They pushed the staff when they were angry. Sometimes they screamed.

This was a place where shoelaces were not allowed on footwear and the doors on toilet and shower stalls were removed. Nurses asked us to stand in lines for medication that we swallowed while they watched our throats bob and checked our tongues to make sure the pills actually went down.

In the mornings, we ate at tables under the monitoring eyes of staff members, our plates piled with lukewarm, processed chicken nuggets and over-salted, mushy vegetables. It was the type of processed American food that, after years of gluten-free, vegan home cooking, made my stomach cramp and roil with nausea.

But the worst part was that exercise was not allowed.

After years of constant movement, I felt insane. I craved the endorphins that came from warming my muscles, running my heart, stretching and working and kneading my body like a mint-flavored piece of gum. It felt like imprisonment to be ordered into stillness. I wanted to climb the walls. But even in my room, where I tried to stretch the anxiety out of my body in secret beside my bed, a fellow patient with whom I shared space threatened to report me.

"I'll tell them you're stretching," she said. "If you don't keep me happy, I will report you. I will find where you live. I will track you down. You can't escape."

It's true that I was desperately sick, that my disordered way of eating was destroying my body. There were doctors who pointed to the things my withdrawn blood and X-rayed bones were telling them: the years of furtive starvation and obsessive vomiting had eaten away at me like a cancer. My bones were weakened; I had early-onset arthritis. The stress fractures that flared like storms in my foot every spring were the result of severe malnutrition. The strange, fuzzy lanugo that grew on my wasted arms and the hair that fell from my skull, the swelling in my face and the rounded distention of my belly, were all stages of starvation.

And it wasn't just physical issues. I had regular bouts of heavy depression and debilitating, radioactive shame. I could not see my beautiful, faithful, miraculous body for the marvel that it was. I had, for nearly as long as I could remember, wanted to escape into a mechanical, un-feeling, un-faltering existence.

I needed help. But the clinic to which I'd been admitted felt like a prison—a place more interested in controlling me than helping me. I couldn't understand the rigid rules and plans they set up for my rehabilitation. Why could I not eat more fresh vegetables and fruit? Why could I not move my body out of stiffness and pain? Why was I given silly stretch band exercises when my triceps wanted to push against weights and my abdominal muscles wanted to tuck me into pirouettes?

I wanted someone to see the pain I was in and help me. But this was a place that didn't seem to see me for who I was at all. They saw me as a diagnosis—a math equation to be stacked vertical and formulaic over a line, then subtracted into a number within the confines of their clinical definitions and preconceptions.

My sister came to see me at the inpatient clinic where I'd been committed. She saw the mumblings of my roommate, the missing doors in the bathroom, the cornered look in my eyes.

"We need to get you out of here," she said.

She and my mom found me an apartment in Boston with university student roommates and a rent I could afford. My sister paid my security deposit, and she got me checked out of the clinic, like someone breaking a prisoner out of maximum security.

Before Boston I had been strong, confident, razor sharp. After years of dedication, I had calibrated every ligament, muscle, and tendon to play in harmony like a well-tuned violin. I was filled with inspiration and artistic purpose. When I stepped into the dance studio, I felt my leg under me, solid as a tree, my toe and toe joint pushing into the ground. Partners thought they were lucky to be beside me, to lift me on their hands or spin me in flashes of tulle and sequin beside them in the spotlight. Audiences across the world applauded me. People respected me. I was a prima ballerina.

But the months I'd spent in America—the unstable housing, the wild spread of my eating disorder, the time I'd spent at the in-patient clinic—destroyed me

My muscles weakened and wobbled. I slouched in corners and waited on couches. My stomach cramped in continual pain from the chemical-laced food. I was watched and controlled, not just in when and how and what I ate, but where I slept, how I moved, when I moved. I had to get permission to stretch, to put on pointe shoes, to jump, to turn. My body felt cornered and exhausted.

So much of my eating disorder was about bypassing stress and shame by imposing a harsh and self-destructive control on what I allowed in my stomach. But the treatment I received in Boston did nothing to heal the things that had hurt me. It didn't teach me how to make decisions to help or be kind to myself; it just took decisions away from me.

Everything about Boston was terrible.

But I can't say I regretted moving there, because Boston is the reason Andrew became part of my life.

Andrew was a person I had known for several years. A mutual friend, who lived in Moscow, had introduced us.

"He's the perfect guy for you," this friend had said. "He's the type of person I want my daughters to marry one day."

I messaged him online, just to make Beth happy. He was polite and friendly, living in America, snowboarding in mountains, playing worship songs on the guitar and piano. He was an entrepreneur who marketed music to churches. He was the type of person I knew my parents would like, the type of person who wouldn't want to be in a relationship with a twenty-something divorced woman.

But it didn't matter what he thought of me. I wasn't interested in him. I lived in Russia. I loved living in Russia. And I was dating someone else. Andrew lived in Boston. He was far away. It wasn't possible to date someone if your futures weren't headed in the same direction.

We met once or twice when I ventured west on trips to guest-perform at a theater in Los Angeles. In person, he was tall with deep-set blue eyes, a wide forehead. For years I couldn't decide if I thought he was handsome. But I liked the kind messages he sent me on Facebook, the ways in which he was easy to talk to.

We messaged on and off for years and sometimes met for dinner when I was passing through a city close to him. He was very Christian, and I, by that time, had moved away from the evangelical church. The judgment and comments over my divorce had been too much. I also couldn't understand the cruelty I'd seen church leaders show toward people who were queer or congregants who didn't live the idealized lives to which they encouraged people to aspire.

By the time I met Andrew, my faith had softened. I no longer waited for God to cleanse or punish me. Instead, I relied on the divine like I might depend on sunlight—as something that warmed me and waited—glowing, approving, steadfast, and kind behind every storm that blew into my life. In Moscow, I occasionally attended an Anglican church. I'd watched my brothers and sisters decide they didn't want to be Christians. I understood them. But faith was still important to me. I just didn't want the judgmental, nationalistic, corporate version of it.

I still wasn't sure which type of faith Andrew ascribed to. But I liked talking to him, and, when I arrived in Boston, he called me. He had moved to California for work but wanted to see me.

"I'm going to be in New York next weekend for a wedding," he said. "I just realized I need a plus one. Do you want to be my plus one?"

I did want to be his plus one. I needed to go to New York anyway to help my grandmother with a construction project at her apartment. Andrew bought me a bus ticket and met me at the station.

By then I had decided. He was handsome. We followed each other around New York—into my grandmother's apartment that floated above the Hudson and the tips of skyscrapers and the green, cotton-candy treetops of Central Park. We wandered the halls of the Metropolitan Museum of Art, gazed at the muscular, windswept pillars of Van Gogh's *Cypresses*. We drove the highways north to upstate New York. We talked about music and composers, and, during the wedding of his friends, we laughed over candles and funny speeches, and I found myself thinking, *This person is amazing*.

Back in New York, he dropped me off at the bus station and said, "I want to keep getting to know you. Can I have your permission to keep texting you?"

Yes.

Andrew found other reasons to visit Boston.

"I'm going to be in town next week," he'd say. "I have a job interview."

But was it a job interview? Or was it an excuse to come to Boston? I didn't ask; I was just happy to see him.

In Boston, Andrew was the only part of my life I liked. I was flummoxed by my American dance colleagues who walked around with ice in their coffee and enormous bottles of water in their hands. I was angry at my theater director for not giving me the roles he'd promised, and I was desperate to return to the level of elite dancing I'd been used to; to be seen, once again, as a person with an entire life—not just an eating disorder.

Andrew saw me as a whole and beautiful person. When he came to Boston, he followed me in the early mornings from my crowded university student apartment to the empty studios at the theater, where he sat at a piano and played music while I warmed up and stretched and did my own barre exercises.

He took me out to dinner and found coffee shops where he could sit across from me, his face lit up, listening to me talk. He flew to Texas to meet my family, charm my mother, sit on the porch steps for long talks with my dad. He put on a suit jacket and followed me to work galas to shake the hands of my colleagues and dance together to pop music under the blue and purple lights that shone at events for wealthy donors. In hotel lobbies and shopping malls, he found pianos to play—places to make music and art where before there had been only silence or the roar of traffic or the hum of people speaking about what they wanted to buy.

He loved art. He loved my dancing. He loved spending time with me. He might, I was beginning to think, love me.

CHAPTER 31

Ranching

Andrew came to visit me in Boston in March of 2020. The winter had begun to thaw, and Boston's lawns were brown.

The city was on edge. You could feel it in the spring-damp streets, the subdued traffic. My phone had begun to feed me a steady drumbeat of news alerts: warnings of a spreading virus; increasingly hyper pleas for regular hand washing; the Lysoling of door handles, countertops, newly purchased vegetables.

But I was nervous for other reasons. I was back at the theater, back up to a healthy weight, back in Boston Ballet's repertoire. I had spent months regaining muscle and cardiovascular capacity after leaving the clinic. I'd been working hard, learning the steps to six different ballets. I was preparing to debut a role in *Carmen*. But I hadn't had enough time to rehearse this newest piece, and my sleep had begun to fill with the anxiety dreams every dancer has about being pushed out on stage, their mind a blank, their body frozen in front of an audience because they can't remember the choreography.

On stage, I rehearsed in an angst-filled rush. But then the director stepped on to the floor, while we waited, still sweaty, for corrections.

"Well done, everyone," he said. "But we actually have to cancel tomorrow's performance. We'll let you know more soon."

At first I was relieved—I wouldn't have to go out on stage unprepared.

Andrew had arrived that day for a visit. He drove straight to the theater from the airport.

"They canceled *Carmen*," I told him.

"Really? For how long?" he asked.

I didn't know. But the next morning we went together to the theater and found it empty. No one sat in the cushioned audience chairs. No one used the Pilates equipment. No one stood in the vaulted two-story studio where Andrew played piano, his back against the mirrors while I, in my black leggings and sports bra, turned pirouettes on a spacious floor.

On our way back to my apartment, the roads were eerily calm, and when we went to the grocery store, we found people rushing around in masks, their carts piled high with canned goods and peanut butter and dried beans. Outside we saw a convertible leaving town, its backseat overflowing with boxes. When we returned to my apartment, I found my roommates nervous, planning to abandon the city.

Andrew was worried too. His parents were the type of people who invested in storage containers filled with ammunition and emergency rations of water and food. They had begun speaking darkly of quarantines and apocalypse scenarios. They warned of cities closing, restricted movement.

After just escaping months of a claustrophobic in-patient treatment center, I was terrified at the thought of being trapped in Boston, or anywhere, against my will.

"If shit hits the fan," Andrew asked me, "where do you want to be?"

His family owned a ranch in New Mexico. It was remote; it was available for us to visit. It seemed like exactly the sort of place you'd want to be if the zombie apocalypse descended.

"Should we go to New Mexico?" he asked.

And I thought, *If work is canceled, why not?*

Andrew bought tickets. We threw our things into suitcases. We locked the apartment behind us.

It will just be for a week or two, I thought.

The ranch owned by Andrew's parents was high in the mountains of northern New Mexico. We found it—a collection of pole barns, horse corrals and wooden lodge buildings—abandoned at the foot of dry brown hills, mounded with snow in the northside shadows, and dotted with bristlecone pine.

The air was still and cold when we arrived, and the buildings were covered with a layer of dust and debris as if the person they'd paid to watch over it had left a window open during the winter months.

We unloaded our rental car, rolled up our sleeves, and got to work.

There were cobwebs and dead birds to clear, grimy windows to wash and fabrics to scrub, gravel driveways to resurface, wood to chop, weeds to pull, floors to mop. It felt like we'd tumbled into a wormhole and landed in a chapter of *Little House on the Prairie*.

I loved it.

In the mornings I woke to a pink sunrise outside a log cabin, laced my tennis shoes, and set off on runs into the mountains. I jogged up gravel roads where the air was so fresh, it tasted sweet. I crossed paths with dark-eyed mule deer and twitchy-nosed gophers. I practiced online ballet classes in the high-ceilinged lodge, holding my hand on wooden bar stools and listening to far-off digital voices calmly move through the familiar routines of pliés, battements, and tendus.

Time didn't seem to apply in this alternate dimension in which I'd found myself. There was just Andrew, confident in the wide-brimmed cowboy hat he began wearing on his head, the pine-scented logs he piled into bonfires, the truck engines he repaired, and the horses he rubbed down with stiff-haired brushes at night. He held my hand on walks through dry grass fields, beside clear, icy streams of water. His parents came to visit, and he and his mother taught me to ride horses, my breast-bone and pelvis aligned with the horse's back, my inner thighs squeezed together like a long-held relevé. Andrew brewed me cups of tea at night and sat with me on the couch, strumming a guitar and singing.

It was the most relaxed I could remember ever being. It felt like I'd disappeared into a normal, slow-paced life—the sort of life I might have had if I hadn't thrown myself into the world of ballet. There were no floor-length mirrors, no cascades of performances to rehearse, no critiques from directors or passive-aggressive feuds with colleagues.

In New Mexico, with Andrew and the horses, I was happy.

I still had a contract with Boston Ballet, but it was suspended. First, I and all my colleagues were put on layoff, our paychecks frozen for what I thought would be a two-week pause to let the virus wash past the city like a wave. But I soon realized the pause would be much longer than two weeks. I saw, in emails that appeared on my phone, that the entire theater season was canceled.

It wasn't just Boston—the whole country had shut down.

Our dancers' union had no solutions—just lobbying they did to get the theater to agree to hold our positions while buildings were closed and public gatherings at theaters, or anywhere else, were prohibited. There was talk of long-distance Pilates classes and pods of dancers who would be able to do daily barre work, rehearse, and eventually perform digital shows together.

I was angry at the way American theaters were funded, the way they treated performers, the way the entire system of health care and transportation and employment functioned in my home country. Yes, there was a pandemic, but even before things had shut down, I'd been angry at a sort of dishonest American optimism that said, "Anyone can do anything!" But, really, what people meant was, you were on your own, constantly unsure, pulling yourself up by your bootstraps.

"In Russia, the government pays for theaters and ballet schools and dancer salaries," I told Andrew. "They invest in the arts—even in the smallest regional theaters."

I was hearing from my friends in Russia by then. They were still getting paid. Theaters were beginning to open, there was talk of a vaccine, there was pay and stability and opportunity for dancers.

"Why is it that the authoritarian countries are better at supporting the arts?" I wondered aloud to Andrew.

By early summer, I was in agony. I missed the forward motion of working a theater season: the opening of curtains in September, the endless repetition of *Nutcracker* at Christmastime, the debuts and pas de deux and morning classes and choreography. I started to feel like a horse that was built to run, but forced to stay in a stable, just looking at the hills.

I had never liked Boston, and, as I spoke to my managers there about what their plans were, when I might start dancing or earn another paycheck, I could not understand when or how things would change. It didn't seem possible to be a ballerina if I stayed in America.

I bought my return plane ticket to Moscow while sitting in the passenger seat of a car, Andrew driving east beside me, his hand wrapped around the smooth curve of the steering wheel.

I had come to love those hands. They were strong, sure, and kind. I had seen them coax music out of the black and white keys of a piano, gentle a hay-scented horse, pass money to a homeless stranger who needed it, repair the greasy metal belly of a pickup engine.

Andrew was someone who was capable and trustworthy. Andrew was someone I loved.

But I didn't tell him about the plane ticket. I double-checked the dates of the flight, made sure the departure and arrival cities were right. Then I scrolled with my thumb to the bottom of the screen of my phone and clicked 'purchase.'

Flight confirmed.

It had been more than four months since I'd last set foot in a theater, since I'd last been fitted for a costume or waited behind the darkened wings of a stage to perform for an audience. I had, in that time, considered my life choices.

Is ballet worth it? Has it kept me from normalcy and happiness? Have I allowed ambition to eat me alive? Would I be happier in a quiet American life, apron around my waist, family filling my home, energy poured into Bible studies, dinner parties, housekeeping, and contentment? Maybe it's time for me to retire and start teaching.

I had met Andrew's family at their ranch, and we had driven cross-country to meet his friends in California, at his old apartment. In the time we'd spent together, Andrew had decided he wanted to leave the friends and life he'd built out west in order to take a job closer to Boston, closer to me and closer to the professional dreams he had for himself.

The people he'd been living with, the friends he was giving up, were beautiful. They smiled at us when we arrived to visit, invited us to community dinners and welcomed us to the life they lived, which was organized around worship songs, outdoor hikes, game nights, and Bible studies. Their words were filled with certainty and conviction about God's plans for them and for the world. For several days, I had imagined myself in their reality—married, committed to church and family, dressed in soft sweaters, planted like a flower in an evangelical American garden.

For hours at a time, that sort of life seemed like a possibility. But deep down, I knew I didn't want it. This was something I understood when I spoke in Russian on the phone to my friends who lived on the other side of the world. Or when I stood alone at the barre in a small-town dance studio; when I felt my muscles warm and stretch and discipline themselves to movements that were like half-remembered songs from a bygone era.

I loved the constellation of artists and performers I had come to know in theaters all over the world. They were both gorgeous and confounding, dangerous and magical. And I loved the art form I had pursued since childhood. It was riddled with a complicated elixir of beauty and dysfunction. But none of it fit in the possible lives I could imagine in America with Andrew.

I had, in the months I'd been living in Boston and New Mexico, received invitations to join theaters in Russia and Ukraine. I had been offered leadership positions in well-funded regional dance companies. My dance partner, Misha, had moved his wife and kids to one of these companies and was filled with excitement for the career possibilities. An old friend from the Bolshoi Ballet was now a director at a newly built theater in southern Russia.

"Come join us," Misha told me. "You would be a principal dancer. This would be a new era in your career."

These were words I had never stopped wanting to hear. I didn't want to be done dancing.

I finally accepted the job offer, in Russian, on the phone, sitting in the car next to Andrew, without telling him.

He had begun to feel uncomfortable during the hours I spoke in Russian beside him.

"I don't know what you're saying," he told me.

"This is me, this is my life," I said. "You can't ask me to not speak Russian."

But the air in the car was very still after I told him I was moving back.

"When?" he wanted to know.

"In a few weeks," I said.

"You already bought your ticket?" he asked.

"Yes. If I don't do this now, I'm going to regret it," I said. "I need to take control of my life."

"But why wouldn't you ask me about this?" he said, his face staring east at the life on the other side of the country he'd been trying to build around our relationship. "We're supposed to tell each other these things. You're supposed to tell me if you buy a plane ticket to move to another country."

"First of all, our relationship is not defined," I said thinking of the mountaintop picnics we'd had, the trail rides we'd taken, the times I'd thought he might ask me to marry him. He hadn't proposed. We hadn't even discussed marriage.

"Second of all, I can decide what I want for my career," I added. "We're not married. We're not engaged. I'm free to do whatever I want."

Part of me was thinking of the amorphous reality of our actual relationship. But part of me was remembering the ways men in past relationships had expected things from me that they hadn't defined, that I hadn't agreed to, that neither of us had ever communicated. Part of me was afraid of being forced into a situation in which I wouldn't be able to stay.

I could see the confusion and hurt and anger on his face in the way his eyebrows knit together and the way his hands gripped the steering wheel.

"I thought"—his blue eyes glanced in question at mine as we drove—"I thought that's where our relationship was headed."

"How can you know that I'm what you want?" I asked him. "You don't really know me, not the real me."

We had started dating when I was sick, when I was living in America, working at a company that gave me lowly *corps* roles. He had fallen in love with me in his world, staying on a ranch while I cleaned house and learned to ride horses. It sounded like the version of life a Hallmark movie heroine might choose: ballerina marries cowboy, moves to the wild west. But the reality of it was something that didn't fit who I was or what I wanted.

Andrew hadn't seen me in Russia. He didn't know what I was capable of, didn't understand who I was.

"I know I love you," he said, his eyes back on the road, his face still and waiting. "I know what I want."

I believed him when he said it. But I also knew he was trying to sign us both up for something he didn't understand. This was a situation familiar to me. In risks I had taken before, in ways I had joined myself to men before, things had gone badly. I had allowed myself to be backed into corners, trapped in difficult situations, turned into a person cut off from the things that made me happiest.

"You can't love me if you don't know me," I told him. "You can't ask me to give up ballet. I've made that choice before, and I'm not afraid to make it again."

CHAPTER 32

Goodbye

Andrew drove me back to Boston, to the apartment I'd abandoned in March. We found it dusty and empty. The roommates I'd been living with were scattered by pandemic restrictions, class cancellations, endings. We confronted the empty rooms, and, just as I'd helped him with his move, he helped me take apart my furniture, pack my belongings, clean out my room, ready my suitcases for Moscow. We moved around that apartment with gentleness, tender to each other, frightened to destroy with our words the kindness and belonging we'd built during our months together.

But eventually, the terrible conversation came. We sat in the empty living room on the black couch my roommate had left behind.

"Joy, if you're leaving, what have the past six months been? Who are we?" Andrew said, his face sadder than I'd ever seen it.

"Of course I want my future to be with you, but you've always told me you're not interested in being long-distance," I said, watching the way his eyebrows knit together on his forehead in hurt.

He was confident and sure-footed in all the scenarios in which I'd ever seen him: at fancy restaurants and parties, in marble concert halls or art galleries; on horseback lassoing a cow, or strumming the strings of a guitar. But I couldn't imagine him following me to Russia. And I had already decided—Russia was the place I wanted to live. I had tried America on like a costume, and it didn't fit. I missed the person I had been in Russia. I wanted to go back to cities where I had friends and job offers. I wanted to live in a country that spent more tax dollars on art. I wanted to be in a place that loved ballet.

I felt tears filling my eyes as I watched him.

"I know I want to be with you," he said. "The reason I haven't brought up marriage is because I know you're afraid of it. But there's not a doubt in my mind."

"But you don't know the real me," I said. "You don't know the Russian me, the me who is strong and resilient, the me who would do anything to dance. You can't make a commitment without knowing me because you don't know what you're saying yes to."

"I know that I love you," Andrew said. "That's something I know for sure. What would you say if I asked you to marry me?"

"But would you be willing to move to Russia?" I asked him. "Long-distance is not what you want. What would happen if I lived on the other side of the world? What would happen if I left for months at a time on dance tours?"

We both cried, sitting in the shadows of an empty apartment on a Boston afternoon in July. We were both in love. But that didn't mean I wasn't leaving.

In New York, before my flight, we spent the dwindling number of days we had left together in my grandmother's old apartment. I introduced Andrew to my New York friends, I took ballet classes, I spent hours on the phone with Misha and Dima, planning the work I'd begin once I arrived at my new theater in the southern Russian city of Astrakhan.

On an afternoon in September, Andrew and I went to Central Park and lay on a blanket in the grass. We watched the water of the reservoir reflect back the blue bowl of sky and the shimmering towers of Manhattan. Andrew had planned the perfect day for us, like an exclamation mark on the end of the perfect months we'd spent in America together. He'd taken me on a helicopter ride over the city, past the raised green arm of the Statue of Liberty. He'd held my hand as we walked in the park on late summer grass past joggers and families out enjoying the warmth of September.

It felt like we were letting our time together go to rest gently, like a mother tucking her child in for the night. It didn't seem possible that our relationship would survive after I moved six thousand miles away to southern Russia and he drove west to Nashville. But we were certain that we loved each other, certain that the end of our togetherness was something that made us sad.

"Let's see how it goes," we'd told each other. Maybe a solution would present itself in future months that would keep us from having to be done with each other.

In the park, Andrew said he had a song to play me on the guitar he'd brought with him. It was a song he'd written for me himself.

"Our love is here to stay," he sang, smiling into my eyes. "I know we can travel the world, and in the end you'll still be my girl."

It was a moment of incandescent happiness, a moment I knew, as it was happening, that I never wanted to let go of. But it was also a moment that was painful, and, as I listened to him, I started to cry because I knew he was amazing and that, when I was with him, I felt safe and loved. And still, I was planning to leave.

Andrew put down his guitar and wrapped his arms around me. We stood and walked to the edge of the water, where the city rose over sparkling blue. I could feel my mascara staining the shoulder of his white T-shirt as I smiled and cried, temporarily safe under his shoulder.

Andrew took his arm off me. Then he sank to his knee and took a ring out of his pocket.

"I love you," he said. "I never want to let you go. I want to take care of you. I want to spend the rest of my life with you. Will you marry me?"

I was already crying, but this made me cover my face and weep. I had been married once before, and I could see the sweet, simple unreality of the type of love he believed in—biblical commitment and worship songs and family values. This was a type of love that I'd heard preached about in churches. But I knew—promises from others were things that fell apart. The only thing that could be relied on was a commitment to yourself and to the pursuit of things that you love, not because they were deemed correct by others, but because they were part of something inside you.

But Andrew's blue eyes were looking up at me, and I knew how kind and good he was. I loved him, and I wanted to be with him.

I said yes. He slipped the ring, sparkling, onto my finger and gathered me in his arms. And the way that I felt then was deeply in love, terrified, exquisitely happy.

That day in New York, I agreed to marry one of the most beautiful humans I'd ever met. And within a matter of hours, I left him and flew to Moscow.

I felt a breath of relief as soon as I boarded my Aeroflot plane to Moscow. There were flight announcements in Russian, attendants in red suits and passengers talking in the low, harsh language for which I immediately realized I'd been homesick. A plane steward with a scarf around her neck showed me to a comfortable seat in business class, poured me a sparkling beverage, and wished me a safe flight.

In Moscow, the Sheremetyevo airport I'd first seen when I'd arrived in the city eleven years earlier had disappeared. It had long since been replaced with a gleaming set of space-age glass and steel terminals that were bright, clean, and efficient. I felt, as I stepped off the plane, rolled my suitcase on the smooth floors, heard the sounds of a calm, overhead voice announcing flight departures in Russian, like hugging one of the burnished-metal support pillars.

Moscow was still in the grip of pandemic restrictions. People wore masks and scanned QR codes at restaurants to avoid touching shared menus or transferring invisible sicknesses with wait staff. But the city was even more beautiful and comfortable than I remembered. After sailing through customs, I stepped seamlessly onto an express train that swept me to the center of Moscow, then glided my suitcases into the marble-walled metro tunnel. I ordered food on my phone to be delivered to my apartment, booked a massage and training session at my gym, then a nail appointment at my favorite salon.

Everything seemed cleaner, more convenient, and more affordable than I remembered. Better than even my beloved New York City. And once I let myself into my tiny apartment and stepped to the window to see the sun shining on the Moskva River and the red walls of the Kremlin, I felt like hugging myself.

I'm home.

I was in Moscow for only a week. I saw my friends, I put my apartment in order, I sat in a cushioned nail salon chair and watched as a Russian woman swiped polish onto the ends of my fingers, then adorned them with tiny swirls of glitter and pinprick rhinestones.

"I'm moving to Astrakhan," I told her.

"Astrakhan?" she asked, incredulous. "Why on earth would you go there? What's in Astrakhan?"

CHAPTER 33

Astrakhan

What was in Astrakhan was a monstrously large and well-funded opera and ballet theater.

The city of Astrakhan itself was not exactly a popular destination. It had been growing into what was now the southern edge of Russia for hundreds of years. Fewer than five hundred thousand people lived in its apartment buildings and ramshackle wooden homes on grids of dusty streets. Compared to Moscow, this city, which was sunk into the Volga River delta on a northern bend of the Caspian Sea, was impoverished—those who had jobs mostly worked in the fishing industry or a gas processing plant.

Astrakhan's single-runway airport was bumpy, and, when I stepped into the terminal after my flight, it felt as though I had landed in 2001. The building was filled with plastic doors and glass cabinets displaying piles of tinned caviar, bear skins, and taxidermized sturgeon. Stray dogs roamed the parking lot, and the asphalt roads were cracked like dry skin in winter.

But the ballet theater for which I'd come rose out of the city center like a green-roofed Russian casino trying to imitate Versailles. It was set in a place of honor in Astrakhan's historic interior, surrounded by a wide swathe of weedy lawn, burbling fountains, and paved-over park land. I was driven there in a rattling van, greeted at a side door by a new colleague, and shown to a hotel room deep within its stone walls.

It wasn't the first time I had been to this particular theater. I'd danced on its stages before during a guest performance with Misha. The theater was incongruous with the rest of the city. It loomed out of dilapidated houses and dusty streets like a gaudy, expensive wedding cake lowered from another dimension. It had been spoken into existence by presidential decree a decade before by Putin himself—a literal gift from the Kremlin to the city of Astrakhan on its 450th birthday.[1]

I knew by then the power of the presidential gaze. If Putin's face shone in your direction, it was like the sun. Grown men were fired or raised to powerful new positions. Cities were paved with granite; bridges stretched across expanses where before there had been only water, sand, and sky. When Putin set his eye on the World Cup, stadiums, airports, and infrastructure bloomed in cities like billion-dollar daisies. Putin was in charge. He had just recently completed a referendum to change the constitution to allow him to remain in power for another sixteen years.

In Astrakhan, no one I knew even spoke about this. Putin was a given. And the people who lived in Astrakhan—city officials, theater directors, shop assistants, and taxi drivers—had all arranged themselves, like a satellite on Russia's southern periphery, to orbit around his gravity of power—a planetary fact of reality that had led the country in stability for more than twenty years.

Surviving or thriving in Russia was all about scrambling to get yourself to a patch of ground on which the Kremlin powers had indicated their attention would shine. And in Russia, I had learned, the sun shone with reliability on ballet.

Ballet was the sort of thing considered patriotic, central to Russia's national identity. And for more than a decade, I had plugged myself into this world of passion, prestige, and myth-making. Ballet in Russia was like ballet nowhere else in the world that I had ever found. It didn't seem to matter where in the country I went: Perm, Ekaterinburg, Vladivostok, Mirny, or the dust-covered streets of Astrakhan. I could find a theater that hallowed the art form to which I had dedicated my life.

I had tried living and working in enough other places to appreciate my circumstances. No matter how poverty-stricken and run-down the Russian city I'd come to might have been, I was deeply grateful to be there.

I was welcomed with open arms in Astrakhan. The theater managers gave me an outsized salary, a well-appointed dressing room, a long roster of prima roles, and a leadership position in the ballet troupe. My former Bolshoi colleague Dima had been given the title of artistic director in this theater. He saw me as someone who would help him achieve a position of honor for Astrakhan on Russia's artistic map. He'd invited both Misha Martyniuk and me to principal contracts, and I'd answered his call. I descended on the theater with suitcases full of gear and permission to perform Balanchine in a city where Balanchine had never previously been performed.

We had big dreams and the license and financial backing to make them come true. We felt, in Astrakhan, like we'd graduated to a plane of existence in which the elite and powerful world of Russian ballet had become our playground.

Dima put me in charge of leading morning classes, giving me the freedom and power to direct learning as I saw best. When I arrived in the mornings to the robin's-egg blue of Astrakhan's high-ceilinged ballet studio, I got to work. Dancers arrived at 9:30 a.m. They wore T-shirts and hoodies, bound their hair with bandanas. When they bent forward at the barre, silver chains with Orthodox crosses or Muslim crescents fell from their necks and swung around their chins. I commanded them to twist their legs into knots, bend their torsos over their knees, flatten their bodies against the floor, plié like frogs against a line on the ground to align their limbs in perfect turnout.

The troupe in Astrakhan had struggled with injuries for years, and my friend Dima wanted me to safeguard their ankles and tendons and hamstrings. I was full of ideas—Master Stretch techniques I'd learned in Florence, Neufit technology applications I'd learned from my mom's colleagues in Austin, vitamin doses designed by my mother that I'd been taking for years. My morning classes became mandatory, and I watched, with a deep sense of pride, as the troupe's injury rate plummeted.

A ballet coach from Perm was in charge of safeguarding me. This was a woman from one of Russia's most famed regional dance schools. She did not bother with niceties, but told me, in short-clipped, plain sentences if she thought my dancing was pathetic or my turnout abhorrent.

"What is that? It's terrible," she would scream. "No, no! Not like that, like this. Why are you so lazy?"

After the gentle methods of the American instructors I'd grown used to, classes with this new teacher were a jolt back to Russian reality. But I could tell this new teacher wanted me to progress. If I performed well, floating across the sky-blue background of the studio like an inverted lavender tulip in my long skirt and leotard, she was frank with her praise as well.

"*Very* good," she would bark, standing in front of the mirrors in her close-cropped haircut. "Super."

I had always appreciated Russians' ability to tell the truth exactly the way they saw it. In Russia, I never had to guess what people were thinking.

The best part of Astrakhan was its stage. It was raked and sprung like the Bolshoi, and it faced a half-drum auditorium with rows of plush red seats and a domed ceiling painted with a pink-and-blue mandala and hung with a glittering chandelier.

It was a place where I was given starring roles, accompanied by an entire orchestra, applauded by a passionate audience. The theater made me its prima. They designed costumes to fit my body and entire ballet performances to fit new choreography created expressly for me. They displayed photos of my performances on their website and in large posters hung around the city. Local TV channels interviewed me and aired segments of my dancing. People threw bouquets at my feet after I took my final bows and met me outside the theater with flowers and requests for autographs.

Teachers, colleagues, choreographers—even the orchestra—listened to me when I made requests for changes in footwork or the tempo of music.

I returned everything I was given right back to my theater. I handed my bouquets to the women who dressed me and cleaned the theater. I spent my hours in classes, trying to fill my lessons with practical tips and encouragement. When people were injured, I dropped what I was doing, rushed through the city, and leaped on stage in their stead.

I'm in charge of the atmosphere and the working conditions here, I told myself. *I set the tone, and I have the power to make this theater a good place or bad place.*

I knew what it was to feel hopeless and discouraged in a career, and I was determined to use the hardship I'd been through in the past to make the Astrakhan State Theater of Opera and Ballet an island of safety and hope for everyone who called it their professional home.

"I'm a prima ballerina," I told Andrew when I called him at night. "I'm so thankful to be here."

Andrew and I had begun arranging the details of our upcoming wedding, and Andrew was applying for a Russian visa. He planned to move to Astrakhan to join me after we were married. I'd found an apartment to rent near the city center. I'd begun attending a local Russian church where people seemed kind and welcoming. I visited nearby nail salons and coffee shops, bought furniture to fill the rooms of our future home. I adopted a poodle, named him Rachmaninoff, called him Rocky for short, and brought him to ballet classes at the theater, where he scampered around and lapped water while I led floor barre.

I began, once again, imagining my future in Russia, where it felt that the sky was the limit. If I wanted to serve art, my opportunities to do so were endless. I could live out my dance career in honored positions at well-funded Russian theaters. And after I was done with the stage, I could teach or direct or rise through the ranks of local and national political positions: to become a regional minister of culture if I wanted.

It made me think of Pat and the Lokkes and the teachers and champions who had made my dreams come true.

If I'm given these positions, just imagine what I could do—the lives I could change through moments of kindness and generosity.

By the time I moved to Astrakhan, I had been a principal dancer for many years. I had captured medals and honors from a myriad of international dance competitions, added them like master's degrees to my title. I was listed in performance programs as a laureate of various international honors.

But in Russia, there were other ladders to climb. In Russia, the best dancers, the career ballerinas, the truly great artists, were awarded medals of honor from the state.

It was a big deal. Like earning a PhD, Rhodes Scholarship, and a medal of valor all in one. Getting an Artist of Russia designation took years of work, excellent performances, letters of recommendation, and signatures from powerful people. But if you managed to jump through all the hoops, you got invited to a palace inside the Kremlin, and Putin himself draped a medal around your neck in a ceremony broadcast on national television. Then your name was hallowed with the "Artist of Russia" or "National Artist of Russia" distinction in every performance and introduction for the rest of your life. You got salary raises, extra bonuses, and privileges at Russian theaters. You became untouchable.

I desperately wanted to become a national artist of Russia. It was something most of the Russian prima ballerinas I admired had received. It was something all my teachers had earned. Misha Martyniuk had an "Artist of Russia" in front of his name. Zhanna, too, had been awarded this distinction.

But I was not a Russian citizen, and I could never receive this honor unless I became one.

Becoming a Russian citizen made sense. It would be easier to pay taxes, easier to stay in the country that felt like home. But the task seemed impossible. I had tried for years to gather the documents I needed. I'd even made friends with the bureaucrats at Astrakhan's immigration office, who were, as it turned out, big fans of ballet. I brought them tickets to my premieres and beautifully wrapped packages of candy. I sat at desks in their office and talked through different combinations of paperwork and legal justifications by which I might qualify. But no matter how we shaped it, there was a list of prerequisites, and now that I was no longer married to a Russian citizen, I just didn't meet them.

"Why don't you just ask Putin to give you citizenship?" This was something my friend Tanya suggested as she sat with me late at night in my apartment.

At first we laughed about it.

"I could be one of those people on the Putin call-in show," I joked, thinking of the annual televised event the Russian president held every year. It was a highly watched and carefully orchestrated tradition—the *Jerry Springer Show* of Russian politics. People from around the country called in with requests and questions, like subjects bringing petitions to a medieval czar.

Children called to ask Putin for fancy new dresses. Middle-aged women rang to ask the president to convince their husbands to allow them to purchase dogs.[2] Journalists and local officials asked about the economy or begged the president to do more to support the sale of the nationally beloved fermented brown-bread drink, kvass.[3]

But the more I thought about it, the more I wondered if a letter to Putin wasn't worth a try. I wanted to live in the country that had made my dreams come true, and I needed Russian citizenship to do that. Putin had the ability to grant it. What did I have to lose?

This is what I was thinking when I sat in the lamplight of my apartment in 2021. I typed out letters to Biden and Putin on my phone. To Biden, I wrote lines suggesting he consider the creation of a new national American honor for artists—something like the Kennedy Center Honor for lifetime achievements. It might encourage more investment in American art. Plus, if I couldn't get a National Artist of Russia designation, maybe I could get an American equivalent.

The letter for Putin I composed quickly, then read it out loud to my friend, half-joking.

"Dear Vladimir Vladimirovich," I wrote. "If you read this, please give me citizenship. I will always pay my taxes on time. I will serve culture here. I dream of becoming a People's Artist of Russia. Please, give me the opportunity to fulfill this dream."

I signed my name. I let him know I was a ballerina, working in Astrakhan, that I'd spent years studying and working in Russia. Then I emailed it to the presidential executive office and promptly forgot about it.

Two months later, I was at home, in my apartment in Astrakhan, when a knock sounded on my door. It was evening, and I was resting after a long day of ballet class and rehearsal, wearing my house clothes. The pounding startled me. I was not expecting guests, and I had not ordered anything delivered. When I opened the door, two men stood in front of me wearing jeans and dress shirts.

"Are you Womack Joy Annabelle?" they asked.

"Yes," I said, my hand clutching a spoon still holding a dollop of yogurt on it.

The two men glanced at each other. "You're an American; you've been living in Russia for a while, haven't you?" one of them said.

They seemed well-dressed, exceedingly well-mannered, nonthreatening.

"A long time, yes," I answered, puzzled.

The men wanted to know what I thought about ballet, about how Russian art compared to American performances.

I was very confused.

How do they know my name? How do they know where I went to school? Where I grew up?

I wasn't frightened, just amused and perplexed. These men were completely in control, calm, unhurried. They stood politely outside the door to my apartment and asked intelligent questions about Russian and American art, and I answered them—all of my sentences ending on an upward note, like, *What is happening right now?*

"We have been looking for you," they finally said. "We're with the Russian Federal Security Services, and we have a letter here from the Office of the President of the Russian Federation."

I stared at them, astonished. They handed me a sheet of paper.

"It's an answer to a request you sent to the president's office two months ago," they explained. "It came to our department here in Astrakhan. We tried to get it to you sooner, but couldn't find where you lived."

I could not have been more shocked if Putin himself had shown up in my stairwell.

"This is the letter you need to submit with your paperwork to get Russian citizenship," they told me.

The men smiled and congratulated me. They wished me well. Then they took off down the stairs, leaving me wide-eyed at my door.

As a rule, people generally do not want to be paid a late-night visit from the Russian Federal Security Services Officers. But to me, that night in 2021, it felt as if I'd been called on by two plainclothes Russian fairy godparents. With a flick of their all-powerful, bureaucracy-dissolving wands, they had granted me the wish I'd been hoping for since I'd moved to Moscow more than ten years before.

CHAPTER 34

American Wedding

We almost didn't make it. There were a few terrible moments when I in Astrakhan and Andrew in Nashville stared at each other in the fuzzy video of our phone screens and wondered, *Is this it? Should we call the whole thing off?*

I wanted him to understand that marriages don't magically work out, and that I was not the wife material I thought he was looking for. I was not like the American girls his friends were marrying. I was complicated and messy. I had committed divorce. I had forced myself to vomit for years. I was insecure, constantly injured, perpetually on the road, and obsessed with dance. I lived in Russia.

I knew what people wanted. I could sense, like a limbic hackle that rose on the back of my spine, the demands people would make of me. Most people wanted to be admired, complimented, flattered. From me, they expected beauty, strength, docility. They wanted me to be needless, eternally capable of accomplishing miracles of physical beauty and wonder out of literal thin air.

I knew how to give people what they were looking for, and I knew all about Andrew. He was a worship leader, a tamer of horses, a writer of songs. His friends had all married women who were beautiful and soft and kind. These were women who wanted to be mothers; their Instagram feeds were filled with smiling photos and Bible verses in curling scripts on gentle watercolor backgrounds. They drank chaga elixirs and regularly attended church.

I wondered if Andrew knew what he was getting himself into, marrying me. I knew how to dazzle people, how to put on a professional show, but I wasn't sure he knew the real me—the weakness and fear I hid behind all my accomplishments; the fierceness I threw at getting done what needed to get done. I kept pressing reality to him, checking to see if he could handle it. Backing away, offering, then threatening to call things off.

But Andrew was steady. He wanted, he insisted, to marry *me*.

When I returned to the United States for my wedding, it felt like a crash landing. I arrived in Austin weeks later than I'd planned, exhausted by a rash of last-minute, hastily organized performances: *Swan Lake*, *Romeo and Juliet*, *Laurencia*. I had danced these at the behest of a disorganized tour manager, and I had danced them with a herniated disc that bulged out of my spine and shot spikes of pain throughout my body when I twisted, landed from jumps, and bent my back in particular ways.

"How are you still dancing?" Mom wondered as she stood next to me in her clinic, reviewing the images that had been made of my spine.

This was the perennial question she asked that I was never able to answer.

Many brides spend the weeks before their wedding rubbing lotions into their faces, curling their hair, receiving massages, meeting with friends for bachelorette parties.

I spent my pre-wedding days lying on my back in a clinic, holding myself still as staffers poked needles into my knees, hips, vertebrae, and ankles. They targeted my pain points, then withdrew blood and marrow before reinserting it into my injured and weary joints.

By the time they were done with me, I couldn't walk. I lay flat, staring at the ceiling and Facetimed Andrew. He smiled but looked worried.

"How are you holding up, my love?" he asked. "Are you going to be able to walk down the aisle?"

I hoped the answer was yes.

I drank water. I slept, I withdrew into a shell for an entire week, like a traumatized snail.

Finally, after days of motionless recovery, after the tingling in my hands and feet had eased, after the medicines had worked on my spine, after I'd slept away the jet lag and exhaustion, after I'd regained the strength to stand, I drove to the airport, got on a plane, and flew north for the mountains of New Mexico.

Andrew met me at the airport, and we drove through the hills to his family's ranch. We found it bursting with green, under a sky piled high with whipped-cream clouds, watered in gentle waves by daily rains. I felt the gravel under my feet, held in my open palm the soft, snuffing noses of horses, and stood in fields of wildflowers under the resinous boughs of pine trees. I felt returned to a place in which I was safe and taken care of.

Our family and friends pulled up the gravel driveway in their rental cars and pickup trucks. They helped us trim the grass, sweep the floors, mow the fields, iron the tablecloths, and unfold the white chairs we had rented into rows in front of an arbor. We grilled our food and ate it outdoors. We sat at picnic tables and reminisced about the places we'd lived: Moscow, California, Boston, Arizona, Texas.

All eight of my siblings arrived from the far corners of the world. We'd each gone our separate ways since leaving California. My brothers and sisters were scientists, artists, and entrepreneurs now. Each of them, in their own way, was indescribably beautiful. I felt honored that they'd left their busy lives to join us. They laughed and played cards and hit Ping-Pong balls across the flat of a table. They made jokes that no one who had grown up outside our home would understand.

My friends from Moscow were there too. They gathered in groups on the steps outside, their faces to the mist-filled valley, and told stories in Russian and English about the cafés we'd visited, the museums we'd seen, the ways Moscow had changed during the years we'd lived there. Andrew's parents smiled and congratulated us. They sat on the couch with my mother and showed my dad how to work the tractor. They transformed their ranch into a place that could host a wedding.

I could tell how much my parents liked Andrew, how thrilled they were at our decision to be together.

I'd struggled to get excited about my champagne gown and lacy veil or the shade of purple I'd chosen for my bridesmaids to wear. I was a ballerina who played dress-up professionally every day. There was nothing special about hair-spraying myself into someone fancy.

But when I saw the bouquet of people who had traveled from around the world and gathered in the hills of New Mexico to watch us marry, I felt so loved and supported and happy. It was perhaps the most beautiful I had ever been.

On the morning of our wedding, I woke early, strapped running shoes to my feet, and set off into the hills. I saw the sun rise pink over the horizon, felt the crunch of pebbled stones beneath my soles as I breathed in mountain air. I'd spent the past year checking with Andrew: Are you sure you want to do this? Are you sure you won't change your mind in two years after you know the true me?

He'd said he was sure, and I mostly believed him, but I also felt frightened. I didn't know what it meant to settle your heart; to prepare for a lifelong commitment before you made it. But that's what I tried to do out in the hills before anyone else woke. My feet pounded the road, and I waited to feel the sort of peace I turned to God for.

Please be with us, God. Please bless this relationship. Please bless Andrew, please bless me. Please don't let it rain.

By the time I was back at the lodge, I was sweaty and clear-eyed and filled with the chemicals that flood the body in moments of exercise. I don't know if I had achieved certainty, but, then again, the future is something about which it's impossible to be certain.

What I do know is that, as I walked down the aisle, surrounded by family and friends, my face set toward a man with whom I was in love, I was very, very happy. The sun shone on green trees, Andrew's conservatory friends bent their bows to violin and cello, my parents' eyes filled with tears, and I promised to spend my life loving a person who became, as we slipped rings on each other's fingers, my husband.

We kissed each other under a blue sky, my veil caught on wildflowers, we cut each other slices of cake in the lodge, and Andrew sat at a keyboard, looked into my eyes, and sang about how much he loved me.

It did, I'm sorry to tell you, rain that day. The water fell from the sky and left splotches of damp on the gray of Andrew's suit-coat shoulders as he picked me up in his arms and we ran for the car.

But later, when it was quiet, when we'd left everyone behind us at the lodge, I gave him the wedding present I'd bought for him at a monastery in Saratov. It was a silver Orthodox cross that hung on a chain, to be worn around his neck—the sort of thing Russians put on after they are baptized.

I wanted to honor the faith that was so important to him—to both of us—and the country that was so important to me. No one ever knows exactly what they are marrying into. But Andrew had, in marrying me, agreed to make Russia part of his future. I couldn't wait to introduce him.

If there's one thing you can say about Russia, it's that it makes an impression. And Andrew, when he saw it for the first time, was in awe.

We flew to Moscow first, where we drove in an expensive car past skyscrapers; office buildings; wide, green boulevards; medieval cathedrals; and eighteenth-century stone palaces. The city center at night was lit up like a Fabergé egg with twinkling gold domes, glowing streetlamps, and a black river that reflected the city's electricity back to the sky like broken glass. The dusty, chaotic city I'd met as a fifteen-year-old, nearly a decade before, had grown up and gotten a makeover.

Andrew and I ate in hipster coffeehouses and walked Rocky down the granite sidewalks past pharmacies, boutiques, and five-story arches carved into imperial-era stone buildings. The whole world passed by us: tourists from Europe and Africa, students whizzing by on electric scooters, families pushing strollers, Russian men who held the hands of their girlfriends and wore T-shirts emblazoned with images of Kalashnikovs.

"Moscow is so big," Andrew said. "It's so cosmopolitan and modern and convenient. This is nicer than Rodeo Drive."

But Astrakhan was different, and when we arrived there just a few days later, a different sort of shock set in for Andrew.

The taxi that picked us up charged less than five dollars to drive us to our new apartment, in one of the city's nicest renovated buildings. It was cozy inside with an exposed brick wall and warm, planked floors. Its front door opened to a still, green canal, its windows overlooked a ramshackle mess of buildings with plastic tarp-covered roofs and disintegrating walls.

Andrew saw, for the first time, a Russian communal apartment building entrance, with its collection of garbage, its overtones of human urine, its creaking and rusting metal door. I could see him trying to withhold judgment and remain open-minded about the country I had chosen as my own.

I took him to my theater, rising from the Astrakhan slums, where he was welcomed like some sort of oil magnate who'd married the city's star ballerina. My colleagues gave him tours of the building, passes to visit rehearsals whenever he wanted. They couldn't understand quite who or what he was—an American, yes, but surely an extremely wealthy one. They couldn't imagine me marrying anyone less than a minor oligarch.

Andrew tried to see Russia the same way I did. I watched the country pass before his eyes: the potholes, the stray dogs, the affordable health care, the theater—gaudy and beautiful, functioning as a world unto itself. He listened to the stories people told about daily corruption: city officials who took money meant to buy medicine for children and purchased

Porsches instead. Or local entrepreneurs who had to factor the cost of bribes into their business expenses. He walked around the city, attached to Rocky by a leash, and wondered, "How did the economy that produced this huge theater also produce these slums?"

He tried to fit his brain around the Russian way I'd come to view the world, but I could see that it felt incomprehensible to him. "This place is like a scene from a postapocalyptic movie," he said.

I waited. Sometimes Russia grows on people. It infiltrates their bloodstreams as they stare, fascinated, obsessed with trying to understand.

Andrew began taking Russian language classes and volunteered to play guitar at the worship services of the nearby Pentecostal church I'd joined. He purchased a gym membership for a few dollars a week and went there for daily massages and visits to the sauna. He took piano lessons with a local teacher and came home at night to tell me about the wonders of Russian artistic talent.

"This pianist in just thirty minutes taught me things I never learned in four years of music school," he gushed. "These people are so talented. They're so good."

He watched me fill Astrakhan's theater stage with dancing. He followed me to Moscow for film debuts, St. Petersburg for days of wandering around art museums, watching ballets at the Mariinsky Theater.

Andrew did his best, our first year of marriage, to make Astrakhan into a place where he could envision a future. He listened to me speak with passion about how much more money Russia spent on the arts, how much more my profession was valued there. He watched me be recognized, greeted, asked for autographs as I walked around the city.

"Things are not as harsh in Russia for dancers as they are in the United States," I told him over and over as he watched me accept invitations from around the country to dance. "In America, the system just spits dancers out. But in Russia, the state literally pays for talented students to study ballet. And then, once you're in a Russian theater, that means something. You're part of that theater's legacy."

"I can see you are protected and honored here," he said. "I can see why you like it."

We both felt safe in Russia, welcomed even. I had found my place in the sun, positioned myself in the rays of official approval. We were there for ballet, we told anyone who asked. We were there for the arts.

I knew what it took to live in Russia. I knew how to play the game.

I never imagined the rules of that game might irrevocably change.

Chapter 35

Flee

Poland in January was overcast and damp. The air in Warsaw filled with flurries of snow that drifted past streetlamps and dissolved in a wet sludge on cobblestone streets.

Andrew and I had left Astrakhan and come to Eastern Europe for two months to film a movie about—there's no other way to say this—me.

It's a strange thing to make a film about your own life. Movies start with years of conversations, negotiations, questions, and emails. You can't publicly talk about any of it—at first because it might not happen. But then, because, bizarrely, it's not your story to tell. You've literally handed the narrative of your life off to a team of people, and you have to wait until the right time to mention it, when marketers and producers and publicists are ready for you to start talking.

We didn't plan to stay in Poland long. The producers assured us it would only take two months to get all the filming done. We didn't bring much with us on the plane: our clothes, a camera, Andrew's work computer, Rocky with his leash and travel crate.

"I'll only be gone eight weeks," I promised my Astrakhan theater director. "I'll be back in March—in time to do *Swan Lake.*"

In Warsaw, the work of creating filmed scenes on a Polish set was all-consuming. There were camera, sound, and light technicians walking around with microphones on poles, wires coming out of their jeans pockets. Producers wearing lanyards scrambled between hallways and wood-floored dance rooms, reminding people what time it was, where they had to be. Directors stood with headphones around their necks, their hands to their chins, frowning behind the black barrels of cameras.

For the two months I worked on *Joika*, I barely slept. Early in the mornings, I rushed to the set, where I strapped a COVID mask on my face and helped choreograph dance sequences, advise wardrobe designers on tulle and bodice colors, coach actresses on their Russian accents, talk to set designers about the suitability of various floors for dancing.

Andrew and I would go without speaking to each other for days at a time. He was asleep at 4 a.m. when I left. In the evenings, when I returned, he was on his computer, attending virtual work meetings in the Western Hemisphere.

In the hours I could escape from set, we walked Rocky in the pale winter sunshine down Warsaw's cobblestone streets.

"After Astrakhan, everything feels like luxury," Andrew said.

There were no stray dogs bounding out from behind corners to snarl at our poodle. The neighborhood where we were staying was filled with artisan coffee shops and vegan cafes. Andrew found a coworking office space to rent that was glassed in with floor-to-ceiling windows, furnished with blond-wood tables, equipped with lightning-fast Wi-Fi. There was no need to purchase and maintain elaborate VPN connections that would allow him to do his work in online confidentiality, safe from the Russian laws that forced people to lower their digital privacy screens.

"I love Warsaw," he said. "Don't you see how amazing life can be outside Astrakhan? I don't understand why you are so obsessed with Russia."

I listened to his comments but did not agree with them. Andrew knew how beautiful Russia could be. We had visited Moscow and St. Petersburg. We'd strolled the arched palace hallways of the Hermitage Museum, the stone embankments of the Neva and the Moskva Rivers. We'd ordered nitro brews and sushi in Russian restaurants.

He still didn't understand what ballet was. He still thought of it as something related to the Saturday morning classes his nieces attended in their adorable pink tutus. He didn't see how the world of elite dance was an echelon of pain and dedication that took an entire lifetime to attain.

I understood what Andrew was saying, and I even agreed with him in some ways. I was willing to leave Astrakhan. I'd actually auditioned at companies in other Russian cities. But I did not want to leave the country that had adopted me, given me citizenship, made me a prima ballerina. Russia was the place that made my life as a dancer possible. Russia was the place that wanted me. Russia was my home.

We stood at the counter of a coffee shop in Warsaw, where the shrill whine of milk being whipped into foam filled the air. Andrew scrolled on his phone.

"Have you seen these satellite images?" he asked, staring at the bright rectangle of his screen. "It looks like there's a lot of military equipment in Belarus, Western Russia, Crimea—it's all right on the border of Ukraine."[1]

I shrugged, reached for a cardboard cup filled with espresso.

"You're overthinking it," I said. "There's been conflict in Eastern Ukraine for years. Nothing ever happens. People just shoot across lines at each other. Maybe this is like a joint exercise between Belarus and Russia. They love to gang up and, like, poke fun. Putin's always doing bait and switch."

"I don't know." Andrew shook his head, slid his phone back into his pocket. "This seems like something new. Both the United States and NATO say Putin is preparing for a full-scale invasion."

I felt the heat of my drink burn the tips of my fingers through the paper shell of my cup. I turned toward the coffee shop door and the clouded light of a February morning.

"There's not going to be an invasion," I said, distracted, confident, not even taking the time to be annoyed with the ways Andrew still didn't understand Russia. "There's going to be something where, like, Ukraine agrees not to join NATO. They're going to sign something, make a concession. Nobody's going to war."

Andrew had decided. He didn't want to go back to Russia.

This is something he told me as we stood facing each other, late at night, under the gray overhead lamp of our Warsaw rental apartment.

Andrew's wide-set eyes were focused, pleading.

"I think we should stay here," he said, his shoulders widened into a line. "If anything happens, we're going to want to be on this side of the border."

"But we need to go back," I said. "Our home is in Russia. All our stuff is there."

I thought of our apartment in Astrakhan: the tall windows we opened to catch breaths of air from the green-water canal. The dusty streets, the pink and blue mandala that bloomed under the vaulted roof of my theater when I danced *Sylphide*, *La Bayadere*. I thought of the Russian audiences that gathered to watch me from cushioned chairs, wearing perfumed dresses and button-down shirts.

"There's no future for us in Russia," Andrew said.

"Actually, my job is in Russia," I told him.

"You could take a *corps* contract with the Warsaw Ballet," he said. "Even temporarily, to get us out of Astrakhan while you look for something else."

He spoke loudly, like an American, like the world was full of possibilities.

"I don't want to do that," I said. "The *corps* is a step in the wrong direction. I'm not going back to that."

I pushed the tops of my toes into the parquet floor to feel the crunch of a stretch, the tension, pain, and relief that come from forcing your body past its normal range of motion.

"Let's go somewhere else in Europe, then. We can find another Airbnb, you could go out on more auditions," he said, as if auditions were magic, as if there was a dance contract waiting for me that I hadn't yet found.

The sides of this argument had become so well-worn between us, they made me dizzy. It was like one of the dances I'd been choreographing in a low-ceilinged studio in Warsaw: a series of turns, one after another, always in the same direction. Each spin slightly different from the last—a hand raised to my face, a leg extended outward, then withdrawn. But no matter how much we twisted these questions over and over, we always ended in the same place.

"We're going back to Astrakhan," I said. Then, to make it crystal clear: "*I* am going back to Astrakhan."

I'd left him once for Russia. He knew that this was what it meant to be married to me.

Andrew turned away, his anger and frustration radiating silently from the other side of the room.

Rocky pranced on the floor below us, wagging his tail, clicking his toenails on wooden parquet, worried. I bent to scoop him into my arms, felt the cloud of poodle fur on my neck. My desperation expanded out into the room around us, then vacuumed back to smolder in my chest, pricking my eyes with tears.

Andrew turned and left, stepping away to our tiny rental kitchen.

He didn't understand. He was the only one in our newborn marriage who hadn't yet developed the callouses needed to survive in Russia. He didn't know what it was to make yourself into a person who could live there. He hadn't experienced what it was to twist the tendons in your hip year after year until your femurs could rotate fully outward in parallel lines. He didn't know the blisters that had risen on the heels of my feet, the skin that had peeled away, the nails that had blackened and fallen from my toes. He hadn't felt his bones break inside of a pointe shoe, hadn't rearranged the neurons in the gray folds of his brain to recognize Cyrillic letters and Russian verbs of motion, hadn't trained his tongue to fit the sharp edges of a Slavic language.

I had tried returning to the United States. He knew this. It wasn't a place I wanted to live. I didn't want cell phone contracts, health insurance premiums, credit scores, suburbs, and smiles that were given freely, without meaning. I didn't want to return to flat stages, to theaters with only decades of history, to cities full of people who didn't cling to art like it was a life raft in a sea of darkness and a never-ending winter of the soul. I didn't want the highlights of my weeks to be trips to Trader Joe's.

I set Rocky on the floor and got into bed, pulled the covers over my shoulders. The herbal tea I'd brewed was cool and still on the nightstand beside me.

I fell asleep angry that Wednesday night in February. Rocky curled at my feet, Poland lying cold and dark around us. The others who slept in the city beyond our windows were as blissfully unaware as we were. But I wonder now—did they feel, even unconsciously, the volcanic pressure gathering to the east? The tanks heavy on the Belorussian border? The violence and slaughter that would break on their neighbor Ukraine in just a matter of hours?

Our sleep was dreamless and tense. When we awoke on Thursday, the whole world had changed.

It began in the Kremlin, where Putin, at 5:30 in the morning, via national television, declared his decision to launch a "special military operation" to "protect" the people of Ukraine.[2] Moments later, Russian Navy personnel swarmed the shores of Odessa, and Russian military troops in tanks and dark green trucks, their sides painted with the bloodthirsty symbolic slash of a Z, flooded over the borders.[3] War vehicles rolled down the long, paved roads of Ukraine from Belarus, Crimea, and Western Russia.[4] Russian planes dropped bombs from the sky onto Kiev, Kharkiv, and Dnipro.[5]

People asleep in their beds across the Texas-sized country of Ukraine were shaken awake by the scream of air-raid sirens, the rumbling thunder of explosions. They fled their homes and cowered in basements and metro tunnels. They called their loved ones. They packed their clothes into suitcases and ran for nearby train stations or drove their cars into gridlocked lines of vehicles, fleeing west.

When Andrew and I awoke in Warsaw, our phones were filled with news of ballistic missiles, swarms of tanks, Russian soldiers moving to wrap themselves around the city of Kiev like a noose.

We stared at our screens for days as we saw images of projectiles blasting into the sides of crowded apartment buildings[6]; terrified families carrying pets across the crumpled ruins of bridges[7]; pregnant women, their faces drained of blood, their limbs raw with open wounds, their bellies protruding like watermelons, being carried from the ruins of bombed-out maternity wards.[8]

I walked around in a daze as friends in Moscow sent messages about their decisions to leave. They threw socks into suitcases and fled for the airport, terrified of being trapped as world airlines ceased flying to and from Russia. They brought their bank cards to ATMs and found they could not access money. They left everything behind them and traveled to Poland and Romania to help Ukrainian refugees flooding across the border.

Some of my Russian friends, the people I'd left in Astrakhan, couldn't grasp what was happening. Russian news stations were filled with anchors discussing the need to free Ukrainians from Nazis. But Ukraine was not a faraway place from Russia. It was a place filled with friends and relatives. It was a place where people's nieces and nephews sent text messages about how frightened they were, how angry they were, how betrayed they were.

"I'm so confused," Russian friends told me on the phone, unable to understand what was true, what was false. "I don't understand what's happening."

I cried in the back seats of Polish taxis on my way to the set of a movie about my life in Russia. I melted into tears in the rental apartment that stood in the center of Warsaw, where our lease was about to expire.

War is not the thing studied in history books years later, complete with maps and narration, heroes and villains. War is confusion, anger, fear, terror, pain, loss, adrenaline, nausea. And in the modern era, war was something I experienced as a series of events viewed through the glowing rectangle of a screen.

I watched on Instagram, WhatsApp, and Signal as my Ukrainian classmates, colleagues, and dance partners strapped bulletproof vests on their chests, traded their ballet shoes for rifles, took their barre routines to underground bunkers, or left the country in a frightened mass exodus.

From Warsaw, I kept calling and texting to check in with friends across the border. Andrew and I scrambled to help them find places to stay at hotels in Poland, cities in America. I introduced the dancers I knew to theater directors, suggested places where they might find a welcome, purchased airline and railway tickets in their names. I met them at train stations, where they stepped onto platforms weary, frightened, in shock.

At first, I was in shock too. I couldn't see the bigger picture; couldn't see past what I'd known for most of my life. Russia had always been there for me. It had given me a type of art, a type of life impossible to find anywhere else. Russia's teachers raised me; its theaters hosted me. Its czar gave me a place in his Kremlin, citizenship in his country. He had welcomed and protected and praised me. When things had not worked out in America, I had always been able to return to Russia, where I was wanted, promoted, supported, appreciated.

When that changed, I saw it but could not, at first, name it. Andrew recognized it before I did. Our return to Russia was impossible.

Epilogue

It is a strange and terrible thing to lose your home, to see the two empires to which you belong, define themselves by becoming enemies.

Andrew and I were spit out across Europe. We traveled to Amsterdam, Finland, Belgium, France, Nashville, England, Australia. I attended audition after audition, begging theater directors to give me a contract.

I watched Russia destroy the things I'd always thought it had held sacred. It dropped bombs onto ballet theaters filled with Ukrainian children.[1] It taught its grade schoolers to prepare for war.[2] Russian dancers I had long admired tattooed their bodies with images of Putin's face.[3] They became members of parliament, joined the United Russia Party, supported the president's campaigns to remain in power, filled their social media accounts with nationalistic posts.[4]

Other artists left their country, made themselves refugees. Some of them stayed in silence. I understood them all. I, too, longed for a Russia that did not exist.

But Ukraine was a line in the sand.

I knew that if Andrew and I kept quiet, if we said we were pro-Russia, if we were neutral or supportive of Kremlin decisions, if we decided to serve the greater good of art, we would have been allowed to return. We would have been welcomed and celebrated.

But we looked at the bombs falling on Ukraine, and we could not do it.

We have not returned to Russia since February 2022. All the belongings we left in our apartment—the exercise equipment, the photographs, the awards, the computers and cameras and wedding presents—are still there, gathering dust in a storage unit. I'm not sure we'll ever see them again.

There are friends and colleagues I used to know and meet in person at cafés or dance studios or metro stops who have now become text messages on my phone, digital voices in my ear. I am not sure if I will ever be with them again.

I still feel a particular kind of grief when I let my mind go over all the "what ifs" and "if onlys." I still lapse into daydreams, longing for things to be different. I miss the ecstasy of Russian White Night summers, the bone-deep friendships forged in ballet rehearsals and apartment kitchens. I miss dancing on Russian stages. I miss the way Moscow feels when you emerge from the metro station to a street glittering with snow and lights. You hurry, wrapped in a frostbitten coat and scarf, over icy pavement, until you step inside a theater filled with warmth and beauty.

There is a quiet place to which you come in life when you wonder what would have happened if you had done things differently. This is the place to which I came after Astrakhan, after Poland, after Brussels, Australia, and Amsterdam, after rejection, after rejection, after rejection.

More than a year after Russia invaded Ukraine, I moved with Andrew to Paris. I had been offered a contract to dance there. It was a contract extended to me by one of the most storied theaters in Europe—the Paris Opera. It was short-term, it was an agreement to dance Balanchine, it was an offer to return to the stage I so desperately missed.

I began, in the months before the start of this contract, after Andrew left for a visit to Nashville, to prepare myself in the way I had for years. I worked my muscles until they were toned, exhausted, in pain. I lifted weights, I ran, I pliéd, I contracted my abdominal muscles into crunches. This was my chance to begin work at a place that was a sort of zenith toward which dancers aspire their entire lives.

I felt nervous about it.

What if I'm not good enough? What if I show up to rehearsal and the directors look at my arms and find them to be too fat?

I went into the bathroom of our Paris apartment, to the cold porcelain toilet to purge and punish myself in preparation. But something stopped me there. It was a thought that had been poking at my brain for years.

What if this is the thing that's holding me back?

I felt a grain of curiosity rise at the back of my head.

What if I don't throw up? What if I let this go? What if I give myself the care and nourishment I need to perform?

I left the bathroom and returned to the living room of our rental apartment. The walls were hung with paintings, and a window opened to a Paris street where stores with glass windows sold silk scarves and leather bags. I did not vomit or starve myself. I sat down at the table and ate a beautiful lunch of curry, my plate covered in multicolored vegetables like a Kandinsky painting.

I will not pretend to you that I no longer struggle with the visceral desire to escape my own body or that I sometimes am not overcome with the need to control things by hurting myself.

But it has been years since I've made myself throw up. And I have grown, inside my muscles and veins and heart, a glowing stamina, a deep satisfaction, a steady strength.

I still come to every ballet as to the edge of a cliff over which I have to throw myself. It is still painful, still difficult, still terrifying. But I have a new cocktail of things I rely on for success: hard work, kindness, piles of vegetables, gluten- and dairy-free desserts, a sense of humor, and life-giving relationships with a rainbow of strange and beautiful people who love me.

I have found, in my marriage to Andrew, in the truth I face when I am alone, that I am someone who is beautiful. I am someone who deserves to be loved and respected and taken care of.

My dancing is better for it; my body is better for it. I am better for it.

I recently stepped onto a stage in Brussels to dance *Swan Lake* with a troupe of international artists who have become my friends. I loved putting on the white costume, feeling the blue lights illuminate my arms and face. I fastened the feathered headdress to my hair and rippled my arms like water in front of an audience—turning, spinning, dipping, rising.

I connected with the floor in a way taught to me by Kuznetsov. I moved my arms in a way I inherited from Zhanna, I held my back in a line demonstrated to me by Bobrova, and I moved with a confidence bestowed upon me by Arkhipova.

I heard, after it was over, the applause of people who'd sat in darkness to watch me. They filled the hall with thunder that resonated deep in my chest. I wondered, as I do after every performance, *Is this my last time on stage?*

When I went behind the curtain, I found an elderly Russian woman waiting for me, her eyes aglow. She told me how beautifully I had danced, how much I had reminded her of the childhood memories she had of ballet. Her words made tears well in my eyes. What more could I want than to be part of the tradition in which I was raised, to carry on the excellence, beauty, and dedication given to me by Russian ballet?

When I left the United States at the age of fifteen, I thought of myself as a fully American person. When I left Russia in 2022, nearly thirteen years later, I thought of myself as a person who had been given the gift of calling herself Russian.

Now I live in Paris, and I see that I am both; I am neither.

In Paris, I walk on cobblestone streets past limestone walls and art galleries and buskers. In the mornings, I take classes at a high-ceilinged dance studio with Paris Opera teachers who have carved atop my Russian school of movement the ornaments of French ballet.

I visit museums; I take my dog on walks down tree-lined boulevards. I meet friends at cafés with tiny outdoor tables that face the pageant of coats and scarves, shoes and faces that pass by on Paris's sidewalks. I cannot believe the glamour and happiness of my life.

I fly to Ecuador, Australia, Belgium, Nigeria, California, to dance and teach. I host Russian, Ukrainian, French, and American friends in my apartment. I am at home in the world with my bag of ballet shoes and stretch bands, my poodle, my husband who fits his work into a computer and follows me back and forth across the Atlantic. I have heard him say that he loves the carousel of travel our lives have become.

There is nowhere in the world like Russia for the discipline of ballet. Authoritarian countries know how to move the arm of power in support of the arts. But I have been all over the world now, and I make my home in the West. I can see, in a way I couldn't from Astrakhan or Moscow, that openness and freedom, diversity and movement are sparks to creativity that are given too little space in authoritarian countries.

From America, I have kept an unreasonable optimism and a belief that miracles—my life being one of them—actually exist.

From Russia, I have held on to an expectation that I will meet suffering. Life is inextricably linked to difficulty and darkness. There is no escaping this. But there is a way in which Russian art handles this truth that is unique. It looks suffering in the eye and accepts it. Not because it's good to suffer, but because suffering is part of the human condition, and if art does not admit that, it's lying.

I used to believe punishment and pain were necessary conditions for making art—that it was normal to kill yourself for art, to "die to yourself to please God," as my childhood church used to preach. I no longer believe this. Punishment is self-sabotage. Dedication and perseverance through suffering, however, can lead to transformation and beauty. God is grace and love. This is what I take with me from Russia.

But I am neither fully Russian nor fully American. I am not thankful to have been forced to leave Russia, but I am thankful to be where I am now—humbled into compassion, open to the world, learning from everyone I meet, creating art shot through, like streaks of gold, with everything I have been given out of difficulty.

Ballet has become my bridge and my passport. I have found my home in the world, in the dance studio, in my marriage to Andrew, and in my friendships. I have found my home in myself.

I still can't believe I get to dance.

NOTES

CHAPTER 4

1. Faculty and Staff, North Ballet Academy, https://www.northballet.com/fac ulty-and-staff.

CHAPTER 5

1. Tatiana Podyablonskaia, "A Voronezh Ballerina Has Conquered Vladimir Vasiliev," *Komsomolskaia Pravda*, June 22, 2008, https://www.vrn.kp.ru/daily/24117 .5/340418/.

CHAPTER 7

1. Peter Bradshaw, "Force of Nature Natalia—Fascinating Study of the Royal Ballet's Star Dancer," *Guardian*, June 6, 2019, https://www.theguardian.com/film /2019/jun/06/force-of-nature-natalia-fascinating-study-of-the-royal-ballets-star -dancer.

2. "Arkhipova," Russkii Balet Entsiklopediia, 2009–2015, https://www.pro-bal let.ru/html/a/arhipova.html.

3. "Bogomolova, Ludmila Ivanovna," Wikipedia, last modified April 25, 2022, https://ru.wikipedia.org/wiki/Богомолова,_Людмила_Ивановна.

4. "Kozhukhova, Maria Alekseevna," Wikipedia, last modified December 11, 2023, https://ru.wikipedia.org/wiki/Кожухова,_Мария_Алексеевна.

CHAPTER 11

1. Alexandra Tomalonis, "Protégés III," Danceviewtimes.com, March 27, 2011, https://www.danceviewtimes.com/2011/03/prot%C3%A9g%C3%A9s-iii.html ?fbclid=IwAR3znGtZdQH3_6wHziSHsxvHDkH6yG7fsZWPGl0ktMhpgfcVlz _uDavn_dQ.

2. Sarah Kaufman, "Dance Review: Promise and Grace from Young Dancers in Proteges II," *Washington Post*, March 27, 2011, https://www.washingtonpost.com /lifestyle/style/dance-review-promise-and-grace-from-young-dancers-in-proteges -iii/2011/03/27/AF9WAokB_story.html.

CHAPTER 12

1. Julia Ioffe, "At the Bolshoi Gala," *New Yorker*, October 31, 2011, https://www .newyorker.com/news/news-desk/at-the-bolshoi-gala.

2. Nastassia Astrasheuskaya and Amie Ferris-Rotman, "Russian Elite Celebrate as Lavish Bolshoi Opens," Reuters, October 28, 2011, https://www.reuters.com/ article/idUSLNE79R04G/.

3. Bolshoi Theater, "The Historic Stage," https://bolshoi.ru/en/about/building.

4. Nastassia Astrasheuskaya, "Russia's Bolshoi Theatre Set for Grand Reopening," Reuters, October 25, 2011, https://www.reuters.com/article/us-stage-bolshoi/rus sias-bolshoi-theatre-set-for-grand-reopening-idUKTRE79O5FN20111025/.

5. Lukas Alpert, "Bolshoi Theater to Reopen after Restoration," October 27, 2011, https://www.themoscowtimes.com/2011/10/27/bolshoi-theater-to-reopen -after-restoration-a10455.

6. President of Russia, "Bolshoi Theatre Opens after Reconstruction," October 28, 2011, http://www.en.kremlin.ru/events/president/news/13260.

7. Bolshoi Theater, "Bolshoi Grand Re-Opening 28.10.2011," March 6, 2012, https://www.youtube.com/watch?v=TtSvnq01Nno.

CHAPTER 13

1. David Hallberg, *A Body of Work* (New York: Atria Paperback, 2017), 182–83.

2. Irina Tkachenko, "Texan Teen to Become First American to Graduate Premier Russian Ballet School," NBC News, April 7, 2012, https://www.nbcnews .com/news/world/texan-teen-become-first-american-graduate-premier-russian-bal let-school-flna678605.

CHAPTER 16

1. Sergei Loiko, "Russia's Historic Bolshoi Theatre Finally Opens," *Los Angeles Times*, October 28, 2011, https://www.latimes.com/archives/blogs/culture-monster -blog/story/2011-10-28/russias-historic-bolshoi-theatre-finally-reopens.

CHAPTER 17

1. The Historic Stage, https://bolshoi.ru/en/about/building.

CHAPTER 18

1. David Remnick, "Danse Macabre," *New Yorker*, March 11, 2013, https://www .newyorker.com/magazine/2013/03/18/danse-macabre.

2. Ellen Barry, "Harsh Light Falls on Bolshoi after Acid Attack," *New York Times*, January 18, 2013, https://www.nytimes.com/2013/01/19/world/europe/ser gei-filin-bolshoi-ballet-director-is-victim-of-acid-attack.html.

CHAPTER 19

1. "Bolshoi Cast Defend Dancer Arrested over Acid Attack," BBC, March 13, 2013, https://www.bbc.com/news/world-europe-21766692.

CHAPTER 21

1. Dmitrii Evstifeev, "American Ballerina Accuses the Bolshoi Leadership of Extortion," *Izvestia*, November 13, 2013, https://iz.ru/news/560562.
2. Evstifeev, "American Ballerina Accuses the Bolshoi."
3. Shaun Walker, "'I Forgive Nobody,' Bolshoi Acid Attack Victim Tells Dancer's Trial," *Guardian*, November 6, 2013, https://www.theguardian.com/world /2013/nov/06/bolshoi-acid-attack-dancer-trial.
4. Walker, "'I Forgive Nobody.'"
5. Evstifeev, "American Ballerina Accuses the Bolshoi."

CHAPTER 22

1. Moscow Kremlin Museums, "State Kremlin Palace," Accessed June 24, 2024, https://kremlin-architectural-ensemble.kreml.ru/en-Us/architecture/view/gosu darstvennyy-kremlevskiy-dvorets-moskovskogo-kremlya/.
2. Julie Miller, "The Crown: Did Prince Phillip Have an Affair with a Russian Ballerina?" *Vanity Fair*, December 8, 2017, https://www.vanityfair.com/hollywood /2017/12/prince-philip-ballerina-affair-the-crown-netflix.
3. Michael Specter, "Galina Ulanova Is Dead at 88; a Revered Bolshoi Ballerina," *New York Times*, March 22, 1998, https://www.nytimes.com/1998/03/22/nyregion/ galina-ulanova-is-dead-at-88-a-revered-bolshoi-ballerina.html.

CHAPTER 23

1. Mikhail Iossel, "The 1980s American Soap Opera That Explains How Russia Feels about Everything," *Foreign Policy*, July 24, 2017, https://foreignpolicy.com /2017/07/24/american-soap-opera-explains-how-russia-feels-about-everything -santa-barbara-trump-putin/.

CHAPTER 24

1. Lucie Steinzova and Kateryna Oliynyk, "The Sparks of Change: Ukraine's Euromaidan Protests," Radio Free Europe, November 21, 2018, https://www.rferl .org/a/ukraine-politics-euromaidan-protests/29608541.html.
2. Andrew Higgins, "An Unfinished Ukraine Palace and a Fugitive Leader's Folly," *New York Times*, February 25, 2014, https://www.nytimes.com/2014 /02/26/world/europe/an-unfinished-ukraine-palace-and-a-fugitive-leaders-folly .html.
3. Patrick Kingsley, "When Rebels Toured the Palace: How Does Ukraine's Presidential Compound Measure Up?" *Guardian*, February 24, 2014, https://www

.theguardian.com/world/2014/feb/24/rebels-toured-palace-ukraine-presidential
-compound-viktor-yanukovych.

4. Luke Harding, "Crimean Coup Is Payback by Putin for Ukraine's Revolution," *Guardian*, February 28, 2014, https://www.theguardian.com/world/2014/feb/28/vladimir-putin-crimean-coup-russia-ukraine.

5. Wojciech Konończuk, "Russia's Real Aims in Crimea," Carnegie Endowment for International Peace, March 13, 2014, https://carnegieendowment.org/research/2014/03/russias-real-aims-in-crimea?lang=en.

6. President of Russia, "Address by President of the Russian Federation," March 18, 2014, http://en.kremlin.ru/events/president/news/20603.

7. Alec Luhn, "Red Square Rally Hails Vladimir Putin after Crimea Accession," *Guardian*, March 18, 2014, https://www.theguardian.com/world/2014/mar/18/red-square-rally-vladimir-putin-crimea.

8. Kevin Liffey, "'Putin the Polite,' Chilling Hero of Russian Souvenirs," Reuters, August 21, 2015, https://www.reuters.com/article/us-russia-politics-wideimage/putin-the-polite-chilling-hero-of-russian-souvenirs-idUSKCN0QQ1PO20150821/.

9. Kevin Leveille, "Russians Flock to Their 'Little Bit of Paradise' in Crimea—and Back Its Annexation," *World*, August 13, 2014, https://theworld.org/stories/2014/08/13/russia-needs-its-own-little-bit-paradise.

Chapter 25

1. Diana Magnay and Tim Lister, "Air Attack on Pro-Russian Separatists in Luhansk Kills 8, Stuns Residents," CNN, June 3, 2014, https://www.cnn.com/2014/06/03/world/europe/ukraine-luhansk-building-attack/index.html.

2. "In Photos: Remembering Boris Nemtsov's life, 9 Years after His Murder," *Moscow Times*, February 27, 2024, https://www.themoscowtimes.com/2024/02/27/in-photos-remembering-boris-nemtsovs-life-9-years-after-his-murder-a84264.

3. "Tens of Thousands Rally in Russia, Ukraine ahead of Referendum," Radio Free Europe, March 15, 2014, https://www.rferl.org/a/ukraine-crimea-rally-moscow/25298167.html.

4. Carol J. Williams and Sergei L. Loiko, "Boris Nemtsov, Prominent Putin Critic, Is Gunned Down in Moscow," *Los Angeles Times*, February 27, 2015, https://www.latimes.com/world/europe/la-fg-russia-boris-nemtsov-killed-20150227-story.html.

5. "Main Witness in Nemtsov Slaying Case: I Didn't See Killer," Radio Free Europe, March 2, 2015, https://www.rferl.org/a/nemtsov-duritskaya-ukraine-girlfriend-witness-killing/26877694.html.

Chapter 27

1. President of Russia, "Russia-ASEAN Summit," May 20, 2016, http://www.en.kremlin.ru/events/president/transcripts/51953.

CHAPTER 29

1. "Medvedev Says 2018 FIFA World Cup Boosted Infrastructure Development in Russian Cities," December 6, 2018, TASS Russian News Agency, https://tass.com/economy/1034667.

CHAPTER 33

1. Astrakhan Opera House, "History," Accessed June 24, 2024, https://www.en.astoperahouse.ru/page/theater-history.

2. Saba Ayres, "'Uncle Volodya, I dream of new dresses': Greatest Hits from Putin's Annual Call-in Show,'" *Los Angeles Times*, June 7, 2018, https://www.latimes.com/world/europe/la-fg-putin-call-in-show-20180607-story.html.

3. Neil MacFarquhar, "Putin, Acknowledging Financial Turmoil, Assures the Nation It's Temporary," *New York Times*, December 18, 2014, https://www.nytimes.com/2014/12/19/world/europe/vladimir-putin-annual-press-conference.html.

CHAPTER 35

1. Christoff Koettl, "New Satellite Images Show More Russian Forces Massing on Three Sides of Ukraine," *New York Times*, February 10, 2022, https://www.nytimes.com/2022/02/10/world/europe/russia-ukraine-forces.html.

2. The President of Russia, "Address by the President of the Russian Federation," February 24, 2022, http://en.kremlin.ru/events/president/news/67843.

3. Jeff Dean, The Letter Z Is a Symbol of Russia's War in Ukraine. But What Does It Mean?" March 9, 2022, NPR, https://www.npr.org/2022/03/09/1085471200/the-letter-z-russia-ukraine.

4. "Maps: Tracking the Russian Invasion of Ukraine," *New York Times*, February 24, 2022, https://www.nytimes.com/interactive/2022/world/europe/ukraine-maps.html.

5. Zoya Sheftalovich, "Battles Flare across Ukraine after Putin Declares War," February 24, 2022, https://www.politico.eu/article/putin-announces-special-military-operation-in-ukraine/.

6. Evgeniy Maloletka, "An Explosion Is Seen in an Apartment Building after Russia's Army Tank Fires in Mariupol, Ukraine," Associated Press, March 11, 2022, https://apnews.com/article/russia-ukraine-europe-aed973d65f3913888e16bd9c1303943b.

7. Associated Press, "Birds, Rabbits, Cats and Dogs: Fleeing Ukrainians Bring Their Pets," NBC News, March 10, 2022, https://www.nbcnews.com/news/world/ukrainians-fleeing-russian-invasion-bring-pets-rcna19562.

8. Mstyslav Chernov, "Pregnant Woman, Baby Die after Russian Bombing in Mariupol," Associated Press, March 14, 2022, https://apnews.com/article/russia-ukraine-war-maternity-hospital-pregnant-woman-dead-c0f2f859296f9f02be24fc9edfca1085.

E<small>PILOGUE</small>

1. Tim Lister, Olga Voitovich, Tara John, and Paul Murphy, "Russia Bombs Theater Where Hundreds Sought Shelter and 'Children' Was Written on Grounds," CNN, March 16, 2022, https://www.cnn.com/2022/03/16/europe/ukraine-mariupol-bombing-theater-intl/index.html.

2. Tim Lister and Katharina Krebs, "From Playgrounds to Parade Grounds: Russian Schools Are Becoming Increasingly Militarized," CNN, September 25, 2023, https://www.cnn.com/2023/09/24/europe/russia-schools-pro-war-parade-grounds-intl/index.html.

3. "Italy Theatre Cancels Show by Putin-Tattooed Russian Dancer," Reuters, December 30, 2022, https://www.reuters.com/world/europe/italy-theatre-cancels-show-by-putin-tattooed-russian-dancer-2022-12-30/.

4. Simon Morrison, "Canceling Russian Artists Plays into Putin's Hands," *Washington Post*, March 11, 2022, https://www.washingtonpost.com/outlook/2022/03/11/russian-artists-canceled-putin-gergiev-netrebko/.

ACKNOWLEDGMENTS

From Joy:

Thank you so much to Elizabeth Shockman. You have walked with me for the past fifteen years. This book has taken so many different winding paths, but it is a testimony to perseverance and to our friendship, which was forged in Russia.

Thank you to my wonderful spouse, Andrew Clay, for loving and supporting me. Thank you to my parents, who have walked beside me.

I couldn't be where I am without Zhanna Bogoroditskaia; the master of humor, Misha Martyniuk; and the late Andrei Petrov.

To Claudia Zaccari for giving me hope and opening doors.

To the estate of Patricia Cloherty—my gratitude knows no bounds.

To my siblings and Grace Womack for taking kind care to always help me.

To the Bolshoi Academy—my teachers, Marina Leonova, Elena Bobrova, Natalia Arkhipova, Ilya Kuznetsov, Anna Malovatskaia. Mario Labrador and my best friend, Masha Beck.

Thank you to Jean Marie Didiere's class—my new home in Paris. Thank you to Westside Ballet, Martine Harley, Francine Kessler, Allegra Clegg, and Jennifer Felkner.

To the Madants family and Klaudia Smieja. To Elizabeth Pewe, Jack Soto, Aaron Orza, the Clay and Leis families, Ghislain de Compreignac, Lewis Gardner, Florent Operto, Marguerite Derricks.

To Alexander Kabanov and Deborah Hoehner for their photographs. To Dina Burlis and Sergey Gavrilov for their work on *Joy Womack: A White Swan*, and for Gavrilov's beautiful camera work. To

Hannah Hamilton for her gorgeous cover designs. To Claire Gerus, Ashley Dodge, and Laney Ackley for their work on this book.

From Elizabeth:

Thank you, Joy, for your many years of friendship and the courage, vulnerability, and beauty with which you approach life, art, and telling your own story. Thank you for answering my endless questions, and putting up with a forty-minute Zoom limit.

Thank you to the dozens of Joy's colleagues, family, teachers, and friends who took the time to give me interviews.

Thank you to Anne Franz, Sarah Ollerich, Bethany Peters, Julia Franz, Eromese Joyce, Jon Collins, Emily Sandmann, Deborah Hoehner, Nastassia Astrasheuskaya, Tiffany Hanssen, Marcheta Fornoff, Britta Greene, and Kara Moen for listening to me talk about this book, in some cases for more than a decade. Thank you for your encouragement, expertise, and editorial reviews.

Thank you to Reuters and Kate DePury for giving me Bolshoi Theater assignments and for locating the bureau just down the street from the Bolshoi in Moscow.

Thank you to my MPR News colleagues for giving me the space and encouragement to step back from full-time reporting in order to finish this.

Thank you to Sarah Chauncey for the proposal edit and expert advice; Bianca Marais and Cece Lyra for the cover letter review; Euan Kerr, Julie Schumacher, John Enger, and Anne Speyer for their kind and timely advice.

In the many years I spent thinking about this book, I read several that helped me better understand ballet and Russian ballet: *Apollo's Angels*, by Jennifer Homans; *Bolshoi Confidential*, by Simon Morrison; *Don't Think, Dear: On Loving and Leaving Ballet*, by Alice Robb; and *Swans of the Kremlin*, by Christina Ezrahi. I didn't draw directly on them in the actual text of this book, but I am indebted to these authors' work and the education I gained from reading them.

Thank you to Claire Gerus for seeing our vision for this book way back in 2013, offering encouragement and keen editorial insights as well as sticking with this project through its many ups and downs before finally landing us with the perfect publishing team.

Thank you to Ashley Dodge, Laney Ackley, Meaghan Menzel, and their entire team for their hard work on and championing of this book. I feel so lucky and grateful to work with you.

Thank you to my family: Maxim, Anna, and William for giving me the time to do this. I love you.

This book touches on themes of self-harm and child abuse. If you or someone you know is struggling and needs help, here are some resources in the United States:

- National Alliance for Eating Disorders Helping: 1-866-662-1235
- National Suicide Prevention Hotline: 1-800-273-8255
- National Sexual Assault Hotline: 1-800-273-8255
- Crisis text line: Text HOME to 741741 or visit their website (https://www.crisistextline.org/) for chat and WhatsApp options

About the Authors

Joy Womack is an internationally awarded ballerina. Originally from Santa Monica, California, she studied dance at the Bolshoi Ballet Academy and in 2012 became the first American woman in history to dance for the Bolshoi Theater. She then went on to dance as a principal at theaters around Russia, including the State Kremlin Palace Theater and the Astrakhan State Theater of Opera and Ballet, until she fled Russia in 2022 at the start of the war in Ukraine. She currently works as a dancer and lives in Paris, France, with her husband, Andrew, and her poodle, Rachmaninoff.

Elizabeth Shockman is an award-winning journalist who met Joy Womack in 2010 while working for Reuters in Moscow, Russia. Elizabeth now works as a journalist in her home state of Minnesota for Minnesota Public Radio and National Public Radio. She lives in St. Paul with her husband, two children, and an overabundance of houseplants.